THE TRUTH BEHIND THE LOSS OF FLIGHT 370

GEOFF TAYLOR - EWAN WILSON

Published by:

Wilson Aviation Limited
14 Hammond Street
Hamilton
New Zealand 3204

www.wilsonaviation.co.nz
www.GoodnightMalaysianflt370.com

Written by Ewan Wilson & Geoff Taylor

Edited by Kingsley Field

First edition August 2014

ISBN 9-780-473-28867-9

Table of Contents

Glossary

AAIB Air Accident Investigation Branch
ACARS Aircraft Communications Addressing and Reporting System
ADSB Automatic Dependent Surveillance Broadcast
AIP Aeronautical Information Publication
AMSA Australian Maritime Safety Agency
APU Auxiliary Power Unit
ATC Air Traffic Control
ATCCS Air Traffic Control Centre
ATSB Australian Transport Safety Bureau
BEA Bureau d'Enquetes at d'Analyses pour La Securite de L'Aviation Civile
BUTTERWORTH Royal Malaysian Air Force. Butterworth Base
CVR Cockpit Voice Recorder
DCA Department of Civil Aviation (Malaysia)
ELT Emergency Locator Beacon
FAA Federal Aviation Administration
FDR Flight Data Recorder
FMC Flight Management Computer
GGCA General Civil Aviation Authority (United Arab Emirates)
GPS Global Positioning System
HCM Ho Chi Minh City
HF High Frequency (radio)
ICAO International Civil Aviation Organisation
ISMS In-flight Safety Monitoring System (usually Star-ISMS)
IFE In-Flight Entertainment (system)
KL Kuala Lumpur
KLATCC Kuala Lumpur Air Traffic Control Centre
LNAV Lateral Navigation System
MAS Malaysian Airline Systems (Malaysia Airlines former title)
MA Ops Malaysia Airlines Operations Centre
MCP Mode Control Panel
n/m Nautical Mile

NTSB National Transport Safety Board (US)
PFD Primary Flight Display
PSU Passenger Service Unit
RAT Ram Air Turbine
RMAF Royal Malaysian Air Force
SAR Search and Rescue
SATCOM Satellite Communications System
SDU Satellite Data Unit
SID Standard Instrument Departure
SITA Society Internationale de Telecommuncations Aeronautiques
SSR Secondary surveillance radar
TAC Thrust Asymmetry Compensation
TUC Time of Useful Consciousness
TRS ThalesRaytheon Systems
UAE United Arab Emirates
ULB Underwater Locator Beacon
UNMO United Malays National Organisation
V1/V2 Important speeds in operation of an aircraft
VMO Maximum operating speed of an aircraft
VAMPI/IGOCU/MEKAR/PIBOS/IGARI Waypoints or geographical locations identified by latitude and longitude along designated air routes.
VHF Very High Frequency (radio)
VSI Vertical Speed Indicator

Foreword

We dedicate this book to the 239 people who lost their lives on MH370 on March 8, 2014, on a flight from Kuala Lumpur to Beijing.

One of our purposes in writing the book was, in some small way to convey the human stories from the tragedy. We hope we have done this without adding upset to the terrible toll relatives and friends are already facing. Our other, more important task was to pursue the truth about what exactly happened. That is one small contribution we feel we can make to this whole terrible affair.

It is doubly tragic that we now also find ourselves dedicating the book to 298 more people whose lives were so sickeningly ended above the skies of Ukraine on July 17. Further on in the book, we will briefly analyse this horrific act and its implications both for the future of the stricken Malaysia Airlines and for the world's commercial aviation industry.

For all of us, the horror of MH17 is still sinking in. Although there were obvious links through the airline, the two tragedies were quite different. The Ukraine crash came from a simple cause. A moment of brutal, callous stupidity which saw the 777 shot down over a war-zone. Although it made the horror no less palpable, within a day it was clear what had occurred. There is no similar clear-cut answer to what happened to MH370. The aircraft is still missing, the relatives still have no closure and no answers. It is the biggest mystery in the history of aviation. For this reason, MH370 is our focus in this book.

Aviation is a highly technical field and is full of its own jargon, acronyms and abbreviations. For the sake of brevity, we use the full title or description in the text and from then on the shortened version, but have included a glossary for the reader's reference. There are also some variations in how some aspects are referred to by people quoted. For example, in the book, the Malaysia Airlines flight is sometimes referred to as MAS370 by air traffic controllers or by its call sign Malaysian 370. The actual flight name is MH370, which is what we use throughout.

As well, we have deliberately steered away from technical references, common in aviation, and tried to keep things simpler for a general audience.

There are many people and many organisations to thank. First, we thank Jahabar Sadiq, chief executive officer of The Malaysian Insider and Martin Vengadesan, news editor of the Star Online for their generosity in making themselves available to us. Others who helped include Asuad Khan and Peter Chong, and also a well-respected 777 200ER pilot who has asked to remain anonymous but you know who you are and we thank you. We have drawn heavily on the expertise of a number of professional reports and news media accounts. These include: Australian Transport Safety Bureau report, MH370 - Definition of Underwater Search; Malaysian Government, MH370 Preliminary Report; Dr Richard E Cole, University College London - An Analysis of the Inmarsat Data from MH370; Air Accidents Investigation Branch Aircraft Accident Report 2/90 (EW/C1094); Transportation Safety Board of Canada, Aviation Investigation Report In-Flight Fire Leading to Collision with Water, Swissair Transport Ltd; GCAS Air Accident Investigation Report Boeing 747 44AF, N571UP, Dubai; Air Accident Investigation and Aviation Safety Board report Helios Airways Flight HCY522 11/2006; National Transportation Safety Board Aircraft Accident Report In-flight break-up over the Atlantic Ocean of Trans World Airlines Flight 300; ATSB - Course manual and notes Human Factors for Transport Safety Investigators Canberra March 2014; National Transportation Safety Board Aircraft Accident Brief Egypt Air Flight 990 Boeing 767-366ER, SU-GAP October 31,1999; New Straits Times, Associated Press, NZ Herald, Weekend Herald, ABC News, AFP, Reuters, CNN, A Current Affair, The Independent, Asia Pacific News, CBC News, The Telegraph, Malay Online, The Economic Times, Perth Now News, Brisbane Times, Brisbane Courier Mail, Sydney Morning Herald, The Daily Mail, BBC, Asia News Network, 60 Minutes, India Today, Borneo Post, Four Corners, Sunday Times, The Daily Mirror, The Daily Telegraph.

We thank the 'old pro', our superb editor Kingsley Field, and the tremendously accommodating teams at Print House and Pan Media. We also owe a debt of gratitude to Gordon Chesterman, Martin Gallagher, Nicola Brennan-Tupara and Deborah Sloan for their advice and Jonathan MacKenzie for his unstinting support.

A special thanks to our incredibly patient wives Julie Taylor and Monique Wilson, and the rest of our families for their love and support. We also thank Charlie, Caesar, Monty and Bruno for their unflagging loyalty.

Lastly, it is possible no one will ever truly know exactly what happened to MH370 down to the last detail. Malaysian authorities - and probably others - are privy to information such as radar data, flight crew records and details of police investigations. We are not. We based our investigations on what was publicly available and on interviews.

We present the various scenarios and attempt by a process of elimination, using logic, analysis of everything we know of MH370, and past evidence from air accidents, to arrive at the most likely conclusion of what happened to the flight. We think we got it right.

But ultimately we leave it to the reader to decide.

Geoff Taylor and Ewan Wilson, July 2014, New Zealand.

PROLOGUE

Wednesday afternoon, July 24, 2014. Eindhoven, Holland.

The planes barely made any noise as they approached the airforce base - a number of people commented on it. Two big military aircraft - a Royal Netherlands Air Force Hercules and a Royal Australian Air Force C-17. They seemed to glide soundlessly in, as if in deference to the occasion. It added to the eerie feel as those first bodies arrived at Eindhoven Airbase in Holland from the flight from Ukraine. Australian freelance writer Daniel Hatch described how it would have been utter silence but for the tinkling sound of the flags flying at half-mast, clattering against poles in the wind. The flags represented the countries which had passengers aboard MH17 - 298 people senselessly murdered near a village in Eastern Ukraine a week before.

Earlier in the day, the coffins had been loaded on to the planes by a military guard of honour at Kharkiv Airport in eastern Ukraine. A nice gesture but too little, too late for many. Churches around the Netherlands rang their bells for five minutes before the planes landed. The coffins were met by members of the Dutch royal family, Prime Minister Mark Rutte and hundreds of victims' relatives protected from photographers by a line of black hoardings.

The aircraft came to a stop on the tarmac. Dutch soldiers formed an honour guard and a bugler played the Last Post, after which there was a minute's silence. Hearses, parked in a line waiting for their sad cargo, got the signal and started moving slowly in a line onto the airfield. They pulled up alongside the guard of honour. Perfectly synchronised, the drivers opened their doors, got out and then opened the rear doors.

One by one, pall bearers unloaded the coffins off the planes. Eight soldiers carried each coffin and lowered them into the hearses with extreme care. Those watching held their breath. It was as if all clocks had stopped. When finally the cortege moved off, led by a motorcade, it passed close by the families. They clapped as the vehicles went by, not knowing what else to do. The scenes when the cortege left the airbase and began its journey through the streets of Eindhoven were surreal. Scarcely believable. Thousands lined the streets in silence, people crying, others with hands gripping their mouths in grief and disbelief.

Eventually the hearses took the coffins to the city of Hilversum, so forensic teams at the Korporaal van Oudheusden barracks could begin the task of identifying the bodies. Holland has taken charge of this task, logical, given that 193 of the victims were Dutch. Already the first of the bodies have been identified but it will be a slow and painstaking task that could take months.

Over the next days in Eindhoven, the same solemn procession was repeated; Thursday the remains of 70 people were brought to the airforce base, Friday 75 and Saturday 38. Each day the crowds turned out to line the route to honour the dead, each time the same despairing expressions on their faces.

The Dutch showed great dignity in their grief. It was a fitting tribute, so very different from those awful corrupt days immediately after the tragedy. The pictures are still ingrained in our minds from that field of debris near the village of Hrabove. The wreckage that one daren't look too closely at in case it revealed body parts, so dreadfully incongruous with the delightful sunflower fields all around.

Nor will we forget the images of hard-hearted men walking arrogantly through the debris, a reminder for us of the lawless land in which those aboard the 777 had perished. Looting was endemic, grieving families forced to cancel credit cards and finding strange men answering their loved one's cell phones when, for some sorrowful reason, they rang their numbers. That the bodies of those poor people have been treated abominably there is no doubt. It makes us re-examine that desire from deep within our core to see our loved ones put to rest with peace and care and attention. Part of us knows they are dead and it makes no difference to them. But it does to us. And the failure of those men swaggering around MH17's wreckage to adhere to this most basic of human decency didn't just horrify us; it scared us and made us wonder what forces were at play here.

Those grim forces have become clearer in the ensuing days. That

298 lives were savagely ended by a surface-to-air missile appears certain. The evidence is not total but it is strong that Russian-backed rebels mistakenly brought down the 777, thinking it was a Ukrainian military aircraft. The flight from Amsterdam to Kuala Lumpur was cruising at 33,000 feet, high enough that only a high-tech missile system could take it down. The only such systems known to be in the area were Buk missiles under the control of the rebels. The day MH17 was shot from the sky, Associated Press journalists reported seeing a Buk missile system in the area. The Economist reported how on July 17 a Buk missile launcher was seen on various social media moving towards Snizhne, about 80km from the rebel stronghold of Donetsk and close to where the aircraft was shot down. Meanwhile, America says a missile was launched from the area just before the aircraft was destroyed. Sources have told media that the same night of the tragedy, the Buk missile launcher crossed the border, back into Russia.

So who was responsible? Three pro-Russian rebel leaders are suspected, based on discussions which reportedly occurred shortly after the plane was shot down. The Guardian named "Igor Girkin", also known as "Igor Strelkov", an alleged Russian intelligence agent dubbed "the rifleman", leading the military forces of the self-declared "Donetsk People's Republic"; and Igor Bezler, a notorious loose cannon who the newspaper says rules the town of Horlivka with an iron fist. A third suspect is a Cossack commander, Nikolai Kozitsyn.

Girkin, more commonly referred to as Strelkov, a moustached, cold-eyed man, is seen as the rebels' military commander-in-chief. Also a Russian citizen, he has served in Chechnya, Serbia and Trans-Dniester in the Russian military. The EU believes he works for Russia's military intelligence - the GRU - and has placed him under sanctions.

Shortly after the plane went down, a Russian social networking page that had been uploading messages from Strelkov, published a post saying rebels had shot down a plane outside Torez, near the location of the wreckage of MH17. The post, which was later deleted, appeared to incorrectly identify the aircraft as an AN-26 military transport plane. "We warned you not to fly in our skies," it read. Rebel leaders later denied their forces had shot down the plane. Ukrainian authorities released recordings of what they said were intercepted phone conversations between rebel leaders. In the first, a voice claimed to be Bezler's says a rebel group had shot down a plane and was investigating the crash site. In the second, a rebel commander reports that Cossacks shot down what was later discovered to be a "100 per cent civilian aircraft" and that documents of an Indonesian student had been found. The first rebels to reach the scene can be heard swearing when they saw the number of bodies and the insignia of Malaysia Airlines. The US has backed the authenticity of these tapes.

Early indications of the data on the 777's black box back up the missile theory. The missile appeared to explode near the aircraft, showering it with shrapnel. CBS News reported that black box data points to a massive explosive decompression with the molten metal smashing open the plane's fuselage.

The loss of MH17 was unusual; it was brought down in a war zone – worse, a no-man's land patrolled by rebels. Rational rules no longer applied. There has been justified outrage at independent authorities' inability to get access to the bodies and to evidence before it was contaminated. BBC News reported that footage showed cranes lifting large sections of the fuselage. A video emerged showing pro-Russian rebels shortly after the crash searching through wreckage and the personal belongings of those on board. Monitors from the Organisation for Security and Co-operation in Europe (OSCE) have visited the site and suggested to BBC World Service that major pieces of the aircraft appeared to have been moved or tampered with and in some cases even "cut into". Normal practice for a crash site - just as with a crime scene - is to secure it so evidence won't be disturbed. Ten days after the accident that still hadn't occurred.

At the end of July when this book went to print, Holland was poised to lead the investigation and the Dutch Safety Board said it would coordinate a team of 24 investigators from Ukraine, Malaysia, Russia, Germany, the United States, the United Kingdom, Australia and the International Civil Aviation Organization (ICAO). Despite the fact that the scene has obviously been compromised the board maintained it would still be able to gather "sufficient relevant information".

Another issue that needs serious investigation is whether the 777 should have been flying the route. On April 25, the Federal Aviation

Authority (FAA) issued a warning about flying over a narrow part of eastern Ukraine. There are many conflict areas around the world and commercial airlines fly over hot-spots all the time without incident. What appears to be lacking is any sort or firm all-encompassing directive. Rather, there is a signal given and the rest is left to airlines' discretion. Different countries interpret protocols in different ways. US carriers tend to be more conservative about the routes they fly over, while Qantas was one leading airline which acted on the warning. MH17 was about 200n/m from the area flagged by the FAA, and The International Air Transport Association, the airline industry's largest global trade organisation, came out soon after the tragedy, stating that the airspace MH17 was traversing "was not subject to restrictions".

But there were other warnings. Earlier in April, the European Aviation Safety Agency (EASA) described the region around Simferopol in Ukraine as an "unsafe situation" and suggested that "consideration should be given to measures to avoid the airspace and circumnavigate". Aviation writer William J McGee points out that also in April, EuroControl - the European Organisation for the Safety of Air Navigation noted that "traffic in the Ukraine has reduced significantly since February 2014." Also ICAO, a United Nations agency that is supposed to develop global aviation standards, said shortly after the downing of MH17 it had issued a prior warning. Its notice pointed out "the possible existence of serious risks to the safety of international civil flights." ICAO also noted "alternative routings are available for those operators choosing to avoid the Simferopol [region]."

Malaysia Airlines could have, if it had chosen to, avoided the route, deviating a little which would have taken longer and cost more in fuel. It is unlikely Malaysia Airlines - or any other airline - will make the same mistake again. The airline must take some culpability - as does the ICAO - for the fact that MH17 was flying so close to a known combat zone.

Some of the Dutch who bought tickets on the flight probably did so with the airline Malaysia Airlines was code-sharing with - KLM Royal Dutch Airlines. The tragedy raises the question of what duty of care the Dutch airline has to oversee a code-share partner operating a flight with a KLM flight number.

International outrage over the tragedy has been swift with Russian president Vladimir Putin the main target. Putin is facing a multi-million-pound legal action for his alleged role, according to Britain's The Sunday Telegraph. British lawyers are preparing a class action against the Russian president through the American courts. Senior Russian military commanders and politicians close to Putin are also likely to become embroiled in the legal claim. London lawyers McCue & Partners have already flown to Ukraine for discussions about how to bring the case and where it should be filed. Victims' families will be invited to join the action. The case will inevitably highlight Russia's role in eastern Ukraine and how rebels in Ukraine came to possess the Buk missile launcher.

Political reaction has been strong too, with the European Union looking to increase sanctions against Russia as feeling builds that some sort of watershed moment may have arrived. Douglas Alexander, British shadow foreign secretary, said Europe faces "a moment of reckoning" in how it responds to Russia.

Russia has responded to criticism from Europe and the US with ominous fighting talk. The Russian Foreign Ministry issued a strongly-worded statement against the United States, in response to White House criticism of "Russian complicity" in the downing of the flight. "Judging by the relentless slander campaign against Russia organised by the American administration, they are being more and more guided by blatant lies when pursuing their foreign policy," the ministry said.

That is about as strong as it gets and should sound some alarm bells about the stability of Putin's Russia. To what degree tensions will escalate from that brutal act in the eastern Ukraine on July 17, we can only guess. The shooting down of an airline carrying civilian passengers has catapulted the Russia-Ukraine conflict into an international context. With so many potential flash points, it needs to be handled carefully or else there is potential for significant escalation in this military conflict.

None of this should detract from the ordeal Holland and its people are going through, nor the many hundreds of other people from around the world related to those killed. As the bodies at last are retrieved, identified and restored to their families, the relatives at least have one small consolation. Their loved ones are mostly accounted for and in time will be accorded a burial. Their death was brutal and horrible, but at least the remains of most will be found.

The same cannot be said for the passengers of MH370. As this book is printed, nearly 150 days since 227 people innocently left a departure lounge and 12 crew members went to work at Kuala Lumpur International Airport, they are still lost. Their families and friends have no memorial at which to visit their loved ones. No certainty where they lie.

They can only wonder.

Chapter 1

The Airport

It's not a night for standing around on the airport concourse.

Passengers dropped off outside Kuala Lumpur International Airport move with a quiet efficiency, subconsciously anticipating the refuge the air conditioning in the terminal will provide.

March 7, late summer, the heat is extreme, suffocating. It reached 36 degrees today and although the temperature has dropped just below 30 the humidity is still deadly.

Despite the late hour - it's after 10pm - the drop-off zone is still busy.

A family unloads luggage from the boot of the car, the children squabbling, vying to be the first to manhandle the suitcases. A grim-faced Chinese businessman with a small suitcase towed behind, obviously a seasoned traveller, passes them without a glance, caught up in his own worries. Behind them a Chinese family repeatedly hugs a young woman who has dropped them off. She farewells them, attentive yet anxious to get moving, aware of other vehicles lining up to get into her spot.

The air is sickeningly still. Forty metres away from the terminal entrance, on the other side of the concourse, two dozen flags signifying the world's airlines hangs limply, as if the heat has got to them too.

Despite the pedestrians straying on to the road and vehicles hovering, looking for spaces, a few cars race past disturbingly fast, as if it's the open road. A cleaner in some sort of uniform; red shirt and black trousers, carrying a small broom and shovel ambles casually across the road, forcing a car at his back to slow down. The driver, perhaps sensing his excessive speed, resists tooting the horn. A policeman, straddling his motorbike parked arbitrarily on the edge of the road, shares a joke with someone on the other end of his cell phone.

One by one, group by group, towing, hauling, shoving suitcases, they all make their way past the big block golden letters KLIA at the entrance of the terminal. Hundreds of others have arrived internally on the train from KL Sentral, swallowed up in this huge airport which processes up to 40 million passengers a year. Their train stops a floor below and passengers take the lift up. Malaysia Airlines Flight 370 - code sharing with China Southern Airlines CZ748 - is due to fly out at 12.40am bound for a 6.30am arrival in Beijing. The definition of a red-eye.

The international terminal at KL Airport makes a statement. It could almost be an opera house with its elaborate swooping timber canopies across the ceiling held up by huge cream darlek-shaped beams. Around the perimeter of the cavernous room are huge glass windows four or five storeys high. During the day, the natural light streams through into the terminal but at night all one sees is sky.

By this time of night, thousands of little lights peppering the ceiling have lit up, giving the magical appearance of stars, and many of the passengers' eyes are immediately drawn to the roof. Children are enchanted by it and point skywards. It's a generous terminal. One is swallowed up by the size of the room. Even at this hour there are more than a thousand people standing or walking in random directions, yet there are few collisions. Passengers or visitors entering the vast arena are immediately drawn into the scene, pulled into the action only an airport can create. The thrill of anticipation of imminent travel to an exotic place, the buzz of hundreds of simultaneous voices, the kinetics of excited children, conversations and laughter in myriad languages and accents drift past the ear; Chinese, Malay, Indian, Arabic, English. People pushing luggage trollies, people standing lizard still, craning necks to departure screens, standing in groups, standing alone, standing in patient lines, pointing, checking pockets, opening wallets, zipping carry bags. All of the buzz augmented by the incessant melodic four-note bong of the PA system followed by a woman's echoed voice repeating a boarding call or the name of a lost passenger.

There's no mistaking where the passengers are tonight. Every third woman wears a hajib befitting this strongly Muslim city dotted with thousands of mosques, from each emanating the Imam's haunting call to prayer repeated from early morning to evening.

Beijing-bound passengers pause at the terminal entrance, then take baby steps as they scan for the holy grail, the relevant check-in area, searching for the familiar red and blue of Malaysia Airlines. They are anxious to get in quick to beat others to the queue, ready to deviate at speed when they spot their target. The correct check-in counter located, they point and accelerate, hauling suitcases, looking back to check loved ones are not lost in the slipstream, beating a path to Malaysia Airlines C1-C18. Economy class check-in.

Malaysia Airlines check-in staff wear green hajibs, one in yellow, probably a supervisor. The women all wear the airline's long trademark eye-catching figure-hugging dresses, teak with a pink floral pattern, drawing men's eyes to them.

By now a large crowd has gathered, queuing for the three open counters, luggage close by and snaking untidily beside them as only baggage in airport check-in lines can do.

Airports are really just a glamorous bus stop or train station. A snapshot of humanity on the move - each person at their own moment on life's path, but for a short time thrust into a group, their being indelibly entwined with hundreds of strangers. All going somewhere. Leaving someone or going to someone. Emotions often run high, paradoxically boredom often pervades. People on their respective journeys, they have a place to go and they just need to get there. Life is fast these days. There's very little choice in the matter. Any hesitation would be met with crooked looks and scoffs. They must trust in the airline they have chosen, they must have faith in the ability and professionalism of the flight crew. All they can do is trust. That uneasy deal sealed with the ticket purchase, they proceed and put apprehension and doubts to the back of their mind. For the time being they will have no control over their own destiny. They suck it in and put their lives in someone else's hands.

The 227 passengers bound for Beijing are heavily dominated by Chinese - 153 of them - and to a lesser extent, Malaysians. Many of the Chinese heading home after holidays reflect the country's burgeoning middle class, these days more open to tourism and experiencing the world.

Some are returning from their first trip abroad. For others, it is just another connecting flight, for another meeting, for another deal to nail down in this busy, increasingly prosperous part of the world.

But take a handful of humanity anywhere and you'll come up with an array of nationalities. There are people from 13 other countries among the bags and trollies hovering around the check-in counter, their voices betraying their nationality to those standing near.

Seven Indonesians, six Australians, five Indians, four French, three Americans, two each from the Ukraine, Canada, Iran and New Zealand as well as passengers from Holland, Russia, Taiwan and Hong Kong.

Eclectic is just a word; it doesn't do justice to the randomness of this crowd of cultures, religions, age and backgrounds: Chinese tour groups, honeymooners, businesspeople, academics, engineers, drifters searching for a better life, young students in love, retired couples following their dreams, and children following their harried parents.

Some of these people's stories have since been broadcast around the world through a staggering array of media organisations.

Many have been the subject of headlines in newsprint and on websites, their faces staring back at us, now vaguely familiar. Faces often smiling, unaware of course of what is ahead. That moment when the reader thinks "if only they knew".

Through the generosity of their loved ones who have shared flakes of their lives, we feel as though we have almost got to know some of them.

Through the skill of so many media organisations we are able to tell some of their stories, just a snapshot of their lives reflected on this balmy night in this manic Asian city.

Loudest by some distance is a group of about 30 Chinese, many of whom are artists. Most of the party has checked in already and are waiting metres away for their colleagues in a chaotic chattering circle. An explosion of high-spirited nasal voices that disconcerts westerners trying to queue in orderly fashion. They had arrived by bus, the Chinese group, earlier than most of their fellow passengers and on a mission to ensure their precious cargo was well packed.

Many of the group are in their 60s or 70s and some are quiet, the length of the day now starting to get to them. They had a big night last night, many up late celebrating with a few too many drinks the end of an immensely successful three-day art and calligraphy exhibition. The Chinese Dream: Red and Green Painting art exhibition celebrated the 40th anniversary of diplomatic ties between China and Malaysia.

The end of the show was worth celebrating. For some artists and calligraphers it was their first venture out of their country and anticipation was high.

It was a lifelong dream for a woman such as Madam An Wenlan, 65, who had fallen in love with painting late in life. The New Straits Times told the story of how the former nurse started to take painting seriously in 2010, after she was rudely prohibited from taking photographs of a peony painting hanging in a restaurant in the eastern Chinese city of Hangzhou. She swore that she would one day paint something just as beautiful. She soon made her way specialising in realistic paintings of flowers like peony and plum blossom. Now here she was among a group of famous Chinese artists, probably barely able to believe where she was.

For most, the exhibition and conference had been memorable. Still, it would be good to get home. On the bus out of KL central business district, they stopped for a meal at a Chinese restaurant. Associated Press told how they deliberately chose a restaurant that served halal food to make things easier on the group's lone Muslim, who had rarely been able to eat with the larger contingent. That man was Uighur artist Mehmet Abula who hailed from the remote city of Kashgar in the Turkish-influenced, far north-west Chinese province of Xinjiang. Kuala Lumpur was his first trip outside China. The 35-year-old oil painter and teacher, married with a young daughter, had had a successful trip and won an award for his work during the exchange.

The group had high regard for Abula who years earlier had pursued his talent by making a courageous trip to Beijing to study for a year at the Chinese Academy of Oil Painting. Think fish out of water. A country boy with dark brooding good looks, adjusting to the push of crowds and the noise of this massive bustling city. Throwing his fears aside to pursue the dream. His art. A CNN report said that during that year he virtually lived off instant noodles because there was no Muslim food. His fellow artists' restaurant choice in his honour would have meant a lot to a humble man like Abula. He was part of the team. He'd been looking forward to going home - last night he called his wife from the hotel in anticipation of seeing his family soon. And the acceptance from his fellow artists has been a fine way to end the trip.

Over lunch, the trip to KL is relived with stories and laughs, and with more drinks digested, spirits and energy levels lift. Chatter and laughter increases in volume as they re-board the bus for the last leg to the airport, savouring the fact that home now is within reach, tantalisingly close. They will have stories to tell when they get there. As the bus driver negotiates the KL traffic where lane changes come without warning or hesitation and vehicles routinely pass within millimetres of each other, the passengers relax; the bus is as safe as a tank amongst the cars. Associated Press reported how Li Rusheng, 76, the charismatic famous calligrapher and elder statesman of the party, leads a singalong. Most are singing and clapping and even the most reserved break the shackles for a few minutes.

It is typical from the larger-than-life Rusheng; a man who, according to the Telegraph, once movingly blogged about the way he wanted to live a "joyous and fulfilling" life after a tough start. "I love to sing and to run in the rain," he had written. "My wife says I am an old child who loves singing, drinking and going barefoot." Life had been hard for him; a terrible childhood caught up in the Japanese invasion of 1938, a number of serious motor vehicle accidents and a bad heart condition. "After these narrow escapes, I have come to cherish life more. I have become more open-minded and more detached." He spoke of how he continued to find new passions as he aged - surely an inspiring example to any retiree. "Even as I am approaching 70, I like new things. In my spare time, I have learned how to drive, how to use a computer, and I study photography and production."

As the bus stops at the airport concourse, the group waits impatiently for their luggage to be unloaded from the hold. The chatter subsides and a sense of purpose takes over. They are feeling the heat and they are anxious to get on with the task of packing their delicate art works with the extreme care needed to avoid any damage during the flight.

In another part of the airport, and in stark contrast to the camaraderie of the Chinese group, New Zealander Paul Weeks is a solitary presence in the Malaysia Airlines Golden Lounge. Weeks transited in from a flight from Perth and rather than having to check in, is having a quiet drink and a snack as he waits for the flight. The 38-year-old's heart is heavy for wife Danica and sons Lincoln, 3 and Jack, 10 months, who are back in Perth. Weeks has been head-hunted for his dream job with Transwest Mongolia. The engineer has 28 days to look forward to in that country; an exciting opportunity - his first fly-in-fly-out job - but with it comes the hollowness of leaving his loved ones for such a long time.

But Paul Weeks wasn't going to go without showing his family how much he loved them all. So, in the last three days he crammed a lot in, taking Lincoln to the zoo, organising a special golf cart ride for the kids around a resort and playing some back-yard cricket. The Daily Telegraph reported how Weeks also hosted a family dinner with his mum and brother, spent almost an entire day bonding with his boys and finished painting the house. Paul and Danica had history and plenty of it. In 2010 the couple made headlines in New Zealand when Lincoln was delivered via emergency Caesarian on the same day of the 7.1 magnitude Christchurch earthquake. Much as he loved their 8ha picturesque property in Oxford, outside Christchurch, the quakes were a huge blow, as they were for thousands of others. Three years on, many of those who stayed in Canterbury are struggling to deal with the trauma. Paul and Danica Weeks weren't going to let that happen. They took fate into their own hands and made a decision to move with their baby to Perth for a new life.

Was it this special shared history of hardship that had made Weeks so aware of the significance of his departure? The day before he left he impulsively handed his wedding ring and watch to Danica. "If something should happen to me, then the wedding ring should go to the first son that gets married and then the watch to the second." Danica was initially indignant but respected his wishes. As Weeks now sits in the quiet business lounge, he takes a moment to send Danica and his kids one last email, telling them how much he is missing them.

Back in the main terminal, also in the check-in line, are nine members of a tour comprising mainly Chinese retired academics, whose story was also beautifully told by Associated Press. It includes three women, avid photographers coming home after a fortnight-long tour of Nepal, the highlight of which was a flight to see Mount Everest. The three women made the most of the trip, putting on bright clothing and scarves, ready for when the plane landed with Mount Everest in the background. "They loved to be photographed, and they were dressed for photos," said Wang Dongcheng, a retired professor of Chinese Literature who was on the Everest flight with the three. "They were very beautiful." One, 62-year-old Ding Ying, had been a cheerful, talkative presence throughout the tour, always telling jokes. Another, Chen Yun, said one of her Everest photos might be the best she had ever taken. The third, Yang Xiaoming, spoke about how much she'd learned in Nepal, and how she was thinking of going on an upcoming tour to England, Ireland and Iceland.

After a lifetime of work, so many carefree adventures ahead.

Check-in queues are never family friendly, and youthful grandparents Dai Shuling and Jiao Wenxue, still in their 50s, are doing their best to help entertain two-year-old Moheng. They take turns picking him up alongside his parents, son-in-law, Wang Rui and their daughter Jiao Weiwei.

Wang Rui works in the Beijing office of Boston Consulting Group and Jiao Weiwei at a software company. New Strait Times told how the couple had told parents at Moheng's day-care centre the family was getting away from Beijing's smoggy air for a while. The family has had an enjoyable month-long vacation in the heat of Malaysia's summer.

Other families are separated and struggling with it. The Economic Times told the story of two working class Sumatrans on the trip of a lifetime. Indonesian couple Sugianto Lo and his wife Vinny Chynthya Tio are far from relaxed. The couple - both 47 - have never been separated from their three children and they are doing it hard. They placed a lot of responsibility in their eldest son Antonio to look after his two siblings. Should they have? The trip is a blessing and a curse. Travel has never been a possibility for the working class couple whose priority has always been getting their children through college. Then suddenly a friend bought them a trip to China and they took it. Only now at the airport is the worry about their children beginning to weigh them down. They both know they should be making the most of this moment and yet still they worry.

Imagine the nerves of a couple who have never yet been on a plane.

But Kuala Lumpur local Norli Akmar Hamid, 33, and her husband Razahan Zamani, 24, have been through hard times after Norli had a miscarriage. The couple, who met in a supermarket and married in 2012, are taking this delayed honeymoon to Beijing partly to help Norli get over the trauma. It is a much-needed journey but also a jump out of their comfort zone.

While many congregate in groups and chatter, Pouria Nour Mohammad Mehrdad is alone and pensive with a backpack and a laptop. He and his older friend Reza Devalar are checking in apart to avoid suspicion; they are both nervous and Pouria wants to avoid standing out in the crowd. The 18-year-old Iranian lad misses his mother Niloufar who two years ago fled Teheran after suffering abuse from Pouria's father. Niloufar took her youngest son Ilia, 14, with her and settled in Germany, but had trouble getting Pouria out of Iran because of his age. He has longed to join her and now, as she battles breast cancer, he can wait no longer. He has left his city of Karaj and taken a stab at freedom. In desperation he and Devalar saved money to pay for passports and tickets that would get them out of Asia and into the promised land of Europe to start a new life. Devalar is hoping to make it to Sweden. Pouria hopes to get asylum once he makes it to Germany.

An Iranian man named Ali was to provide Austrian and Italian passports and tickets; the pair needed to go to Kuala Lumpur and wait for someone to deliver them. They'd expected the process to take a few days but it dragged on for a week, during which time they grew more agitated and struggled with money. Eventually, they needed another place to stay for a night for free. Pouria contacted Mohammad Mallaeibasir, an old school friend from the same year during his Teheran days. He was hugely relieved when the good-natured Mallaeibasir agreed and on Thursday night before the flight Nouria and Reza gratefully crashed at Mallaeibasir's house.

They spent most of the evening watching movies in the lounge with Mallaeibasir and his room mate, and during the evening went into the kitchen to call Ali. He had what they needed.

Late on Friday night Mallaeibasir drove them to the airport.

Pouria's plan is to transit through Beijing and then fly onwards to Amsterdam and then Frankfurt. He has emailed his mother his plans and she will meet him at the airport in Frankfurt. What a joyous moment that will be. He tries not to look behind to search the line for his friend and breathes deeply so that his anxiety with using his new passport doesn't overtake him. He must stay calm. This is his one and only chance. He and his friend have no idea about the reliability of the passports they have paid for. If they aren't what they are supposed to be they could look forward to a hellish trip back to Iran and a future that doesn't bear thinking about. His life will be over. He is terrified.

Chapter 2

Departure Time

There's a liberation in checking in and being handed one's boarding pass. Everyone feels it. There's a moment of concern as the tickets and passports are checked. Maybe there's something wrong? But then the transaction progresses normally. Soon they will be flying. You can see it in their body language, the way they wheel away from the counter, liberated of luggage and ready to explore the terminal.

There is no exception tonight. The Chinese artists are splintered into four or five noisy groups, drifting towards shops behind the queue they've been part of. Some stand and wait, others go over arm in arm to look at them. Sembonia, a clothes shop, attracts most of them, while a couple buy something at the Chocolate Fantasy stand. Once checked in and free of suitcases, most passengers waste little time gathering themselves and heading through to the first passport and boarding pass check; no-man's land where only passengers can pass. It's a natural instinct to keep moving now that their access has been approved.

But four Australians in their fifties don't seem to be rushing. All checked in, they now browse shops on their way through the airport and enjoy a joke. These are times to savour. Rod and Mary Burrows from Brisbane and their friends Bob and Cathy Lawton from Springfield Lakes are enjoying each other's company as they prepare for the trip they had planned together. Here are four friends doing what solid hard-working people should be able to do at this age: travel and explore. Love life.

Rod and Mary Burrows from Brisbane, have three adult children, two daughters and a son, and are expecting their first grandchild in April. Rod Burrows planned the trip to China after being laid off last year, and Mary took long-service leave from her position with the

Queensland Police. The couple plan extensive travel, and want to head to the United Kingdom later this year. Meanwhile the trip is a special one for the Lawtons who are passionate travellers. Cathy has serious health problems. Bob told his boss at Sharp Plywood he was taking five weeks' long-service leave to give Cathy a trip to Malaysia and China to celebrate her birthday "before she lost her eyesight".

They are only a week into the trip, having started in Malaysia. After Beijing they are going to Hong Kong to take a cruise down the coast of Vietnam. Long-time friends of theirs, Les and Karen Stonehouse had been to Vietnam and media reported how shortly before the Lawtons left they visited the couple and looked at their photos. It was exciting to see what was in store for them. The Lawtons had a thing about eating chicken in China. They joked with the Stonehouses that eating chicken there was their biggest concern; they wouldn't be going near it.

After going through passport control, the passengers head down an escalator to a floor below.

At the immigration desk, a large queue forms in economy. This time, bags and people are X-rayed. Past the scrutiny of airport officials, passengers pick up their carry-on bags and laptops. There's something disconcerting about filling up plastic trays with laptops, carry bags, wallets, keys, cellphones. Once through, passengers regroup, pat their pockets and triple check in case they've forgotten something. They find themselves face to face with a Duty Free Shop and indecision. Is this their best chance to get what they need for gifts back in Beijing or will there be a better opportunity? Some travellers take the plunge and Duty Free staff approach to help and make a sale, while their friends wait. Others walk on.

On their left is a series of wooden cases, much like bookshelves, where little models of planes are mounted on orange silk. Walk a bit further to the right and passengers come across much bigger models of planes, a metre in length, mounted on steel tripods. The various airlines showing off their latest models. Shiny, immaculate, all the different airlines' colours represented. A young boy's paradise.

As they walk past all of this, anticipation is sweet for Gu Naijun and Li Yuan. They are excited and they deserve to be. They are going to see their gorgeous daughters back in China. Theirs is a story of two people who fell in love, worked hard, took a chance and got dealt a bad hand from life. All the same they are fighting back and still full of optimism. The Sydney Morning Herald described how the couple, who took the anglicised names Carlos and Carrie, met as university students in Sydney, fell in love and married. The couple bought a home in the southern Sydney suburb of Sylvania, and the Metro petrol station at nearby Miranda in 2007. But their financial situation turned bad following a terrible accident at the petrol station, when an electrician was electrocuted after he fell from a ladder while installing an air conditioner. The business went under and the bank repossessed their home, forcing the couple to move into a smaller, rented apartment.

This plucky couple didn't give up. Li Yuan branched out into a software business. Temporarily, as they re-established themselves, their daughters went to stay with their Chinese relatives. For these hard workers who refuse to be beaten by bad luck, seeing their gorgeous girls again will be just reward for their stoicism. There's an unmistakable speed in their steps as they make their way to the next stage of their journey.

As the passengers continue further they start splitting up to go to various fingers of the terminal. H, C, G, A and D. Beijing-bound passengers need to take a short train ride to C. A big group waits for it to arrive, lining up behind the yellow line, anxious not to miss out on a place, some ditching their trollies hurriedly as they do so. They pile on. It's a strange little train; there are no seats which momentarily surprises passengers. A couple of the Chinese laugh to each other. It's standing only. You just stand with little hand holders attached from the ceiling. The train comes out from under the terminal and they get a clear view outside across the expanse of runways. The train then slips underground, taxiway above their head. They come out into the open again and now they can see C on their left, including their own gate C1. Planes are parked outside and they can see bright orange lights from the maintenance and baggage vehicles. Two or three families point, arguing about which big Malaysia Airlines plane is theirs. They never resolve it before the train goes underground again and ends its three-minute ride in a clear plastic tunnel where they are disgorged into a new lounge. Members of clubs such as Qantas or Malaysia Airlines go upstairs to the Malaysia Airlines Golden Lounge to relax before it is time to go their gate. On the immediate left is a bar, while there are several places to get food and hundreds of vacant comfortable seats around tables. Some economy passengers take the opportunity for a quick bite at Burger King, while others check out the shops below it; perfumes and cosmetics, Bobby Brown, Hermes - a bag and shoe store, Ralph Lauren, Versace, Salvatore Ferragano, Victoria's Secret.

Somehow, the-top-of the range shops sweeten the moment. They are getting close, it's getting exciting for them. The last obstacle now is one last boarding pass check followed by a security check. Some waste little time making their way to the departure lounge, as if willing the flight to come sooner so they can sleep on the plane and be home before they know it. Others take their time.

An hour before the flight and the departure lounge for C1 is crowded. It's a nice well-turned-out long rectangular lounge; orange carpet with yellow patterns, black padded vinyl seats in six rows and a couple of large flat screen TVs. Of the 200 people in the lounge, a quarter have their heads down examining smart phones or tablets. Some are talking quietly, making calls to loved ones on their smart phones, others have used the two pay phones right outside the departure lounge. Indonesian couple Sugianto Lo and Vinny Chynthya, still fretting about their children, have already called twice from the airport. Now they are still busily backing it up with a text to their oldest son Antonio to ensure he will come home early enough in the evening to look after his younger brother and sister. Uighur painter Abula, who teaches art at Kashi Normal School back in his home province, finds a quiet moment away from the group of artists and calls a friend of his. "How are you guys?" he asks. "We are all at the school, waiting for your return," the friend said.

Chennai resident Chandrika Sharma, an NGO worker heading to Mongolia for a conference, always calls her mother before flying. Chandrika, director of the International Collective in Support of Fishworkers, is married and has a daughter at university in India. Earlier, she called her mother to tell her about the trip she was on the point of taking, and now she calls from the departure lounge to remind the 88-year-old to take her medicines.

Just before midnight, the flight number is called and with a buzz of anticipation and movement the passengers are asked to board in the usual fashion; business class first and then groups of rows are called. Some passengers rise to their feet immediately, others look around in confusion, not having heard the announcement properly, while a few decide to wait it out and relax a few minutes more, knowing their moment will come to board soon anyway.

Gradually the attractive departure lounge empties out. Flight MH370 to Beijing will soon be on its way.

Chapter 3

Take-Off

Flight attendant Mohd Hazrin Mohamed Hasnan sits back in the Malaysia Airlines Crew Lounge in the terminal and composes himself. He's a good-looking muscular young man. He doesn't say a lot but is quick with a smile and tends to be popular with women. Not anymore though. He's married with a three-year-old daughter, and his wife Intan Maizura Othaman, also a flight attendant, is due to give birth to a baby in May. The crew lounge, a place for cabin crews to relax and get ready before entering the aircraft, is crowded. Hazrin is a little late. The Malaysian media told the story of how Hazrin a couple of hours earlier, had missed the bus provided by the airline for its staff. It was unusual for him to even be on the flight; he usually flew on the European and Australian routes but was called in to replace a colleague on MH370. Hazrin was supposed to fly off to Paris on Sunday, but instead tonight he found himself on the Beijing red-eye.

Annoyed with himself for missing the bus and anxious not to be late for the flight, he had to ask his heavily-pregnant wife to take him to the airport. She didn't hesitate and he was grateful. They chatted in the car and when they arrived Hazrin held her hand and kissed it. "I love you", he said. Now with some of the other members of the mainly male flight crew, he sits in the crew lounge and moves into work mode.

In another part of the crew lounge Kuala Lumpur local Foong Wai Yueng is her usual bubbly self. Anyone not feeling at their best gets an instant lift when they see her arrive. The attractive flight attendant with a short bobbed hairstyle and an engaging smile is in her element. She loves to fly, she loves to travel and Malaysia Airlines has been her life. Foong Wai married her first boyfriend Lee Khim Fatt. They have been together for 20 years and now have a 10-year-old son and four-year-old daughter. She doesn't like being away from the kids at nights but she doesn't let it change her demeanour. Foong Wai joined Malaysia Airlines 18 years ago as a bright eyed 18-year-old. She still has those same bright eyes.

Chief Steward Angri Nari is highly organised and looking immaculate as always in his grey suit and waistcoat, blue tie and spectacles. The well respected 49-year-old is a veteran and has been with Malaysia Airlines for 25 years now. Nari, from Sibu, Sarawak originally, is well liked. Married to a former flight attendant, he has two children.

He is a mad Liverpool football fan and is enjoying the Merseysiders' return to form this season as for the first time in years they are in contention to win the English Premier League. He loves his German Shepherd and his music. Anyone who loves Dire Straits and Pink Floyd is the man you want to be sitting next to at a dinner table. But there's another side to Andrew Nari; he's also an intensely religious man, a man with some depth.

Brought up in the Roman Catholic faith, he worked as a tourist guide before studying to become a Catholic priest. He spent two years with Kuching seminary, before deciding it wasn't for him. Instead, he opted for something completely different. In 1989 he became a flight attendant with Malaysia Airlines.

Nari has done well with the airline. Fluent in English, he often flies to Western destinations such as Los Angeles and London. Tonight's the short trip to Beijing which he takes in his stride; he's a true professional. With the others ready, Nari leads the smart-looking group of flight attendants out of the crew lounge and into the terminal on the way to the C1 boarding gate. The good-looking group's progress doesn't go unnoticed as tends to happen with cabin crews. The women's classy tight dresses and the men in their well-tailored grey suits draw lingering looks from members of the public. The six-hour overnight flight to Beijing is not a particularly popular one, not one crew would go out of their way to volunteer for. It's tiring. Crew are only allowed to sleep on shifts of 12 hours or longer and there's a 24 hour turnaround before the staff have to fly again. The best part is getting a chance to shop in Beijing with the prospect of picking up some bargains to bring back to Malaysia.

Upstairs the flight crew, Captain Zaharie Ahmad Shah and his co-pilot Fariq Abdul Hamid, have headed to the pilot briefing room. They are an odd couple; they don't know each other very well. Zaharie, 53, is bald and stocky but it somehow suits him, adds to his appearance of authority. Zaharie is a 30-year-veteran pilot with Malaysia Airlines with 18,365 hours of flight time. He is obsessed with aviation and immensely experienced. In years gone by he has also flown Boeing 737s, Fokker F50s and Airbus A300s. As a pilot Zaharie is well respected. He is a certified flight simulator examiner with Malaysian Department of Civil Aviation, and today he is flying with a baby-faced 27-year-old who has been with the airline for seven years. In recent months Fariq has been transitioning to the 777, and has just been signed off after completing five flights under supervision. It's been an arduous few months. The ground course was hard work learning all the systems of the 777, followed by a number of flights in the highly sophisticated flight simulator in which he has had to endure numerous exams and mock simulated failures. Now it's time for the real thing. Tonight is his first as a fully-fledged 777 co-pilot but he's well ready for it.

It's a doubly exciting weekend for Fariq. On Sunday when he returns to KL he is due to sign up for an Audi 4 he has recently bought. Life is good.

In the pilot briefing room, a despatch officer who is managing a number of flights hands Zaharie a flight briefing envelope. It contains the flight plan; the route they will fly including waypoints which are imaginary signposts in the sky to guide aircraft. The flight plan includes the planned altitude and details on weather they will encounter on the flight and at the destination. It also includes fuel requirements, cargo manifest and passenger numbers.

The pair have a look through it and talk briefly about it. They don't know each other at all; they didn't request to fly together but were assigned for this flight. Zaharie is the old campaigner with the airline and all that entails; experience and at times an air of disillusionment. Fariq is at a completely different place on the curve; excited, ambitious and confident. Cocky enough that two years earlier he blatantly broke airline rules and brought two young women into the cockpit during a flight from Phuket to Kuala Lumpur where he and his co-pilot smoked and chatted them up. He got away with it. He's keen and excited about tonight's flight. Zaharie tells Fariq he should fly the sector. It makes sense, it's Fariq's first big flight in this role. A sector involves take-off and climb, enroute and then descent and landing. Fariq nods contentedly. Just what he wanted. The flight despatch officer also hands the pair information from the Operation Performance Tool for take-off. Thrust setting and V speeds for take-off have already been downloaded from flight despatch into the 777's Flight Management Computer (FMC). They're ready to go. Without a lot of talk the pair walk briskly through the final security clearance, raise their arms as they are checked and go through the gate at C1. Zaharie first and then Fariq.

About half an hour before the flight, Zaharie, wearing a green high visibility jacket does the walk around inspection of the plane. He walks up to the nose and goes methodically out to a wingtip, blocking his ears because of the roar of the auxiliary power unit at the back of the aircraft. Zaharie looks at the undercarriage, goes to the back of the plane and out to the other wingtip before, satisfied, re-entering to the cockpit where Fariq is waiting. The pair are then informed of final passenger numbers, confirmation of fuel upload and the aircraft's weight and balance to ensure the centre of gravity is correct. They check the maintenance technical log which lists any snags - technical issues that have been found on previous flights and what steps engineering has taken to fix them.

Airlines are obsessed with process. For the sake of safety and risk minimisation they live and breathe standard operating procedures. This involves check lists which Zaharie and Fariq now start systematically going through. Fariq calls out the item and Zaharie completes the action or confirms it has already been done.

They check that the flight plan has been correctly loaded into the FMC via the Aircraft Communications Addressing and Reporting System (ACARS), including tonight's standard instrument departure (SID). They check pilot oxygen masks, oxygen pressure in case of a depressurisation and that cabin pressurisation is set to automatic. Zaharie inspects the maintenance release, a document signed by the ground engineer showing the aircraft is fit to fly from a maintenance point of view.

Later during the taxi and as part of the pre-take-off checklist they do a take-off briefing in which Zaharie sets out tonight's SID procedure such as initial heading and altitude once airborne. He sets out that in case of an emergency, he takes over control. Lastly, Zaharie checks that the appropriate flaps setting for take-off has been selected. Out in the aircraft's cabin there is the usual pedestrian process as passengers board, clog aisles as they hesitate, craning their necks to find their seats and struggling to get hand luggage into the overhead lockers. The cabin crew watch patiently, direct lost passengers to seats and help others with their luggage. Slowly passengers begin to settle in. There is order. Finally, seats taken, seat belts clipped, passengers sit back impatiently and wait for the plane to take off.

Shortly, cabin crew will take passengers through the usual safety drills, content if they can get a third of the heads to look up and take notice.

At 12.25am Zaharie, who is doing communications while Fariq prepares to taxi, checks in with Air Traffic Control.

"Delivery MAS 370, good morning."

Ten seconds later ATC asks 370 to stand-by while it clears a flight to Frankfurt.

And then 17 seconds later ATC is back.

"MAS 370 request level." ATC asks what altitude they want.

"MAS 370, we are ready, requesting flight level three five zero to Beijing."

Air Traffic Control issues a standard instrument departure clearance, heading to the waypoint PIBOS, a departure with initial clearance to an altitude of 6000 feet, and assigns 2157 as the unique four-digit identifying code, known as a squawk code, which Fariq enters into the transponder, a radio transmitter in the cockpit that works with ground radar. When the transponder receives a signal from the secondary radar it returns the squawk code revealing the aircraft's position and altitude which will allow radar to identify and know it is 370.

At 12.27am, 370 is passed over to a new communication as per usual practice; Kuala Lumpur ground which will guide 370 on its taxi to runway 32R.

Also at 12.27am, as a tug attached to the nose-wheel pushes the 777 back into position - what's known in the trade as push back - one engine is started, followed quickly by the second. The tug then disconnects.

At 12.36am Kuala Lumpur Tower takes over transmission and at 12.38am allows 370 to enter runway 32 at Alfa 10.

"370 Line up 32 Right Alfa 10."

Fariq is doing the taxiing so Zaharie reads back as per protocol "Line up 32 Right ALFA 10 MAS370."

At 12.40am, Lumpur Tower clears MH370 for take-off.

"370 32, right, cleared for take-off . Good night".

"32 right, cleared for take-off MAS370. Thank you, bye," is the response from Zaharie.

Fariq handles the take-off and slowly increases the throttles, monitoring all engine gauges and set take-off thrust. As the speed builds at 80 knots Zaharie calls out "80 knots". Fariq confirms.

When the 777 reaches V1 speed, about 162 knots, Zaharie calls out "V1", and they both know at that point that they are committed to take-off. Zaharie announces VR (about 170 knots) and Fariq gently rotates the aircraft's nose upwards to take the 777 airborne.

When Fariq is satisfied that the aircraft is climbing appropriately he calls out "positive rate of climb, gear up" at which point Zaharie reaches across and pulls up the lever to start bringing the undercarriage up. Moments later, Zaharie contacts the departure controller who confirms that 370 is identified on secondary radar.

Control immediately passes over to Lumpur Approach, an operator based separately from the airport.

"Malaysian Three Seven Zero, good morning identified."

The operator gives 370 a slightly differing route from the standard instrument departure originally planned, a common enough event. On this occasion it's a direction to turn right towards a waypoint known as Igari to take a more direct route to Beijing. Zaharie acknowledges.

Passengers ease back in their seats. The momentary anxiety at the lack of control at take-off, gives way to the implacable faith all passengers must place in the giant bird transporting them. As MH370 ascends, window passengers see Kuala Lumpar's billions of lights below. It's not like some cities' blankets of never-ending lights. KL's lights are punctuated by pockets of darkness, areas of bush or waterways.

The lights fade from view. MH370 is on its way to Beijing.

At 12.46am MH370 is passed over to Lumpur Radar and the aircraft is cleared to 18,000 feet.

"Malaysian 370 Lumpur Radar, good morning. Climb flight level two five zero."

The cockpit reads back to acknowledge.

MH370 is now cleared to climb to 25,000 feet.

At 12.50am the operator asks 370 to continue its climb to an altitude of 35,000 feet.

The cockpit reads back to acknowledge.

At 1.01.14am MH370 reaches the required altitude and levels off: The flight crew confirm to Lumpur Radar that the aircraft has reached its initial cruising altitude, called top of climb. Twenty minutes have elapsed since take off.

The confirmation response from the operator: "Malaysian Three Seven Zero."

As the weather is good, the seat belt sign has been switched off. The cabin is darkened for take off but the window shades remain open. A few passengers have turned on their individual reading lights. As the aircraft settles into cruising altitude the crew start to prepare the galley for a drinks round followed by a late supper service. It's not unusual for the crew to keep the cabin quite warm on these night flights to encourage people to try to get off to sleep. Pillows and blankets were placed on their seats when they boarded and some now are using them. Most would have eaten while waiting for the flight in the terminal, saving themselves for a good sleep until breakfast service, two hours from arrival.

In business class, welcoming drinks are served about 20 minutes after take off. Snack and breakfast menus are distributed by the cabin crew but many of the passengers, having eaten in the lounge beforehand, turn it down. Paul Weeks, seated in a window seat in row 2, right at the front of business class, is one of them. They've all been given pillows, blankets and noise-cancelling headphones and most passengers indicate to the cabin crew they want to be woken for breakfast. Until then, they plan to sleep.

In economy, about 40 minutes into the flight, cabin crew members on both sides of the aisle are starting to bring the drinks trolley through the cabin. The Lawtons have window seats on the left-hand of the cabin, about half way down, seats 21A and C. The Burrows are directly behind them but it's hard to turn and talk over the seats so both couples are doing their own thing. Pouria - Christian Kozel according to his passport - is too excited to sleep. He's pinching himself that he has really has got on this flight and it really is in the sky. Pouria is in 30C while his friend, Luigi Maraldi, alias Reza Delevar, is four rows back. Throughout the flight they intend to keep up the pretence they don't know each other. It's too soon to drop their guard.

Some of the Chinese artists are sitting in row 31 in the middle seats and in the right window seats. Others are behind them, all the way back to Madam An Wenlan who has a window seat near the back in 40K.

Most passengers in business class are curled up in the dark but the few passengers who have chosen to eat have had their table dressed and snack delivered.

MH370 is flying over the South China Sea now.

At 1.19.24am it is time for the operator to pass MH370 over to the Ho Chi Minh City operator and he gives the appropriate frequency.

MH370 is about to enter a grey zone; a vulnerable area between the two nations' air traffic control. If there was a will to do so, it is the perfect place for an aircraft to disappear.

At 1.19.29am comes the response to KL, repeated around the world so many times since: "Good night, Malaysian Three Seven Zero."

The words come from Captain Zaharie Shah.

Chapter 4

Disappearing Act

At 1.21.13am - 90 seconds after Zaharie gives the final farewell, just after MH370 passes from Malaysian Air Traffic Control into Vietnamese airspace, the aircraft's two transponders stop working and MH370 disappears from the secondary radar screen at Lumpur Radar ATCC.

The weather is good and MH370 sends out no warning or distress signal. It just vanishes.

Minutes go by. After the KL operator hands MH370 over to Ho Chi Minh City control, MH370 is supposed to have checked in with Ho Chi Minh City Air Traffic Control Centre (HCM ATCC) but it has heard nothing. This is virtually unheard of. Normally the check in with the new air traffic control is done immediately as a matter of course.

Former chief pilot at Malaysia Airlines Nik Huzlan told Australian documentary Four Corners, a pilot wouldn't even hesitate. "Any pilot worth his salt, any pilot anywhere in the world. When you hand it over you switch frequency and in the case of a 777 you probably already have switched to a new frequency. I tell you, it's all done in one swoop."

No further radio communication is made by MH370 which either means all radios on board fail, or are deliberately switched off. It is important to note the 777 is a highly technical aircraft equipped with multiple communication devices including 3 VHF radios, 2 HF radios, 1 SATCOM unit and the two transponders.

What follows next is a bewildering delay in reacting to the loss of communication with MH370.

That Ho Chi Minh City (HCM) didn't contact Malaysia Airlines ATC within three or four minutes is astounding. That it took a full 17 minutes before, at 1.38am HCM finally tells KL ATCC that verbal contact has not been established with MH370 and the radar target has been lost is a travesty.

Apparently during this 17-minute period the Civil Aviation Authority of Vietnam has made its own efforts to contact MH370 and with no success and suspecting some sort of communication breakdown directly between MH370 and Vietnam Control, asks the pilot of another aircraft to try to make contact. The pilot is to relay a message to MH370 to contact Vietnam ATC.

Just after 1.30am a pilot of an aircraft bound for Narita, Japan, attempts to make contact and hears a weird mumble or noise seemingly coming from a stuck microphone from MH370. The pilot, who asks to remain anonymous, tells the New Straits Times that his plane was able to make contact using an emergency frequency.

"We managed to establish contact with MH370 just after 1.30am and asked them if they have transferred into Vietnamese airspace.

"There were a lot of interference ... static ... but I heard mumbling from the other end.

"That was the last time we heard from them, as we lost the connection."

At either HCM or KL's instigation, multiple attempts are made by other aircraft to contact MH370 but no response is received.

At 1.37am a signal revealing monitoring of the engines' performance that should have been transmitted from MH370's ACARS (Aircraft Communications Addressing and Reporting System) is not received at Rolls Royce in the United Kingdom and at Malaysia Airlines Operations. Signals are supposed to be half hourly, indicating that ACARS was turned off or somehow stopped working sometime between 1.07am and 1.37am.

Even once Ho Chi Minh City finally contacts KL ATCC at 1.38am there doesn't appear to be undue urgency.

In fact this is only the start of the dithering and incompetence.

At 1.41am KL responds that MH370 did not return to KL frequency.

The conversation continues until at 1.57am HCM informs KL that there was officially no contact with MH370. Attempts on many frequencies and by aircraft in the vicinity received no response from MH370. What follows is a delay during which there is confusion about whether MH370 has entered Cambodian airspace, a suggestion prompted by a Malaysia Airline source. Why it should have been even suggested is a mystery. MH370's flight plan has no mention of going into Cambodian airspace. It was an horrendous, unforgivable and also inexplicable mistake.

At 2.03am KL ATCC confirms with HCM that there was no radar contact and no verbal communications. Then KL ATCC relays this strange information received from Malaysia Airlines Operations (MA Ops) that the aircraft is in Cambodian airspace.

At 2.15am KL ATCC watch supervisors query MA Ops who inform them that MH370 was able to exchange signals with the flight and it was flying in Cambodian airspace.

By 2.18am HCM has checked and Cambodia advised that it had no information or contact with MH370. It was a red herring and a costly waste of time.

Despite this, the ridiculous misapprehension continues.

At 2.35am MA Ops even give MH370's supposed co-ordinates in Cambodian Air Space, despite the fact that they hadn't even tried to call MH370.

At 2.39am they finally try to do so on a Satellite phone - unsuccessfully.

Bizarrely, until 3.30am the myth about MH370 being in Cambodian air space is allowed to persist until MA Ops finally correct this and explain it had only been a projected position for the aircraft. Belatedly, KL ATCC contacts other air traffic control centres at Singapore, Hong Kong and Beijing to see if they have had any contact with MH370.

At 5.20am a Singapore staff member accurately states that based on known information "MH370 had never left Malaysian airspace". According to the transcripts in the preliminary report released by the Malaysian Government on May 1, it is not until 6.14am that KL ATCC queries HCM if SAR is activated. Hopelessly behind the 8-ball, Vietnamese authorities had initiated a search at 5.30am.

Four hours went by between the moment MH370 failed to report in when it was supposed to and the decision to mount a SAR operation.

The response was so cumbersome and hamfisted it was almost as if authorities had all decided to go to bed and worry about MH370 in the morning.

By 5.30am, the time when a SAR is finally initiated, MH370 is long gone. In fact it is still flying hundreds of miles to the west over the Indian Ocean.

At about 5.30am a desultory SAR effort is beginning on the path of its flight route along the South China Sea to Vietnam, Cambodia, Laos and China. The delay from the moment MH370 disappeared at 1.21am to the initiation of a SAR operation at about 5.30am is an abysmal failure. There appears to have been no real effort by authorities to explain this delay. Perhaps this is understandable. How can one explain the inexplicable?

Initially, a feeble attempt was made to cover up this four-hour gaffe. When questioned on the day by media about the delay, Department of Civil Aviation (DCA) chief Azharuddin Abdul Rahman said it was too dark to operate before that.

"We lost contact with the aircraft at 1.30am, and checked with air traffic controllers in the region who also confirmed that it was not on their radar. We then informed MAS (Malaysian Airline Systems) at 2.40am.

"We activated rescue control at 5.30am because we had to gather information and assistance from neighbouring countries. At 5.30am it is still dark. We went to the area (where the plane was last spotted on radar) at first light," he said.

It was the start of a fruitless search. They were quite simply searching the wrong sea. And the searches would continue valiantly but hopelessly for the best part of a week, all in vain.

The response to MH370's disappearance from the respective countries' air traffic control was clumsy and lethargic. It almost certainly wouldn't have saved their lives but passengers of MH370 were tragically, profoundly let down by air traffic control staff's appalling reaction to the aircraft's disappearance that morning. The one thing that could have helped them - a quick response from Malaysia's Air Force to its military radar - didn't. The military was nowhere to be seen.

Air traffic controllers were left floundering and were made to look ridiculous. But it is not all their fault. The biggest culprit in this sorry response to an aircraft's disappearance is Malaysia's military and it's monitoring of and reaction to what it saw on its primary radar. It is, quite simply, a scandal.

Chapter 5

The Radar Disaster

Primary radar was developed in the 1930s by a number of countries and first put to use by the British in the Second World War as a device to protect its shores. Broadly speaking, it sends out pulses of electro magnetic radiation that collect reflections which bounce off aircraft in the sky. According to some in the media modern systems can reach up to only 100 nautical miles (n/m) and it can't identify what an aircraft is but can plot its course and its rough altitude. The actual primary radar of the Malaysian defence force installations are naturally not openly discussed. After all, it's a matter of national security. But we do know they have confirmation that the last primary radar return of MH370 was 200n/m on the 295 radial from Malaysian Air Force Butterworth base. Clearly more than100n/m.

Air traffic controllers rely instead on secondary radar which is considerably more sophisticated. It sends out a signal to the aircraft which interrogates the aircraft's transponder. The transponder responds with a signal - the unique squawk code which identifies the aircraft, its height and course.

On March 8, MH370's transponders had stopped working, almost certainly deliberately turned off. The aircraft vanished from secondary radar at 1.21am and never reappeared. Much of the route to Beijing is well covered by secondary radar, but once the transponders were turned off, the only way initially to find MH370 was through primary radar.

The 777 aircraft operating MH370 is equipped with an Automatic Dependent Surveillance Broadcast function (ADSB), an innovation allowing an aircraft to interrogate a Global Positioning System (GPS) satellite and confirm its exact location in the world. The aircraft then send that information through to land-based stations. MH370 had

ADSB as part of its transponder suite but once the transponders were switched off it was disabled as well.

But MH370 wasn't invisible for long. As part of its responsibilities to the United Nations, Malaysia is part of the International Civil Aviation Organisation (ICAO). A central requirement is that Malaysia has its own Aeronautical Information Publication (AIP) which sets out its responsibilities with regard to aviation and in particular radar. Malaysia's AIP says except for some lower levels on the eastern cost, radar coverage in the Malaysian Peninsular is all but complete. The AIP lists in detail Malaysia's secondary and primary radar capability. In regard to primary radar, its assets include a 60n/m primary radar facility located to the south of Kota Bharu-Sultan Ismail Petra Airport runway and a 50n/m terminal approach radar at Butterworth in Penang. Within 50 or 60n/m these radar are accurate enough to be able to help aircraft to descend, but although accuracy drops away, their range is nearly twice that. At 100n/m they will probably be able to identify a target, and in fact we know that the primary radar based at Butterworth tracked the aircraft until it was some 200n/m from the base.

According to the Australian Transport Safety Bureau's (ATSB) Definition of Underwater Search report, at 1.25am, Malaysian primary radar, presumably based at Kota Bharu Airport on the east coast, picked up an unidentified aircraft - MH370 - making a turn over the Gulf of Thailand and heading back towards Malaysia.

Having picked up the blip on its radar, there's no reason to doubt that Malaysian authorities would have continued to watch the mysterious aircraft as it tracked from east to west towards Malaysian shores. The blip belonged to no filed flight plan yet it was allowed to head unmolested across the country. Near Kota Bharu, the aircraft turned south-west and flew along the Thai and Malaysian border and across the peninsula, travelling towards the southern tip of the island of Penang. The aircraft then turned north-west and we know from what little information was released by the Malaysian DCA that it was identified by primary military radar flying over Pulau Perak Island at 2.02am, some 89n/m from Butterworth base on a radial of 279 from Butterworth and along the Malacca Strait towards the Andaman Islands.

Near waypoint VAMPI the aircraft turned slightly more west and travelled towards waypoint MEKAR and the Nicobar Islands. Near waypoint MEKAR the aircraft turned again slightly and tracked further north-west towards waypoint IGOGU. The last primary radar location confirmation is at 2:22am on the 295 radial 200n/m from Butterworth base. From 1.25am until the time MH370 was lost from radar at 2.22am there is no evidence that any proactive contact was made with the DCA or that the matter was pushed up the chain to senior military command. If it was, they did nothing.

The first big question is why, when the aircraft didn't respond to attempts to communicate with it, were fighters not scrambled to follow the unidentified aircraft? It was a question raised by Emirates president Tim Clark at the International Air Transport Association annual meeting in Doha in early June.

"If you were to fly from London to Oslo, and then over the North Sea you turned off and then went west to Ireland, within two minutes you'd have Tornadoes, Eurofighters everything up around you," Clark told the Australian Financial Review.

"Even if you did that over Australia and the US, there would be something up."

The first suspicion is that Malaysian radar capabilities are not what they should be. Was the aircraft tracked at all or was radar not being monitored in real time? Was it only when military authorities checked their radar data later in the morning that they discovered the unidentified aircraft blip? Or were the radar operators asleep on the job?

The New York Times reported that there was a four-person team monitoring radar at Butterworth base. Perhaps they were playing a game of poker?

Significant investment appears to have gone into Malaysian radar systems in recent years. In 2010, the country's Defence Ministry announced that it had bought two Czech-made Vera-E passive surveillance radars for RM7.2 million three years earlier.

Deputy Defence Minister Abdul Latiff Ahmad told the Malay Mail at the time, the purchase of the highly-advanced Vera-E, to detect aircraft, ships and ground vehicles, was "to protect the country's air space."

Zetro Aerospace is one of Malaysia's biggest defence contractors specialising in avionics. It holds three government contracts for maintenance and repair of aircraft radios, airborne radar, air traffic control and air defence communications, radar and navigational aids. It received a RM43 million contract to modernise the radar systems at two Royal Malaysian Air Force (RMAF) bases in Kuantan and Butterworth in 2005. More recently, last year, ThalesRaytheonSystems (TRS) heralded that it had provided the Malaysian Ministry of Defence with an enhanced national command and control system.

"The C2 system we've executed in Malaysia represents technological integration at its best," said Kim Kerry, CEO of US Operations for ThalesRaytheonSystems.

However, there is more to a top-notch radar system than just possessing the equipment, according to an analyst.

"Equipment does not equal capability," Tim Huxley, executive director of Singapore-based security think-tank the International Institute of Strategic Studies - Asia told the Wall Street Journal. "There are so many other elements: logistical support, training, morale, integration capacity."

Jahabar Sadiq, chief executive of the news website, The Malaysian Insider, is cynical about how well-organised the country's radar defences really are.

"The military guys are pissed off because the world knows the extent of their radar capabilities," he said.

Malaysian Opposition leader Anwar Ibraham has also said he is baffled that even a sophisticated Marconi radar system that he authorised as Finance Minister in 1994 would have failed to track MH370. He told the Telegraph it is "not only unacceptable but not possible, not feasible" that it could travel across "at least four" Malaysian provinces undetected.

"They had the capability to detect any flight from the west - or from the east to the west coast, from the South China Sea to the Indian Ocean," he said.

In an opinion column in Free Malaysia Today, commentator Kua Kia Soong is highly critical of the failure but puts it down more to human error than faults in Malaysia's radar capability. He quotes a four-year-old Malaysian Defence Review which states: "As a whole, the

RMAF currently possesses total radar coverage save for some gaps at certain height levels, details of which are classified."

Kua Kia Soong goes on to say: "Apart from the millions spent on our radar systems, MH370's erratic route should have activated our Sukhois and F18s to be scrambled to prove their worth. Unfortunately, they were idle when they were most needed."

Sadiq indicates that at that hour of the night the nation's military is less prepared than most people might think. He doesn't even believe the military have jets on standby.

"No fighter jet was scrambled. We don't have a policy of keeping a fighter jet on standby. From what I know we've never had a jet on standby."

However, it is extremely difficult to believe that if the need arose, a fighter couldn't be mobilised with 45 minutes from Butterworth base. What is also perplexing is the lack of meaningful communication that took place between the Malaysian military and the DCA. Here was a 777, an international airline flight belonging to Malaysia Airlines and with 239 people on board, missing and yet there was virtually no communication between DCA and the military. It beggars belief.

Malaysia's Defence Minister Hishammuddin Hussein told Australia's Four Corners programme that the Malaysian Civil Aviation Authority called the military asking them to keep an eye on the plane. The military doesn't appear to have broken into a sweat trying to help. This is even more of an indictment. This indicates the military were actually warned to be on the look out for the plane. Still, they did nothing, even when they spotted an unidentified aircraft, albeit totally off course.

Malaysia Airlines' commercial director Hugh Dunleavy is also highly critical of delays in getting vital information from the authorities, even in the days after MH370's disappearance. He told the Evening Standard he first heard about the military's radar tracking of MH370 through the media.

"I only heard about this through the news," he said. "I'm thinking, really? You couldn't have told us that directly? Malaysia's air traffic control and military radar are in the same freakin' building. The military saw an aircraft turn and did nothing.

"They didn't know it was MH370.Their radar just identifies flying objects, yet a plane had gone down and the information about something in the sky turning around didn't get released by the authorities until after a week. Why? I don't know. I really wish I did."

The consistent line of the Malaysian Air Force and the Malaysian Government is that the aircraft was tracked by the country's primary radar facilities that night but they weren't sure what they were looking at. Therefore they didn't know how to respond.

Malaysia's Defence Minister Hussein, indicated to Four Corners that a conscious decision was made not to send military planes to check on an unidentified plane which appeared on their radar.

"It was commercial, it was in our air space, we were not at war with anybody," Hussein said.

When questioned further about the lack of military intervention he said: "If we are going to send it (jets) up, are you going to say we were going to shoot it down?"

It is a disingenuous response and a ridiculous one. The jets need not have shot anything down but getting an accurate fix on location would have prevented more than a dozen countries' aircraft and vessels searching in the wrong sea for a week. In a CNN interview Malaysian Prime Minister Najib Razak insisted the military radar spotted the plane and some sort of judgement not to react was made. He said the blip was deemed not be hostile.

"Now the military radar, the primary radar, has some capability. It tracked an aircraft, which did a turn back. But they were not sure - exactly sure - whether it was MH370. What they were sure of was that the aircraft was not deemed to be hostile."

The politicians are not necessarily to be believed. They had two options when trying to defend Malaysia's failure to act on the radar sighting of MH370. They could either say they didn't pick it up on primary radar that night because of incompetence, thus opening themselves up for ridicule and showing weakness to potential enemies. One wonders if it wasn't until the radar records were hastily reviewed in the cold light of day that the military picked up what had occurred. Or they could try to defend the indefensible and say they saw the blip on the radar but deliberately chose not to act. This argument isn't a winner either, yet it's the one they have chosen to pursue. Quite simply, it makes the authorities and the military look lame.

Anwar Ibrahim was quick to point out that by not scrambling fighter planes to track the unidentified aircraft the military had completely breached the standing operating procedures.

"The air force will be alerted and will have to then be flown to that area to either ... guide the plane to land or to leave the Malaysian airspace. They're standard operating procedure and this was never done," he said.

What would sending up a pair of fighter planes have achieved?

Light would be difficult at night but you would dispatch highly-qualified pilots, flying a sophisticated aircraft with their own tracking capability. Even if the 777 was deliberately trying to avoid detection the jets have their own primary radar.

In a modern military situation the aircraft would easily be vectored into the area where they get a primary radar return.

Malaysia's AIP gives clear rules for aircraft being intercepted by aircraft in these situations. Initially they would try to establish radio communication, using the emergency frequency if necessary. The fighter planes would observe the 777 closely, looking for signs of life in the cockpit.

A jet would flash its navigational lights and rock its wings to signal the aircraft has been intercepted and should change its course and follow. The 777 would rock its wings and flash its navigational lights to show it understood and would comply. Next, the jet would make an abrupt break-away manoeuvre from the intercepted aircraft consisting of a climbing turn of 90 degrees. The 777 would rock its wings to show it understood. Lastly the jet would lower landing gear, show steady landing lights to indicate the aircraft should land at a nearby runway. The 777 would respond by lowering its own landing gear or, if it had a problem with the runway selected, lifting the landing gear while passing over it.

In this case, there may have been no response from the 777, and as it continued on north-west towards the Andaman Sea, the fighters would have had to abandon it and return to base to refuel. At the very least, the operation would have clarified exactly where MH370 was and helped SAR teams immeasurably in their grim job. Surely a huge advantage when one considers that more than four months on, MH370 has not been located.

Failure to act on the radar sighting, if indeed it was picked up in real time, was a colossal mistake and one that notably wasn't even mentioned when the Malaysian Government released a preliminary report on MH370 on May 1. What made the mistake worse - criminally worse - was the military's refusal to act decisively on its findings for days afterwards.

Chapter 6

Aftermath

MH370 was due to land in Beijing at 6.30am, and Asia woke to the realisation that a state-of-the-art airliner routinely carrying 239 people appeared to have crashed.

Word spread quickly about the 777's disappearance but with agonisingly little information available. At Beijing International Airport in the city's north-east it was obvious that something was terribly wrong. At the airport, no one had to say anything - it was visible on the drawn faces of Malaysia Airline staff. MH370 sat at the top of the airport's arrivals board in stark red with the words 'delayed' beside it. Hundreds of families were waiting in the arrivals hall and becoming increasingly distressed, the reality closing in that there was nothing routine in this delay. As relatives stood waiting, tempers would suddenly erupt, only for a family member to pull the loved one back and quieten them down. They all suspected the worst but desperately hoped for otherwise, alternating between denial, sorrow and fury, particularly if they got a hint airline staff were holding out on them.

Terrible jarring scenes began to unfold. A sad counterpoint; distressed family members and stricken, scared airlines staff trying to hold them at bay. The tension was exacerbated as photographers and TV camera crews descended on the arrivals area, prompting near hysterical reactions from some relatives. Distraught family members had their grief played out in the most cruel way possible for millions of viewers around the world.

And the overriding frustration continually repeated: "No one knows anything, no one knows anything."

"They keep saying there's no information," Zhai Le told Fairfax correspondent Philip Wen, explaining through tears that she had a friend on board the flight. Chang Ken Fei, a Malaysian waiting at Beijing airport for friends to arrive, told Reuters: "At first I thought the plane was just delayed as normal, so I came a bit later. I've just been waiting and waiting."

One woman was crouched down on the floor sobbing, before a male companion and police led her away. Another man appeared shell-shocked as he explained he had been waiting to pick up his boss when he heard the news. ABC News quoted a woman as saying her son was on the plane.

"My son is only 40 years. He is so kind," she said, weeping uncontrollably. "Please take my life, and give my son back. What am I going to do? My son, Malaysia Airlines, you are killing me."

Another relative told The New Straits Times that he was awoken by news on Saturday morning that his niece Bai Xiaomo, who was in her thirties, was on the flight. He rushed immediately to the airport but had not been able to contact Bai as yet.

"Her parents and relatives are now all gathered at home and crying so we're here just to get some information."

Eventually - hours later than it should have been - a decision was made to get the relatives and friends off-site to protect them from the media scrutiny. The dithering has been criticised. Robert Jensen, president of Kenyon International Emergency Services told CBC News that the first thing Malaysia Airlines should have done is contact the airport and ask it to take the flight off the arrivals board, set up a reception area for families and bring relatives into that protected area before news broke to protect them from the media onslaught.

"We're not protecting families. We're not giving them a space. We're not giving them a shield, if they want it, from unwanted attention," said Jensen.

It's easy to criticise authorities' handling, although in fairness, a lost aircraft is something most airport authorities would never expect to experience. Airport staff had no script for what was occurring. And it was not as if there was anything useful to tell the poor relatives. There was precious little information available. There was simply nothing they could tell them. Nothing.

Finally, police and airport staff escorted relatives to the nearby

Beijing Lido Hotel to wait for news, even as flustered family members continued to arrive at the airport, desperate for information. A whiteboard next to an information booth in the arrivals hall offered those who had just come transportation to the hotel where they were promised more information. One woman, boarding a shuttle bus to the hotel, wept as she spoke on a cell phone. "They want us to go to the hotel. It cannot be good," she said.

By 10.30am, four hours after the plane was due to arrive, most people waiting for it at Beijing International Airport had left. The arrivals board still listed the flight and it wasn't until 2.13pm that the flight was finally removed. By late afternoon, many relatives had been waiting for hours in a hotel ballroom guarded by police. Those contacted by Chinese media said they had not been given any updates. Some relatives were screaming in frustration that they had not been able to speak to an airline official and all they could do was wait helplessly. About 20 people stormed out of the room at one point, enraged they had been given no information.

"There's no one from the company here, we can't find a single person. They've just shut us in this room and told us to wait," said one middle-aged man. "We want someone to show their face. They haven't even given us the passenger list," he said.

Another relative, trying to evade a throng of reporters, muttered: "They're treating us worse than dogs."

Worse, The Lido Hotel was no shelter from media who had camped outside the ballroom, forcing relatives to push through a corridor under police guard.

"I know nothing, I really don't have anything to say," one man whispered through a crush of reporters, squeezing the hand of an elderly man trailing behind him. A woman in her twenties entered the room frantically crying, ignoring questions from the horde. A man in his 60s wiped tears from his eyes with a handkerchief as he entered the room. He hit a cameraman in the face who tried to film him as he walked by, as a security guard shouted, "Don't you all have families?"

At Kuala Lumpur the grief was also palpable as distressed families began arriving, desperate for news. They started gathering from about 10am at the fifth floor of the departure hall. Reporters were prevented from interviewing the family members, who were shielded by five security guards.

One of those gathered at the Kuala Lumpur International Airport to wait for the latest development was news portal Ant Daily employee Lokman Mustafa, 40, whose sister, Suhaili, 31, was among those on the flight bound for Beijing.

"She was in a flight with 15 of her colleagues. They were going to be in Beijing for a month to look into setting up a factory there. She lives with my mother," said Lokman. "I lost one family member while there are those who lost four of their family members at one time. You should interview them, not me," he said, trying to evade more questions from the media as he rushed to the elevator heading to the car park.

Malaysia Airlines told passengers' next of kin to come to the airport with their passports to prepare to fly to the crash site, which had still not been identified. But the assumption was that a crash site would soon be known. Vietnam seemed to be the site on people's lips. Two family members of each passenger would be allowed to go on the special flight. Lokman said he was rushing home to get his passport and other documents.

Putih Idris from Kajang said her daughter-in-law was on the flight. She said she was notified about 9am when Malaysia Airlines called her house.

"I am not going to the site but a few others are going," she said.

Malaysia Airlines released its first statement at 7.24am, confirming that MH370 had lost contact with Air Traffic Control.

"Malaysia Airlines is currently working with the authorities who have activated their Search and Rescue team to locate the aircraft."

It promised regular updates and gave families a contact number. Malaysia Airlines had staff in a room calling every relative of passengers they could get to, but they didn't get to everyone before the plane's disappearance hit the media. In Subang, Zaharie Ahmad Shah's wife Faisa was one of those who found out about the flight's disappearance from 8am television news. Faisa knew Zaharie was operating one of the flights to Beijing but wasn't sure which of the two flights that night he was on. She went in to check the roster and quickly realised it was his flight that was missing.

There was grief all around yet everyone was in a strange kind of holding pattern. There was no news, no confirmation. At times, it was hard to believe. Didn't no news mean there was hope?

It was the start of a bizarre emotional roller coaster for relatives throughout the world and the public of Malaysia and China.

Martin Vengadesan, news editor of the Star Online, says he was called into work from home on Saturday morning and it was the start of two manic days in the newsroom. It was also the beginning of what would become an obsession for the experienced journalist. The mystery of MH370 would play on his mind to such an extent that he would dream about piloting the plane himself and could barely think of anything else.

Jahabar Sadiq, chief executive officer of Kuala Lumpur news website, The Malaysian Insider, was on deck when Malaysia Airlines' first statement came through and vividly recalls the website "flashing it up" online as quickly as they could.

"It (an airline tragedy) had never happened to Malaysia so we didn't think too much of it. 'Ah this plane is missing.' We thought maybe they crash-landed, belly flopped. The day went by normally. I think the media and the authorities were in the same kind of state: 'We'll find it at the end of the day. We'll find it, a few people may have died but we're not sure'. But as the day dragged on something was not right. There were a lot of rumours about people sighting things, but nothing."

At 9.05am Malaysia Airlines released a second statement: "We deeply regret that we have lost all contacts with flight MH370 which departed Kuala Lumpur at 12.41am earlier this morning bound for Beijing. The aircraft was scheduled to land at Beijing International Airport at 6.30am local Beijing time. Supang Air Traffic Control reported that it lost contact at 2.40am (local Malaysian time) today." Malaysia Airlines would later clarify that contact time to 1.30am, when the pilot of another plane made some sort of contact with the aircraft. In fact 1.21am, when the transponders went off, was the real final point of contact.

The release stated there were 239 passengers and crew and that passengers were from 13 different nationalities.

"Malaysia Airlines is currently working with the authorities who have activated their Search and Rescue team to locate the aircraft. Our team is currently calling the next of kin of passengers and crew."

While real information about what had happened was in desperately short supply there was no shortage of misinformation and loose theorising. The first reports started dribbling in of the plane being traced off the coast of Vietnam.

Vietnamese search personnel reported they had detected an Emergency Locator Transmitter (ELT) signal about 20n/m south of the coast of Ca Mau. Tuoi Tre, a leading daily newspaper in Vietnam, quoted Navy Admiral Ngo Van Phat, Commander of Region 5, as saying that military radar reported that the plane crashed into the sea at a location 246km south of Phu Quoc island. The Navy later said the admiral only referred to the position of the last radar contact with the aircraft.

The director of Vietnam's Maritime Search and Rescue Centre in Vung Tau clarified the situation with Reuters.

"We have been seeking but no signal from the plane yet," said Pham Hien. The information on local media about the signal near the Cape Ca Mau was inaccurate.

At 9.40am a Senior Malaysia Airlines official was quoted on CNN as saying that the jet was carrying about 7.5 hours' fuel and they feared that it had now run out.

"At the moment we have no idea where this aircraft is right now," Malaysia Airlines Vice President of Operations Control, Fuad Sharuji, said.

Some of the rumours flying round were downright idiotic and devastating for passengers' loved ones. A story spread mainly on Chinese social media that the aircraft had made a safe emergency landing in Nanning, China. One Twitter user posted that he or she had "some inside news from a pilot uncle that MH370 has emergency landed somewhere in China! Hope everyone is safe." If ever there was the ultimate indictment on the petty idiocy of the twitterverse, this was it.

The rumours picked up steam, with some local Malaysian media outlets publishing similar stories.

Adding to the confusion, some of the incorrect rumours cited Nanming, Vietnam, not Nanning, China, as the landing site.

Vengadesan remembers the reports of the landing in Nanning and is thankful the Star "didn't go with it - although others did."

"Right through the morning we had various sightings and reports all over the place - (such as) Vietnam's airforce commander saying it had been (found) in the South China Sea," he said.

"It was a pretty emotional time, especially with all the false reports. One of the things that annoyed me was a lot of cyber space people creating false statements when we were looking for the truth."

At 10.30am in a chaotic press conference in Kuala Lumpur, Malaysia Airlines CEO Ahmad Jauhari Yahyain, read a third statement.

"Ladies and gentlemen, we are deeply saddened this morning with the news of MH370. Malaysia Airlines confirms that flight MH370 had lost contact with Supang Air Traffic Control at 2.40am today (again the incorrect time). There has been speculation that the aircraft has landed at Nanming. We are working to verify the authenticity of the report and others."

He released the breakdown of nationalities on the plane and released the names, ages and flying hours of the pilot and co-pilot. The world was introduced to Captain Zaharie Ahmad Shah and Fariq Abdul Hamid.

By the time Malaysia Airlines released its fourth media statement, at 4.20pm, there wasn't a lot more to report other than to re-iterate there was no news.

"Malaysia Airlines is still unable to establish any contact or determine the whereabouts of flight MH370. We are still trying to locate the current location of the flight based on the last known position of the aircraft. We are working with international search and rescue teams to locate the aircraft. So far, we have not received any emergency signals or distress messages from MH370."

Searches had been launched along the estimated flight track of the aircraft from the Gulf of Thailand, Vietnam, Cambodia, Laos to China. The passenger manifest would not be released until all families of passengers had been informed.

Meanwhile, in the South China Sea, the start of the biggest search in aviation history had begun. At 7.20pm Malaysia Airlines released its fifth media statement of the day, saying search and rescue teams from

Malaysia, Singapore and Vietnam had failed to find evidence of crash wreckage. The sea mission would continue while the air mission would recommence at daylight. At last, with all next of kin notified, the airline was able to release the passenger manifest.

As the day grew more chaotic a Vietnamese aircraft spotted an oil slick on MH370's flight path which Lai Xuan Thanh, the director of the Civil Aviation Administration of Vietnam, said was suspected of being from the crashed Boeing aircraft. More conjecture followed. News organisations assumed it to be the case. The Airline Reporter website said MH370 had most likely crashed 153 miles off Vietnam's Tho Chu Island. It seemed a sure thing.

"The location information comes from the Vietnamese Navy, using radar telemetry that is most likely accurate. Also, a 12-mile oil slick discovered in the area points to the idea that the Boeing 777-200ER was lost here."

A Chinese coast guard vessel was reported to be rushing to the waters where the oil slick had been seen. There was no confirmation that the slicks were related to the missing plane, but the statement said they were consistent with the kinds that would be produced by the two fuel tanks of a crashed jetliner.

Jahabar Sadiq said that with all the speculation it was difficult to know where to send reporters.

"We were thinking of sending a reporter down to Vietnam because everyone assumed it had crashed between Malaysia and Vietnam."

He eventually sent two photographers to a spot from where they would be able to access the Vietnamese coastal waters with the Malaysian coast guard.

"They found nothing, of course."

At an evening press conference Malaysian Prime Minister Najib Razak vowed that search and rescue operations to locate MH370 aircraft would continue for as long as necessary.

The Prime Minister also reiterated that no signs of any wreckage had been found, despite numerous rumours that the Boeing B777-200 aircraft had crashed off the coast of southern Vietnam. Somewhat futilely, Razak pleaded for an end to the relentless speculation on the fate of the Beijing-bound flight. Given the nature of the unfolding tragedy and the chaotic communications from Malaysian and Vietnamese authorities throughout the day, Razak may as well have been urging the waves not to roll into the shore. Malaysian authorities were under siege and nothing would change with the passing of the night.

Chapter 7

Sinister Motives Emerge

Sunday morning was to be all about the search off the coast of Vietnam as a mini flotilla approached the area targeted as the location where MH370 may have crashed into the sea, a target reinforced by Vietnam Air Force's sighting of an oil slick.

There was huge expectation that recovery of the aircraft's wreckage was imminent. There was no reason to believe there would be any major delay in finding MH370. Discovering its wreckage and all that came with such a discovery, seemed an inevitability, as was the grief that would follow. Vessels from Malaysia and Vietnam as well as two Chinese warships were also on route to Phu Quock Island. But events overnight, stemming from the release of MH370's passenger manifest had already distracted media attention. As Malaysia had tried to sleep through its nightmare, there was action occurring in Europe - none of it good.

A story emerged of up to four people boarding MH370 with false passports, raising the immediate prospect of some sort of terrorist act. On Sunday morning the Associated Press quoted Malaysia's Transport Minister, Hishammuddin Hussein, as saying: "All the four names are with me and have been given to our intelligence agencies. We do not want to target only the four; we are investigating the whole passenger manifest. We are looking at all possibilities."

Until this point, hijacking or terrorism had never entered most people's minds. Some sort of mechanical, electrical or structural catastrophic event had been assumed to be the cause of whatever had happened to MH370. That was still the main assumption - but 9/11 has ensured that concerns over terrorism are always quick to surface, even with flimsy evidence. The spectre of some terrorist act being involved with MH370's disappearance racheted up the story several notches.

While concerns were initially raised about four of the passengers, this was later discounted and most of the interest focused on two Europeans who were listed in the passenger manifest but were not actually on the plane at all. Overnight, Italian news agency ANSA called the home of Luigi Maraldi in the northern Italian city of Cesena, acting on the fact that an Italian with his name was on MH370's passenger manifest. They got no answer. Maraldi, 37, would ultimately call his worried parents after reading news reports of the missing flight.

"I'm alive - I'm in Thailand!" he said.

Maraldi had reported his passport stolen six months earlier when it went missing from a motorbike rental shop on the tourist island of Phuket, when he was on holiday. He apparently left his passport at a rental shop in Patong, the resort island's tourist centre, only to discover when he later went to collect it that the shop owner had handed it over to a man who looked "similar". Passports are often requested in exchange for car and motorbike rentals in Phuket - visited by 12 million tourists every year - but the steaming hot tourist island is a hotbed of identity theft, and complaints of stolen and lost passports are rife. Meanwhile, it emerged that Christian Kozel, the 30-year-old Austrian citizen listed on the flight's manifest, also had his passport stolen two years ago during a flight from Phuket to Bangkok, according to the Austrian Foreign Ministry.

Initially, incorrectly, Malaysia Airlines played down the use of two stolen passports, saying that any passengers headed to Beijing would have had to apply for a Chinese visa.

"To get a visa you need to submit your passport to the Chinese authorities and they get validated at that stage," said Hugh Dunleavy, Malaysia Airlines commercial manager.

However, the Telegraph confirmed with China Southern, the codeshare airline which made the economy-class bookings for the men travelling under the names "Luigi Maraldi" and "Christian Kozel" that both were merely transmitting in Beijing and did not require a visa. Worse still, as Interpol was quick to point out, both missing passports had been added to their database of 40 million across 167 countries which airlines are supposed to consult to check travel documents. It was obvious that border control officials hadn't bothered to check it, which Interpol chief Ronald Noble described as a "grave concern".

He warned that "only a handful of countries" routinely made such checks and said authorities were "waiting for a tragedy to put prudent security measures in place at borders and boarding gates."

The revelation was obviously embarrassing and annoying for Malaysia Home Minister Ahmad Zahid Hamidi who criticised border officials for letting the men through when they had European passports but Asian features.

"I am still perturbed," he told Bernama news agency. Can't these immigration officials think? Italian and Austrian (passport holders) but with Asian faces?"

He promised a probe of the officers who were on duty that night.

The whimsy continued the following day when the reference to Asian faces was refuted at a Malaysia Airlines' press conference by Malaysian Civil Aviation chief Azharuddin Abudul Rahman. Rahman told reporters in Kuala Lumpur that the men were "not Asian looking" and may have been part of a stolen passport syndicate. CCTV footage showed they completed all security procedures but hijacking couldn't be ruled out. When prompted by reporters to describe the two men, Azharuddin said: "Do you know a footballer by the name of Balotelli?" referring to AC Milan striker Mario Balotelli, who was born in Italy to Ghanain parents.

A reporter then asked, "Is he black?" and the aviation chief replied, "Yes."

No one asked whether the two imposters on MH370 also sported a mohican and had diamond studs in their ears. To Rahman's credit he later pointed out that all he was trying to do was highlight that a person's appearance was no indicator of their nationality. He shrugged his shoulders and ignored the media's attempts to make fun of him. Just why the men posing as the Italian and Austrian would have used the false documents was still unclear to authorities. While terrorism was the first possibility that leapt to mind, people trying to flee the Middle East or Asia for a better life as we know Pouria and his friend Reza were doing, was already authorities' favoured scenario.

Such attempts were hardly unusual, particularly through accomplices in Thailand where hundreds of passports are thought to be lost or stolen every year in a black-market racket. Six Syrians hoping to seek refugee status in Sweden had recently been picked up by authorities at Phuket International Airport after attempting to fly to Stockholm via Beijing on Greek passports. Local media suggested the group had said the route to Sweden through Phuket and Beijing was a regular path. Thailand's role as a place to obtain stolen passports was under the spotlight. The revelations triggered a terror probe by Malaysian authorities, who began working with other intelligence agencies including the FBI.

The stolen passports weren't the only terrorism scenario being fuelled. The presence of two Uighur passengers was suddenly being raised in Chinese social media as a factor, given a recent terror attack in the south-western city of Kunming that killed a number of people. Ethnic Muslim Uighurs make up 45 per cent of the western Chinese province of Xinjiang, and the horrific knife attack had caused shockwaves in China. Painter Mehemet Abula with the Chinese painting group and a Turkish-based Uighur academic, Dr Mamatjan Yasin, were now under scrutiny. Chinese social media wasted no time on picking up on the rumour.

"I am afraid the incident was launched by Xinjiang people," read one such conjecture posted by @Chen Lei on the Tencent social media platform. "It is time to investigate Xinjiang and kill those who should be killed."

Reports that Dr Yasin had once taken flight simulator training caused particular alarm. According to his online CV dug up by media outlets, besides extensive teaching and research experience in electronics, biomedical, and digital communications, the man had also spent slightly less than a year in 2004 as a researcher at a training and simulation centre in Sweden. The Chinese Government ultimately dismissed the possibility, saying its background checks on the Chinese passenger had revealed nothing of concern. There were also reports of an email sent to journalists by a member of the Uighur Separatist Movement, although these were dismissed as opportunistic and troublemaking.

Also on the Sunday, came the first revelation that MH370 may have changed its flight path. Out of the blue, the Royal Malaysian Air Force suggested that there was a possibility that MH370 could have attempted to turn back, based on military radar records. Whether this came from the military guessing they had missed a crucial sighting overnight and hurriedly revisiting their radar data records, or from a guilty conscience at not having acted is still unclear and may never be known. At a 1pm press conference, air force chief Rodzali Daud decided he needed to mention that they had recorded the unidentified blip on the radar and they were considering the scenario that MH370 had made some sort of "turn-back".

"What we have done is actually look into the recording on the radar that we have and we realised there is a possibility the aircraft did make a turn-back," he told reporters at a news conference. "At this juncture, we are still trying to collaborate with civilian radar and other international agencies and with this collaboration, probably we will get a better picture," he said.

Malaysia Airlines chief executive Ahmad Jauhari Yahya explained that such a turn-back is done when an aircraft could not proceed on its original course, and procedures dictate that the pilot has to report this to air traffic control. However, no such report was received, nor distress calls of any kind.

"We are also baffled that there is no signal from the (aircraft's) emergency locator transmitter (ELT)," Rodzali added, referring to emergency beacons that can be activated manually by the pilot or automatically in case of impact.

As a result of these revelations the search was expanded to a degree to not just take in the large expanse of sea between Malaysia and Vietnam but to the west over Malaysia's east coast. The revelations prompted new speculation about what could have occurred, and John Goglia, a former board member of the National Transportation Safety Board (NTSB), the US agency that investigates plane crashes, said the lack of a distress call suggested that the plane either experienced an explosive decompression or was destroyed by an explosive device.

"It had to be quick because there was no communication," Goglia said.

This was contradicted by a report in the New York Times quoting a Pentagon official.

"Preliminary surveillance data" examined by the Pentagon suggests the missing Malaysia Airlines jet did not explode over the South China Sea. The newspaper cited a U.S. government official who spoke on the condition of anonymity as suggesting "a system that looks for flashes around the world" had not identified any sign of a blast.

Meanwhile the search for wreckage off the coast of Vietnam had turned up nothing. The air force's suggestion of a turn-back had been somewhat equivocal and vague, and most energy and attention from search and rescue teams still focused on the area around MH370's flight path. By now, an armada of ships and aircraft was approaching : at least 40 ships and 22 aircraft from Vietnam, Malaysia, Thailand, Singapore, Indonesia, China and the United States were participating. But all that anyone was coming up with was a series of dead ends. Samples of oil slicks spotted on that first night after MH370's disappearance had emanated from ships rather than an airliner, and no debris had been found relating to initial sightings.

The biggest excitement came from a series of sightings from aircraft of some sort of debris field off the east coast of Vietnam. A Vietnamese marine police aircraft and passengers and crew on a Cathay Pacific flight spotted debris, including an orange object floating near Tho Chu Island. Vietnam Search and Rescue Control Centre released a photo of an object which it said was believed to be part of the aircraft. There were suggestions it was either a door or part of the tail of the Boeing 777. In time these hopes were dashed too. Vietnam's Search and Rescue Centre later announced that vessels arriving at the position of the debris did not find any objects. There were high winds and large waves; the debris possibly drifted away. A Thai cargo ship in the area was asked for assistance and found nothing. A second vessel asked for assistance also turned up and left empty-handed.

In another injection of farce into the proceedings, reports surfaced - and even worse, photos - of co-pilot Fariq Abdul Hamid and a colleague entertaining two young women in a cockpit during a flight two years earlier. Headlines proclaiming him a "playboy" flooded around the world. Fariq and a colleague were photographed posing and smiling alongside the attractive young women, having blatantly broken Malaysia Airline rules when they invited passengers Jonti Roos and Jaan Maree to join them in the cockpit for the one-hour flight from Phuket to Kuala

Lumpur. Roos told Australia's A Current Affair she and her friend posed for pictures with the pilots, who smoked cigarettes during the mid-air rendezvous.

"Throughout the entire flight they were talking to us and they were actually smoking throughout the flight, which I don't think they're allowed to do," Roos said. "At one stage they were pretty much turned around the whole time in their seats talking to us. They were so engaged in conversation that he took my friend's hand and he was looking at her palm and said 'Your hand is very creased. That means you're a very creative person,' and commented on her nail polish."

Fariq had apparently picked out the South African nationals as they waited in the boarding queue at Phuket Airport in December 2011. As they took their seats on the aircraft, a flight attendant approached the women and invited them to join the pilots in the cockpit. Despite pictures exposing the gross misconduct of the distracted pilots, Roos said she wasn't concerned for her safety.

"I did feel safe. I don't think there was one instance where I felt threatened or I felt that they didn't know what they were doing," she said. "The whole time I felt they were very friendly. I felt they were very competent in what they were doing. We wished they (would) stop smoking because it is such a confined space. But you can't exactly tell a pilot to stop smoking."

The pair apparently wanted Roos and Maree to change their travel arrangements and extend their stay in Kuala Lumpur and join them on a night on the town. It was another embarrassment for Malaysia Airlines which issued a statement about the incident the next day.

"Malaysia Airlines has become aware of the allegations being made against First Officer, Fariq Abdul Hamid which we take very seriously," the statement said. "We are shocked by these allegations. We have not been able to confirm the validity of the pictures and videos of the alleged incident. As you are aware, we are in the midst of a crisis, and we do not want our attention to be diverted. We also urge the media and general public to respect the privacy of the families of our colleagues and passengers. It has been a difficult time for them."

And not just for them. Malaysia Airlines was taking a battering not only in the media but in the financial markets. By Monday, when trading began in the Malaysian Stock Exchange, the airlines' shares plunged 18 per cent to a record low. They recovered a little during the day but it was obvious the already embattled Malaysia Airlines brand was in free-fall. As an international airline Malaysia Airlines was on life-support well before the disappearance of MH370, being highly unprofitable and needing constant government bailouts to survive. The airline never seemed to have been able to make the transition that other legacy airlines have made to become more efficient and profitable. Part of the problem is with the mix of aircraft type within their fleet. The airline's management has been unable to make efficiencies from economies of scale. The variety of aircraft requires duplication within spare parts, training processes and different maintenance tools. The airline has also been known to carry a lot of dead wood. Historically, politicians would reward people with jobs with Malaysia Airlines when they had very little competence or expertise.

Furthermore, Malaysia, as both a destination in its own right and as a stop-over, lacks the appeal of some of its rivals such as Singapore with its carrier Singapore Airlines and Hong Kong with Cathy Pacific.

While Malaysia Airlines' reputation and shares in the stock market took a further pummelling Boeing, the maker of the missing 777, was keeping a low profile. On March 8 the massive Chicago-based company released the following brief statement: "Boeing offers its deepest concern to the families of those aboard missing Malaysia Airlines Flight MH370. Boeing is assembling a team to provide technical assistance to investigating authorities."

The conservative response from the world's largest aircraft manufacturer was predictable. As an aircraft manufacturer based in the most litigious country in the world it has accumulated considerable experience in how to act and conduct itself following the loss of an aircraft. Which in essence is to say very little, and to provide any assistance possible to the carrier and whoever else is involved in pursuing the cause of the accident while quietly preparing itself for the lawsuits that frequently follow which are often more fishing expeditions than for any justified legal grounds.

The legal ramifications of an air accident are complex. However, they are governed by a convention, one tenet of which is that the normal payout for human life is approximately US$175,000. The bill falls to airline insurers who, of course, then try to ensure other parties accountable contribute according to their share of culpability. Airline investigations tend to take a long time, which is not surprising given their complexity and the scale of the task, not to mention the implications of the outcome. If negligence or deliberate action can be proven then the constraints of the convention are quickly pushed aside and whoever is proved culpable suddenly finds the door is opened for massive multiple class-action suits that could drain the financial coffers or any airline - and any government behind the airline.

Boeing's careful response to MH370's loss was not at all surprising.

Meanwhile, Malaysian Police at last had some good news to report as the two Iranian men travelling on stolen passports were ruled out as suspects in any terrorism attack. Pouria Mehrdad, the brave 18-year-old desperate to link up with his mother, was named by Malaysian Police, as was his motive, while Ronald Noble identified the other as Delavar Seyed Mohammadreza, 29. Noble said he did not believe the disappearance of the Malaysia Airlines plane was a terrorist incident. Authorities were sure the two men had no links to extreme groups.

Noble said: "The more information we get, the more we are inclined to conclude it is not a terrorist incident."

A touch of farce came with the revelation of the men's identities when police released photos only to have accidentally spliced one man's legs over the other in a photocopying error. The lower halves of their bodies were identical, prompting social media trolls to suspect foul play and accuse them of doctoring evidence.

"Why did they try to photoshop the legs on the released photo of the Iranians?" one person asked.

"Photoshop failed! Same legs on those pics. Are they for real??" another posted.

"It was not done with malice or to mislead," police spokeswoman Asmawati Ahmad told AFP, adding that it had been explained to some journalists when the photos were handed out.

Away from all the distractions, the grim truth was sinking in that it was days now since MH370 had disappeared and it was becoming increasingly obvious that whatever had occurred, no one could have survived. Relatives of passengers were closeted away, and the agonising wait for news was slowly morphing into an excruciating understanding that whatever followed now could only be tragic and awful. The plane and its passengers were surely lost. Still many seemed to be holding on to vain hope. At makeshift memorials at the Kuala Lumpur International Airport and at The Pavilion shopping centre in the central business district people were urged to "Pray for 370".

Meanwhile, scores of Chinese relatives camped in the Beijing Lido Hotel still seemed to cultivate some belief in the unbelievable. And who could criticise them for that?

Star Online news editor Martin Vengadesan said that by Monday morning he knew a sad milestone had been reached.

"I had this idea from the start really that after 48 hours if we hadn't found it, if nothing had turned up, no sign of them at all, well after that no one was alive. I thought after 48 hours there was no hope."

Chapter 8

The Real Search Begins

On March 11, through a mixture of media reports and information grudgingly provided by Malaysia's Air Force, the turn-back theory began to get some momentum. Some much-needed light was at last shone on MH370's true flight path on the morning of March 8, with or without the air force's assent.

A media report emerged suggesting air force primary radar data showed the aircraft may have turned west over the Gulf of Thailand and flown past the east coast near Kota Bharu and the west coast of Malaysia near Kedah. The pro-government Berita Harian newspaper quoted General Tan Sri Rodzali Daud as saying the RMAF Butterworth airbase had detected the location of the airliner as indicating that it turned back from its original heading in the direction of Kota Bharu, Kelantan, and was believed to have passed through the airspace of the east coast of the northern peninsula of Malaysia. The last time MH370 was detected by the air control tower was in the vicinity of Pulau Perak in the Straits of Malacca before the signal "disappeared without a trace".

Malaysia Airlines subsequently released a statement announcing that the search had expanded beyond the scope of the flight path to the Malaysian Peninsula and into the Straits of Malacca. The newspaper's story was extremely accurate so it was no surprise that in one of many incidents of contradictory statements and straight-out lies, the commander of Malaysia's Air Force sent out a statement denying saying what was quoted.

"I request this misreporting be amended and corrected to prevent further misinterpretations of what is clearly an inaccurate and incorrect report," he said in his six-paragraph statement. Berita Harian's report remained on its website.

A meeting with Malaysian officials and families of missing families in Beijing revealed "All right, good night" were the last reported words from MH370's cockpit. This would later be corrected to "Good Night Malaysian 370", but not until March 31. Bizarrely, Malaysia's Department of Civil Aviation (DCA) officials stressed at this meeting that they did not have any indication that the aircraft may have turned back or deviated from the planned route. The aircraft "suddenly disappeared".

In the evening of March 12 the commander of Malaysia's Air Force confirmed in a media conference that an unidentified radar target was last seen about 200n/m north-west of Penang at 2.15am. As the primary radar did not identify which aircraft, it was not clear whether the unidentified target was MH370. This radar observation, however prompted Malaysian authorities to expand the search into the Malacca Sea and the Andaman Sea. Uncertain or not, it had been enough to persuade them to look elsewhere.

The conflicting messages about whether MH370 turned back prompted a well-deserved broadside from a Chinese Government Minister, Qin Gang, who said China had asked Malaysia to check conflicting information about the change of course of the jetliner.

"It's pretty chaotic, so up to this point we too have had difficulty confirming whether [information is] accurate or not," said Qin, responding to conflicting information provided about the flight path of flight MH370.

"[China] has requested Malaysia to verify the 'turn-back' rumours and act accordingly," Qin later said in a statement on the ministry's website, "and notify the situation to China timely (sic)."

Guo Shaochun, head of the Chinese Government task force in Kuala Lumpur, added his voice, saying Beijing "requests that Malaysia releases authoritative and substantial information" on the missing plane.

And then the Wall Street Journal threw the cat amongst the pigeons with a report claiming American investigators suspected the aircraft stayed in the air for about four hours past the time it reached its last confirmed location. The business publication said this raised the possibility that the Boeing 777-200ER jet could have flown on for hundreds of additional kilometres.

Aviation investigators and national security officials believed the plane flew for a total of five hours, based on data automatically downloaded and sent to the ground from the Roll Royce engines on the 777 as part of a routine maintenance and monitoring programme, the paper said. That raised a host of new questions and possibilities about what happened. While the Wall Street Journal was actually correct about the fact that MH370 flew on and on, it was incorrect in its methodology about how this was detected. The report indicated the readings were from ACARS, but in fact ACARS had been shut down many hours earlier.

Malaysian authorities were able to refute the Wall Street Journal's story. The next day Malaysia's Transport Minister, Hussein, said in a televised press conference, that the last ACARS transmission was received from the aircraft at 1:07am, and there were no later transmissions via ACARS. The last transmission received from the aircraft indicated all systems were operating normally. Boeing, Rolls Royce, and the US National Transport Safety Bureau (NTSB) confirmed the last data transmission received from the aircraft was at 1.07am.

But there was another method of confirming that MH370 had indeed flown on for many more hours than suspected, an automated communication link between the aircraft and a satellite used by British company Inmarsat. This automated communication was the product of a communication and data service that Inmarsat offers via a company called SITA which bundles voice communication and data products and sells them to airlines but which Malaysia Airlines had not subscribed fully to. Still, however, the satellites were sending out interrogation signals - "pings" - to link up with the service user's SATCOM. It explained that if the ground station did not hear from an aircraft for an hour it would transmit a 'log on/log off' message - a 'ping' - and the aircraft would automatically return a short message indicating that it was still logged on, a process described as a 'handshake'. Inmarsat had discovered that a satellite recorded hourly 'handshakes' with MH370 recorded by a ground station in Perth, after its last known contact with air traffic controllers. Inmarsat found there had been seven handshakes - an hour apart - until one last partial handshake at 8.19 on Saturday morning.

Inmarsat had provided the information to SITA which had contacted Malaysia Airlines and in turn the Malaysian Government with its findings, but found the authorities reluctant to listen or divulge details of MH370's last know position based on their radar data. A charitable interpretation is that the Malaysian Government was embarrassed by the radar breach and concerned about the impact on its security.

While Inmarsat was quietly going about its work and contacting the Malaysian Government to try to get it to listen to it, the penny was dropping outside Malaysia. Western media began joining the dots and concluding that through a mixture of secretiveness and contradictory statements Malaysian authorities were presiding over a costly and time-wasting search for MH370 in the wrong sea.

The Malaysian Government was the emperor wearing no clothes.

On March 14 Inmarsat released the following statement on its website: "Routine, automated signals were registered on the Inmarsat network from Malaysia Airlines Flight MH370 during its flight from Kuala Lumpur. This information was provided to our partner SITA, which in turn has shared it with Malaysia Airlines. For further information, please contact Malaysia Airlines."

Inmarsat had informed the Malaysian Government that its routine automatic communications between the Inmarsat satellite and MH370 could be used to determine several possible flight paths. In addition to being able to establish the length of time MH370 had remained in the air, Inmarsat developed a second technique that took into account the velocity of the aircraft relative to the satellite and the resulting change in signal frequency, known as the Doppler Effect. Inmarsat was able to calculate the range of the aircraft from the satellite, and the time it took the signal to be sent and received, to generate two arcs of possible positions for the aircraft - a northern and a southern corridor.

This it had presented to the Malaysian Government to a mixed reception, and it was struggling to get any traction. The statement on its website was making it clear to Malaysian authorities that it was time to act. Inmarsat had the information to solve this riddle and get search and rescue looking for MH370 in the right place. It must have felt it had a responsibility to the passengers and their relatives to get the information acted on.

Even by Friday, March 14, the Malaysian Transport Minister Hussein, was still saying the unidentified westbound radar contact had not been definitely accepted as being MH370, so he was reluctant to switch the multinational search effort entirely to the west and to abandon the Gulf of Thailand.

As the sixth day since MH370's disappearance dawned it was clear that the real story was coming out whether the Malaysian Government liked it or not. The White House accelerated proceedings when a spokesman stated during a routine press briefing that the search for the missing flight might be expanding to the Indian Ocean based on new but inconclusive information about the aircraft. Western media reports were suggesting the disappearance of 370 could be a deliberate act rather than a catastrophic failure.

Still stubbornly, Malaysia Airlines stuck to its guns. Its last statement that day, at 2.45pm, it said it had 'nothing further to add' to the information although it was fully aware of ongoing media speculation. But behind the scenes there was plenty to add. The Malaysian Government was having its arm twisted to accept the truth and act on it however unfamiliar it may be with such a concept and whatever embarrassment and anger that course of action was bound to create.

Saturday March 15, exactly a week after MH370's disappearance, proved to be a dramatic day as the inevitability that had been brewing culminated in a dramatic announcement. Malaysia's Prime Minister Razak called an emergency press conference at 10pm - the late hour a sign there was something big afoot. The event was hastily arranged at the Putra World Trade Centre. Here he announced that Malaysia would call off the search in the South China Sea and Straits of Malacca. And most dramatic of all, Razak's statement confirmed the suspicions of many, that in some shape of form MH370 had indeed been hijacked. It was the moment where MH370's disappearance moved definitively into a new, dark realm.

Razak announced two vital new pieces of information. The plane's communication systems were systematically disabled after take-off, and after its last contact with air traffic control over the South China Sea it was probably flying for about another seven hours. The plane was diverted back across the Malaysian Peninsula and flew off in a north-westerly direction.

"Based on new satellite communication we can say with a high degree of certainty that the Aircraft Communications Addressing and Reporting System was disabled just before the aircraft reached the east coast of peninsula Malaysia. Shortly afterwards, near the border between Malaysian and Vietnamese air traffic control, the aircraft's transponder was switched off," said Razak.

Movements of the aircraft until it left Malaysia's primary radar coverage were consistent with deliberate action by someone on the plane. The primary radar target, so far believed but not confirmed to be MH370, could today be identified as MH370 with the help of new data received from the satellite data provider. The aircraft could have flown on for seven hours. The last trace of the aircraft was identified at 08:11am.

"Due to the type of satellite data we are unable to confirm the precise location of the plane when it last made contact with the satellite," Razak continued. "However, the investigation was able to determine that the last communication was in one of two corridors: the northern corridor stretching approximately from the border of Kazakhstan and Turkmenistan to northern Thailand, or the southern corridor stretching approximately from Indonesia to the southern Indian Ocean. In view of this latest development the Malaysian authorities have refocused their investigation into the crew and passengers on board."

The revelation about deliberate action wouldn't have surprised many; the signs were there - all of the evidence revealed to this point suggested it, but to have it confirmed by Malaysia's PM was still a sobering moment. Barring pilots taking charge because of some unknown and catastrophic technical problem, hijacking of some type was now the most likely cause of MH370's disappearance. Police needed to renew their investigations into the 227 passengers and 12 crew members on board.

They were reported to be looking into four possibilities: hijack, sabotage, and personal and psychological problems. And as the "deliberate" actions involved disabling the plane's communications, and then diverting it onto a new course, clearly requiring detailed knowledge of the Boeing 777, interest has inevitably focused on the pilot and co-pilot. Police immediately made a big show of the fact that the homes of Zaharie and Fariq in the city of Shah Alam were searched. A police van with a large contingent of officers passed through a security gate at the entrance to the luxury compound of Laman Seri where Zaharie lived with Faisa.

In what appeared a very stage-managed operation, police apparently spent two hours inside the home, and left carrying small bags, similar to shopping bags. Suddenly, the flight crew was in the frame.

Police were reportedly looking into the political and religious backgrounds of the pair. Two lap-tops had apparently been taken from Zaharie's home - one thought to contain data from his flight simulator. Aviation experts were quick to weigh in with their views. Consultant Chris Yates told the Independent: "It's increasingly clear that the hand of some form of terrorism is at play here, whether from a group or one skilled individual. The levels of specialist aviation knowledge on display here cause me to cast my mind back to 9/11 when hijackers had acquired a level of technical and flight training."

David Gleave, a former air crash investigator, added that any terrorist seizure of the plane "would have required one hell of a piece of planning".

Phil Giles, a former air safety investigator who worked on the Lockerbie bombing, told Asia Pacific News: "Taking over a Boeing 777 without experience or skill is akin to some Somalian bloke in a tiny boat trying to take over a super tanker and captain it. Unless the hijacker has a fair amount of technical and aviation knowledge he would have to rely on putting a gun to the pilot's head."

An unnamed Malaysian Government official was quoted in media as saying that investigators had concluded that one of the pilots or someone else with flying experience hijacked the missing Malaysia Airlines jet. Another extremely sobering realisation was that the search for MH370 had just got harder. The search area now involved was utterly massive.

Malaysia Airlines followed Razak's announcement with a statement: "This is truly an unprecedented situation, for Malaysia Airlines and for the entire aviation industry. There has never been a case in which information gleaned from satellite signals alone could potentially be used to identify the location of a missing commercial airliner. Given the nature of the situation and its extreme sensitivity, it was critical that the raw satellite signals were verified and analysed by the relevant authorities so that their significance could be properly understood. This naturally took some time, during which we were unable to publicly confirm their existence. We were well aware of the ongoing media speculation during this period, and its effect on the families of those on board. Their anguish and distress increases with each passing day, with each fresh rumour, and with each false or misleading media report. Our absolute priority at all times has been to support the authorities leading the multinational search for MH370, so that we can finally provide the answers which the families and the wider community are waiting for."

If Malaysian authorities were hoping this would head off the criticism they were wrong.

China's state news agency attacked Malaysia's handling of the investigation.

Xinhua said: "Massive efforts have been squandered, and numerous rumours have been spawned, repeatedly racking the nerves of the awaiting families".

The report cited reluctance to share information "in a full and timely manner" which was intolerable for the relatives.

Chinese media accused Malaysian authorities of "squandering" precious time and resources by releasing dramatic information on the plane's fate a full week after it vanished.

"It is undeniable that the disclosure of such vital information is painfully belated," a scathing editorial by China's state-run Xinhua news agency said, noting the "excruciating" seven days it entailed for relatives of the missing. It suggested Malaysian officials were guilty of an "intolerable" dereliction of duty.

There was particular anger and frustration that Malaysia had taken so long to cancel search operations in the South China Sea if it already knew the plane had doubled back and flown towards the Indian Ocean.

"And due to the absence - or at least lack - of timely authoritative information, massive efforts have been squandered, and numerous rumours have been spawned," the Xinhua editorial said. "As the leader of the international search and rescue mission, Malaysia bears inescapable responsibility," it added.

The Chinese Government and state-run media's hard line stance on Malaysia's handling of the tragedy was predictable and understandable. Throughout, the Chinese Government had been forceful and had allowed Chinese relatives the same scope. It was not an easy situation for Chinese leaders who, despite sending nine ships to the initial search area, were seen to be failing to get traction from Malaysia in finding the truth about what had killed 153 Chinese nationals. Chinese leaders found themselves facing outrage from the public as evidenced by an explosion of anger on social media. Users of micro-blogging network Weibo - China's version of Twitter - made their views crystal clear.

"The Malaysian Government's behaviour in this affair can be summed up in one word: 'deceptive'," said one typical comment.

But criticism wasn't limited to the Chinese. There was condemnation internationally. Security and aviation experts rightly continued to question why so many resources were deployed in searching the South China Sea for so long, and how the Malaysian military had failed to identify the plane as it backtracked over the peninsula.

"It is an astonishing failure of security," said Ajaj Sahni, executive director of India's Institute for Conflict Management in New Delhi. "And it seems an astonishing failure of technology in every aspect that something like this could happen."

Terence Fan, an aviation expert at the Singapore Management University, said Malaysia's crisis management was flawed and had tested public confidence.

"Why did they need days to 'corroborate' from their own radar images that the airplane could have turned west?" Mr Fan said. "Couldn't they have known from day one that the different communications systems on the aircraft were turned off at different times?" he added.

The Malaysian Insider's chief executive Jahabar Sadiq says the criticism was deserved.

"The world was acutely aware that something was not right because the Malaysian guys, they didn't know what to do. Stolen passports, terrorism, everything. They were just clueless."

But nor does he really blame the authorities who he suggests were out of their depth.

"They are mediocre internationally, that's the best they can do. The whole world now knows what we know. That these guys are incompetent. Having said that, that's the best they can do."

The Star Online's Martin Vengadesan thought criticism was over the top and he emphasised the scale of the tragedy, which was not easy for any country to handle.

"I did feel certainly the international media was trying to get this angle that the Malaysian Government was bungling it all up, which I think was unfair. Every country has its crisis. New Zealand had the miners and Korea had its ferry, and the difference between this and other crises is that you haven't found the wreckage so that gives rise to many conspiracy theories. In this case, until this point we haven't, and we may never find out for sure what happened."

On the positive side, the Malaysian Government's decision to at last take a stand inspired a constructive reaction from other governments. The size of the task at hand demanded this. Malaysia's statement had come a week too late, but it at least was a call to action for interested countries. The Government called upon all the countries to the north-west, as far as Turkmenistan and the Caspian Sea, to check their primary radar records for unidentified contacts in their airspace in the seven hours after the 777 went missing. Depending on the actual track the aircraft followed, if it had headed approximately north-west this could include some - if not all - of the following countries: Thailand, Myanmar/Burma, China, Bangladesh, Bhutan, India, Nepal, Pakistan, Afghanistan, and Turkmenistan.

But the big problem was the sheer size of the search areas - especially to the south. If the aircraft went north it would be found sooner or later. If it went south there was no guarantee, given the vastness of the southern Indian Ocean. Hussein, the Malaysian police chief, said that the number of countries involved in the search for Flight MH370 has risen from 14 to 20. Reuters reported that Malaysian officials briefed envoys from about 20 countries on progress in the investigation. Logistics of a new, far more difficult search, needed to be put together. Still, only one week into the loss of MH370, and with the momentum created by the new information and a new direction, there was optimism the families' grim wait would soon be ended. It was optimism which would soon prove to be totally unfounded.

Chapter 9

The Vast Indian Ocean

The search had changed dramatically for good and for bad. Cooperation between countries had never been so good, but the job had never been so difficult, with a search area of 2.24 million square nautical miles. By now 25 countries - nearly twice the number as before - were sharing roles in a dual search of the northern corridor stretching approximately from the border of Kazakhstan and Turkmenistan to northern Thailand, or the southern corridor stretching approximately from Indonesia to the southern Indian Ocean.

Malaysia's Transport Minister, Hussein, acknowledged the size of the mountain to be climbed. The diplomatic liaison job with so many countries had become huge. Areas of land in 11 countries were being searched while primary satellite data - always a sensitive subject - was being requested from any country which could help. Search aircraft and ships were also requested.

Three investigators from the French Bureau d'Enquetes at d'Analyses pour la Securite de l'Aviation Civile (BEA) who helped with the search for Air France flight 447 in the Atlantic four years earlier, arrived in Malaysia to help out.

On March 18 Australia's Maritime Safety Agency (AMSA) confirmed they were coordinating a search for MH370 in the southern Indian Ocean. The first search area was about 1500n/m south-west of Perth, and aircraft from Australia, New Zealand and the USA took part. Also on March 18 Thailand's Air Force reported they did pick up a primary target of an airliner on March 8, one that departed Kuala Lumpur towards Vietnam. However, they had no subsequent contact with such a target. The information was passed on to Malaysia. Further clarification came that an intermittent signal of an airliner was picked up at 1.28am as it headed towards Kuala Lumpur from the South China Sea, turned right towards Butterworth (Malaysia) and was lost from radar. That signal was only acknowledged after a specific request by Malaysia. Thailand's authorities added that the signal was never observed within Thailand's airspace. Northern corridor searches were drawing a blank also. On March 22, Hussein said that China, India, Pakistan, Myanmar, Laos, Kyrgyzstan and Kazakhstan had reported no sightings on March 8 of unidentified aircraft on their radar.

Progress on a police investigation of Zaharie's flight simulator didn't appear to be yielding much. The logs apparently had been cleared and media reports indicated that there were no findings of any significance.

The action was occurring in the southern Indian Ocean. On March 20, with scores of aircraft and 18 ships scanning the waters along the southern corridor, came the first of a whole series of debris sightings. Analysis of satellite images by Australian Geospatial-Intelligence Organisation showed two pieces of debris about 1350n/m south-west of Perth, adjacent to the defined search area. Prolonged searches failed to come up with anything significant. On March 22 China released a new satellite image identifying an object floating about 63n/m south-west of objects identified two days earlier. The same night an Australian aircraft spotted objects including a wooden pallet, and a buoy was dropped to track its movement. The sighting sparked interest because the lost 777 was carrying wooden pallets.

The next day, Hussein said Malaysia received new satellite images from French authorities showing potential objects in the vicinity of the current search area in the southern corridor. The images were forwarded to Australia and vessels from several countries including China and Japan helped the search out of Perth. An Australian vessel carrying a remote-controlled submarine vehicle was on the way to the search area.

Meanwhile, Indonesia was leading the search into the northern part of the southern corridor. On March 24 there were further sightings of floating objects from Chinese search planes. An Australian search plane saw a circular grey or green object, and a rectangular object in a different area.

But at the end of a frustrating few days, none of these sightings turned out to lead anywhere. Day by day, the realisation of the enormity of the task ahead was becoming more evident. But searchers were in the right place - or at least in the right ocean - of that authorities were now becoming sure.

Inmarsat had been doing more calculations, and working alongside the UK-based Air Accident Investigations Bureau (AAIB) had reached a new conclusion which they had been sharing with Malaysian authorities. Through extremely complicated analysis and calculations Inmarsat was slowly narrowing down its understanding of the route MH370 had taken.

Chapter 10

More Pain

On March 24, Malaysia's Prime Minster Razak called another unscheduled press conference at 10pm. Relatives were called into briefings half an hour before the press conference; in Kuala Lumpur to the Sama Sama Hotel next to the airport, and in Beijing back to the ballroom of the Lido Hotel, the scene of so much chaos on that first terrible day.

Between about 9.30am and 10am cell phones belonging to relatives in both locations starting to beep as they received text messages. The message they received read: "Malaysia Airlines deeply regrets that we have to assume beyond any reasonable doubt that MH370 has been lost and that none on board survived. As you will hear in the next hour from Malaysia's Prime Minister, we must now accept that all evidence suggests the plane went down."

While relatives tried to deal with what they had just received and while in the Lido many could not understand the message because it was in English rather than Chinese, Razak's press conference started.

Razak stated that AAIB experts had briefed him, stating that the satellite experts had done further computations on data using methods never used before. Based on the new computations Inmarsat and the AAIB had concluded MH370 flew the southern corridor with its final position west of Perth, Australia, at a remote area of the Indian Ocean with no landing sites.

"It is with deep sadness and regret I must inform you that, according to these new data, Flight MH370 ended in the southern Indian Ocean," the Prime Minister stated.

It was then that the screaming started.

In the minutes that followed, relatives stumbled out of the room one by one, blinded by grief, into a media frenzy of flashing cameras and microphones. The New Straits Times told how in the Lido some relatives started crying hysterically and others smashed chairs. After the announcement, some family members came out of the room crying uncontrollably, supported by other family members. Loud sounds of crying in the room could also be heard.

"Why were they hiding the truth? Why did they not tell us everything earlier? Don't they have children?" one man shouted. Another woman said: "The way they told us the news is too cruel... They should come out and talk to us... Malaysia is too cruel. Tell the world for us!"

"I'm devastated, devastated, devastated," wailed one elderly woman, repeating herself over and over, her mind frozen, reported The Telegraph. After a few minutes, a policeman gently ushered her back inside, away from the madness.

Another woman refused to believe the news. "The information they released is wrong! Those governments just keep lying to us!" she screamed. "How can you talk about human rights, human rights? Do they have children? Their children must be dead."

The mood inside the Beijing hotel had reportedly been volatile from the beginning. Distrustful of all officials, the relatives cycled between anger and despair, sustained each other's false hopes and conspiracy theories, and lashed out at Malaysian officials. Now as the emotions among the relatives began to run out of control, a stream of policemen flowed through the narrow marble-floored lobby into the room to keep order. At least six stretchers were brought in for those who fainted. One man and one woman were wheeled out for more medical attention in the ambulance at the hotel entrance.

Media reports described how inside the room, many sat silently, the men smoking, the women with faces pale with grief. Outside in the cool night air, one group of relatives stood quietly away from the media, weeping silently. Some lost control. Two men rushed out of the room, their target, members of the media outside.

"Murderers! Murderers!" one man screamed as he was dragged away by the police, the veins in his neck popping as he lunged at the journalists.

"Get out of my way!" another snarled, kicking and swinging at the journalists, trying to knock the whirring and flashing cameras to the ground.

Later, Malaysia Airlines claimed they had told "the majority" of the relatives the news in person, not by text. There may be some truth in this, although it appeared as though most of those gathered in Beijing had not been briefed before their phones buzzed.

The use of a text came in for widespread criticism, but Malaysian Airlines CEO Ahmad Jauhari Yahya defended the move, saying at a press conference the next day that the company's "sole motivation" for informing passengers' family members of their findings through text message was to ensure "the families heard the tragic news before the world did".

Relatives at the Lido Hotel conference room hunkered down into the early hours of the morning as they absorbed the news. Partly they were there to comfort each other, and partly because, with only an empty hotel room to return to, they had nowhere else to turn. Then, just after 2am, representatives of the families faced the media and delivered a statement.

"Eighteen days have passed during which the Malaysian government and military constantly tried to delay, deceive the passengers' families and cheat the whole world," they said. "This shameless behaviour not only fooled and hurt the families of the 154 passengers but also misguided and delayed rescue actions, wasting a large quantity of human resources and materials and lost valuable time for the rescue effort. If the 154 passengers did lose their lives, Malaysia Airlines, the Malaysian government and military are the real executioners who killed them. We the families of those on board submit our strongest protest against them."

At around the same time Malaysia Airlines released its own statement to the relatives. It read in part:

"Malaysia Airlines deeply regrets that we have to assume that MH370 ended in the southern Indian Ocean. As you will hear in the next hour from Malaysia's Prime Minister, new analysis of satellite data suggests the plane went down in the southern Indian Ocean. On behalf of all of us at Malaysia Airlines and all Malaysians, our prayers go out to all the loved ones of the 226 passengers and of our 13 friends and colleagues at this enormously painful time. We know there are no words that we or anyone else can say which can ease your pain." The next day, Chinese relatives held a protest outside the Malaysian Embassy in Beijing. Around 200 family members, some in tears, linked arms and shouted slogans including "The Malaysian Government are murderers" and "We want our relatives back" as they slowly walked the four kilometres from the Lido Hotel to the embassy. Scores of black-clad uniformed police officers were on duty, blocking traffic, their walkie-talkies abuzz.

Meanwhile the Chinese Government, feeling it needed to act on behalf of its citizens, demanded that Kuala Lumpur hand over the satellite data that led it to conclude MH370 ended in the Indian Ocean. The event and more fury over the next few days, marked the nadir in Chinese reaction to Malaysia's handling of MH370 leaving some observers surprised by their vehemence. Chinese social media railed against Malaysia and was full of conspiracy theories involving either Malaysia or the US shooting down the airliner or diverting it to a remote island.

Government censors appeared remarkably relaxed about the outrage, but as the days went by authorities wanted to clamp down on the angst. After a week, the Chinese Government began to distance itself from some of the behaviour. An Associated Press report quoted Chinese Ambassador Huang Huikang branding some of the relatives' viewpoints "radical and extreme," and "somewhat irresponsible" and not representative of China's view. He emphatically stated Beijing's support for Malaysia's handling of the crisis.

American woman Sarah Bajc, whose partner Philip Wood was on the missing plane, said the way some Chinese relatives were campaigning was not helpful, particularly as they were being put up in hotels throughout the ordeal. She said pressuring Malaysia to devote staffers and resources to the Chinese relatives "is like having baby sitters for a bunch of spoiled brats throwing a tantrum".

"All the Chinese are doing is hurting themselves," she was quoted as saying. "They're interfering with the investigation. They're losing face. They're losing confidence in front of the world's eyes."

The story quoted the views of Zhan Jiang, a journalism professor at the Beijing Foreign Studies University, who accounted for the reaction by the fact that "Chinese people are generally distrustful of authority and more prone to believe conspiracy theories, or that people in charge are hiding things".

Martin Vengadesan felt some of the Chinese reaction was over the top.

"I honestly feel that China didn't do much to stem that. They allowed everyone to be angry," he said.

He suggested China was perhaps deflecting the fact that two Uighar people were on the flight and there was suspicion about their role.

Nor was China in a position to throw stones.

"I think China itself has at least 5 to 10 situations where the Government suppressed the nation regarding national disasters or crackdowns, and I think that in itself makes Chinese people suspicious. I just feel that based on my colleagues (what they say) in China, I felt it was something that was allowed to be fuelled. The Chinese media were whipping up a frenzy."

It is all too easy for TV audiences to watch such scenes of raw grief with the benefit of distance and from the comfort of an armchair, and judge that it doesn't seem real or legitimate to them. It's a salutary reminder of just what distress these people were going through when one witnesses it or hears it first hand from a bereaved family member.

A young Chinese man who lives in New Zealand but had returned to China for a month's holiday in late April told the authors of this book at his shock when his father broke the news that his uncle was on the plane.

"He said 'There is something you should know. Your uncle was on that plane, the one that went missing.' My mind went blank for about 30 seconds. And then my father said, 'Now we go to the Lido Hotel, where the Malaysia Airline family support centre is, to see if there are any updates.'"

The young man said that when they got to the Lido they passed through a heavy police presence and security check to get into the hotel meeting room.

"There were notes and banners all over the wall. Some of them were official press releases, some of them were personal messages from the victims' families to pray for the returning of the plane and their loved ones. There was a heart-shaped display made out of candles on a table. At this moment, I could not hold my emotion any more. I felt I was surrounded by darkness, so many faces floating randomly around me and yelling at me. Some of them were the passengers on the plane, some of them were family members. It was just like the moment before you wake up from a nightmare. I couldn't hold my tears any-more and started to kick those tables over until my mum stopped me and accompanied me out of the room."

Jahabar Sadiq says Malaysia was guilty of being slow to understand the nature of the grief Chinese relatives were feeling.

"I think a lot of us didn't understand the context of grief in China. Because of their one-child policy most of the chaps on board the plane, some had their fathers and son and grandchildren there. Three generations of families wiped out. We couldn't relate at first. Once you finally comprehend we killed a lot of clans, entire generations of families. It was a dissonance between their culture and ours that we didn't understand."

Bereaved family members' distress goes a lot wider than the Chinese. Danica Weeks is a spokeswoman for Voice 370, an international committee set up to represent families of those on board MH370, driven by frustration at the unsuccessful search and cynicism about whether Inmarsat's conclusions are correct. Voice 370 wrote an open letter, signed by Weeks and 10 others, to the leaders of Malaysia, Australia and China appealing for help to find their loved ones. It said: "Our purpose is to support each other, with the sole intention of finding MH370 and our loved ones. Due to the lack of physical evidence that MH370 ended in the southern Indian Ocean, the families are in urgent need for the conclusion based on Inmarsat data analysis that the aircraft's flight ended in that ocean to be reconsidered to confirm its accuracy. Further, if Inmarsat's analysis is unable to rule out other flight paths as a possibility, that fact must be acknowledged. Given the lack of tangible evidence of what happened to MH370, in our view data analysis that only indicates a probable southern flight path is an insufficient basis to support a definitive conclusion that no other flight path was possible."

Voice 370 asked authorities to release the raw satellite data "so that it can be subject to broader analysis by relevant experts".

"The satellite data is the only lead we have and is key in identifying MH370's flight path... In view of the lack of emergency locator transmitter activation, zero detected debris and the lack of convincing 'pings', we feel it is necessary that the data be subject to independent third-party review. It is our hope that with out-of-box thinking the whole world can help to look for the plane."

The Malaysian Government agreed to do so and issued a 45-page report, and Voice 370 sent the data to various experts and posted a link on its Facebook page. Weeks told the Weekend Herald in New Zealand Voice 370 was happy with the release as it was "a step towards transparency", but "we are not sure why they held on to it for so long".

"There does not seem to be anything in there that would have held back its release. We are grappling with completely changed lives and ... trying to fight to get transparency at the same time. We have been through enough," she said. "Until we find out what happened, we cannot move on, we cannot grieve, and it consumes our thoughts 24/7; it's a harrowing, distressing and frustrating road."

More recently, Voice 370 launched a crowd-funding campaign to reward whistle-blower information with $3.22 million cash. Weeks said families would try anything to uncover vital information they believe is being withheld by authorities.

The international fundraiser "Reward MH370: The Search for the Truth" launched on website Indiegogo. In addition to the $3.22m reward, the group aims to raise $2.35m for a private investigation into the plane's disappearance.

"We are desperate, we really are," Danica Weeks told the Herald on Sunday.

"There are things they are refusing to tell us. We want them to be transparent and we will try any avenue possible to get the answers.

"Someone knows something."

Weeks said she had emailed questions to Malaysia Airlines but had been given the runaround.

"We have been cut off at the gate so many times we are getting frustrated - that is why we have started this," she said. "Every time I ring now, I feel like we have become an inconvenience."

The website reads: "The first aspect of the campaign will be to fully fund a reward that is sizable enough to change someone's life. Our target remains $5 million and we realize this may take a little longer than anticipated and require funds generated outside of the Indiegogo campaign.

"The second aspect of the campaign will be to engage a professional, licensed private investigation company to follow up on all leads we had prior to the commencement of this campaign and rule out those which are not worth pursuing.

"The third aspect will be to continue to fund the investigation of leads received through the reward program. This would be a requirement for the larger pledges to be secured. The more we raise, the more investigation we can do."

Said Weeks: "We believe there is a person or persons who know the truth about what happened, and know where the plane is. We want to encourage the truth to come out by offering a substantial reward."

The Reward 370 initiative is led by a governance team of six people. Four of the group had family on the flight. They include Frenchman Ghislain Wattrelos, whose wife Laurence and two of his teenage children, Hadrian and Amber, were on the flight; Philip Wood's partner Sarah Bajc; Indian K.S. Narendran who lost his wife Chandrika Sharma; and Pralhad Shirseth, whose wife Kranti was on the plane.

Two others, Maarten Van Sluys, a Brazilian whose sister died on Air France 447 in 2009, and Ethan Hunt are in the group for their fundraising and private investigative experience.

When this book went to press Reward 370 had raised nearly US$90,000.

Chapter 11

No Black Box, No Luck

The traumatic announcement by Malaysian Prime Minister Najib Razak marked a new chapter in the search for MH370.

Inmarsat's analysis based on radar data and satellite communications placed MH370 on a huge arc in the southern part of the Indian Ocean. The initial search area decided by a joint investigation team was 600,000 sq km in an area about 2500km from Perth. Australian Prime Minister Tony Abbott branded the area "as close to nowhere as it is possible to be". With a 30-day deadline for the black box's battery looming over the search team creating even more pressure, the odds of searchers striking gold were astronomical. Everything was against them.

As the ATSB's Definition of Underwater Searches report sets out, success for an over-water search normally is dependent on a number of factors. These include position information from ground-based radar systems, position information automatically transmitted from an aircraft, position reports from crew, re-tracing of the flight route and eye witness reports, often from other aircraft or ships.

In the case of MH370 there had been no radio notification or a problem from crew and no radio communications after 1.19am on March 8. The final secondary radar position was midway between Malaysia air space and Vietnamese air space at 1.21am. At 1.25am the aircraft deviated from its planned flight route and the final primary radar fix occurred at 2.22am near the Andaman Islands in the Malacca Strait. The satellite communications log indicated the aircraft had continued to fly for another six hours until at least 8.19am. There were no confirmed eye witness reports and no emergency locator transmissions received and lastly, the Australian-led search was beginning 10 days after the aircraft went missing.

The scale of the problem for searchers in finding MH370 only comes into context when compared with Air France 447 which crashed on June 1, 2009, killing all on board. The ACARS system on that aircraft was reporting more parameters (and it was switched on) than MH370 and programmed to automatically transmit its position every 10 minutes.

The last Air France flight position report occurred at 2.10am and 24 maintenance messages were received via the same satellite operated by Inmarsat over the next five minutes. The impact time was based on the fact that a message had been expected to be received within one minute and hadn't, narrowing the time the flight ended to between 2.14.26am and 2.15.14am. This narrowed the search area hugely and the first wreckage was found on June 6. The actual aircraft wreckage was not located for nearly two years.

A huge search effort for MH370, coordinated by the Australian Maritime Safety Authority, was mounted along the specified area in the southern arc from March 18 involving an international fleet of aircraft and ships generally moving from south-west along the arc to the north-east.

On April 2 there was some hope when UK defence vessel HMS Echo, using a hull-mounted acoustic system, detected a ping in an area further to the north-east than Australian vessel Ocean Shield's area of highest probability. But HMS Echo tracked pings for two hours and 20 minutes before losing it and then tracked pings on three more occasions. Ocean Shield moved away from the area pinpointed by Inmarsat to be the most likely final resting places for MH370 to join the hunt and employed a Towed Pinger Locator, an implement towed 1km deep looking for signals.

On April 4 there was another glimpse of hope when Chinese vessel MV Haixun 01, operating a Benthos pinger detector, also picked up a ping, repeating at one ping per second. Ocean Shield made its way to the area and with the Towed Pinger Locator detected the ping three times but never again after that.

A US Navy robotic submarine Bluefin-21 was used extensively in a search of the seabed but found nothing. Bluefin-21 required 16 missions to complete its search of the 314 square kilometre area around the detections made by the Towed Pinger Locator. Subsequently, doubts have been cast about what the "pings" picked up by these vessels actually were, but there appears to be widespread agreement they were nothing to do with MH370. A US Navy source told CNN that the pings were more likely from some other man-made source, possibly a ship or even from the electronics of the Towed Pinged Locator. No debris from MH370 was found either from the surface search, acoustic search or the ocean floor search near where pings had been heard. The ocean floor search was ended on May 28.

The day after the search ended, a statement from the Joint Agency Co-ordination Centre summed up the conclusion: "The Australian Transport Safety Bureau (ATSB) has advised that the search in the vicinity of the acoustic detections can now be considered complete, and in its professional judgement, the area can now be discounted as the final resting place of MH370."

In its report on June 26 the ATSB said refinements of the analysis of flight and satellite data had been continuous over recent months and a team of experts from the UK, US and Australia had reached a consensus in identifying a priority underwater search area for the next phase of the search for MH370. The priority area of about 60,000 sq km with a width of 93km is further south and still about 1800 km offshore from Western Australia. The new search area has not been mapped and Chinese and Australian ships are mapping the sea floor. This is expected to take three months.

The search will be able to start properly in August and could last for 12 months.

Chapter 12

Kuala Lumpur Moves On

If you're looking for some sort of shadow hanging over Kuala Lumpur as a result of MH370 you won't find one.

Three months on from the loss of the 777 - before the incredible tragedy was repeated with the shooting down of MH17 over the Ukraine - the city's mood has noticeably lifted.

As journalists begin re-interviewing anyone with the slightest involvement as they build up towards their "100 days since MH370" features, KL International Airport appears not the least bit tense and uptight that such an atrocity could have occurred from within. You don't even need to fill in an immigration card when you arrive and the bag search is minimal if, non-existent.

KL is at once a paradox; it is a strange combination of laid back and friendly and downright manic. Sunday night at 11 o'clock and the narrow street near the hotel at KL Sentral is chaotic. Throngs of people are out and it's noisy, incredibly hot and the nose is accosted with a variety of smells all at once - some delicious, some horrific; spicy curries and something akin to sewage meet in one odour. The sidewalk tables outside makeshift flimsy shop fronts, tailors, a plethora of food stores and garish jewellery stores, have all spilled out on to the street, and hundreds of men drink tea and talk and laugh and shout while an armada of scooters dexterously thread their way through the cluttered street. It's a weird arrangement. Although it's a narrow street, angle-parking is provided. Then, just to really tax the available space, cars are idly parked behind them.

"Double parking, it's the Malaysian way," observes the taxi driver.

It's a city of contrasts and incongruity; Malays, Indians and Chinese co-existing. Chinese-style architecture hard up against mosques, two buildings down from a brand new high-rise. The perennial Asian contrast between rich and poor, clean and filthy, old and new; look out the tinted windows of a new hotel to decaying buildings and yards. Clothes hang off makeshift lines while a monorail hums past. Roots of tropical jungle sprout up wherever concrete and steel and glass hasn't squashed the life out of it.

After the first trip in a taxi in which the driver quotes 14 Ringits for a journey and changes it to 40 when we arrive at the destination, one realises that taxi drivers without meters are to be avoided at all costs. Kuala Lumpur society is complicated, even to locals who try to explain it. Newspapers aren't neutral. They're either pro-Government or anti-Government or somewhere in between, depending on who owns them. Even journalists are high-ranking members of political parties.

The Muslim influence is everywhere, the tone set around 5.45am with the enchanting call to prayer from the local mosque's Imam. And as a visitor, you'll always be within earshot as there's always a local mosque. A bit like a British pub, there appears to be a mosque on every corner. The eye quickly adjusts to women wearing hajib. Although it's all relative; from the attractive Malay who smiles genuinely at you on the train to the fully covered married woman in a Middle Eastern restaurant who requires her husband's escort to the bathroom and a screen brought across to cover her table so others can't watch her eat.

Such behaviour jars with the western culture that infiltrates almost insensitively. At the hotel's rooftop café we watched a fully covered Muslim woman sit with her husband at breakfast while a sleazy Miley Cyrus croons through the stereo in the background. Some days there's a haze across the city, the top of the Petronas Towers lost until the extreme heat burns it off and builds throughout the day. Then huge downpours wash away the swelter in the late afternoon. One remembers images of candle-lit vigils and memorials with written messages "pray for MH370" but across the city now this emotion seems to have dissipated and given way to fatigue.

We couldn't find any MH370 memorial at either the airport or in the Pavilion Shopping Centre in the CBD. Both appeared to be gone. The main feature in the shopping centre was a Batman 75th exhibition.

While pressure from the West eventually forced the conniving Malaysian Government into open dialogue over MH370, one realises that nothing has changed for the people of KL. The Government has locked down all information on MH370, we're repeatedly told.

At a café in Bangsar, south west of the CBD, Jahabar Sadiq, the amiable chief executive officer of The Malaysian Insider tells how on the Monday after the tragedy, everything related to the aircraft was sealed up and given to the DCA.

"They got everything. All the recordings, passenger and cargo manifests - everything."

Although some of this was subsequently released in the Government's Preliminary Report, vital information such as detailed primary radar readings from the night of March 8 are still buried. But there's also a belief that the investigation is going nowhere. Sadiq tells a story of a maintenance engineer he knows at the airport who has been interviewed four times by investigators, each time with a virtual identical line of questioning.

"He's told them the same story each time."

Sadiq doesn't rate the ability of Malaysian authorities to investigate what happened. Police were initially criticised for allowing Zaharie's wife Faisa too much time before interviewing her, and it was suggested it was a cultural thing in Malaysia not to invade someone's grief. Not according to Sadiq who puts it down to incompetence.

"Not so much a cultural thing. I tell people our guys are not equipped to investigate. They are not technically, they have no idea."

The frustration at the lack of information has bred a deep suspicion about analysis of where MH370 has ended up. The inability of searchers in the southern Indian Ocean to recover or even locate any wreckage of the 777 has increased the cynicism of even intelligent journalists about whether Inmarsat's theories are correct.

"A week ago we wrote a story about doubts over the final resting place of MH370," says Sadiq. "I got a call from a senior diplomat at the British High Commission saying 'you can't say there are doubts, we are sure of these things.'" But can we be? There is no physical proof, no debris, all we know is the electronic data."

Sadiq says many media have become frustrated at the lack of answers and tried to change the focus of their stories.

"I think we were just disgusted by what happened and no closer to finding out what happened. We've been following this every day but at about 50 days we thought screw the search, let's just focus on the families. Let's tell their stories."

Sadiq refers to a story the Malysian Insider did two weeks earlier about flight attendant Mohamad Hazrin's wife giving birth to their second child. Star Online news editor Martin Vengadesan agrees an element of fatigue has crept in for Malaysian people.

"Most Malaysians are very sad about it. But with any tragedy, particularly if you don't have a personal involvement you will move on. Now it's almost three months. In March it was the predominant thought in everyone's mind, but now I guess people have moved on."

He admits a similar frustration to Sadiq at some of the stories run by international media and suggests there is more to it than legitimate sources.

"When information is released you wonder who are they and what is the agenda."

There's a degree of annoyance at international attacks on Malaysia and even on the Government.

"Often when people attack you from the outside it's one way of unifying people. People are trying to run down Malaysia. It's our home, it's a beautiful country. Even if you support the opposition you may not want to see your country's Government run down."

Both Zaharie and Fariq lived in Shah Alam, a city 20km west of Kuala Lumpur. It's almost exclusively Muslim and a taxi driver tells us with a smile "there's no cinemas and no one complains".

Fariq's neighbourhood in section 7 of Shah Alam is pleasant and relatively spacious when one considers the rest of the city's housing. He couldn't be closer to a mosque if he tried. The dowdy Surau Al-mawaddah mosque is barely 30m away. Fariq lived on a lane just opposite. The mosque looks well visited; a cat shades itself beside a parked motorbike.

Born into a middle class family in 1987 as the first of five children, Fariq excelled at studies, enjoyed sports, played the guitar, and showed a flair for drawing and aviation, classmates say. Things came easy for the boy and he progressed effortlessly to be able to follow his chosen profession of flying. He graduated from HM Aerospace, a private flying school in Langkawi and hadn't looked back since. He even enjoyed some notoriety recently when he was the subject of a CNN documentary when on a flight from Hong Kong to Kuala Lumpur, a CNN reporter sat in the cockpit to observe Fariq guide the aircraft in what his supervisor described as a "textbook landing".

Fariq had an eye for women and wasn't above pushing his credentials to meet them as his secret flirtation with two South Africans in a cockpit two years ago has showed. He had apparently been in a relationship with another young pilot, a first officer Nadira Ramli who flies for AirAsia, the daughter of a pilot herself. There are stories that an engagement was imminent but whatever the case, it was a serious committed relationship.

The two-storey houses are similar. It's no gated community - still middle class - but the next best thing is a tall gate in front of every property. They are big houses on small sections with two or three upmarket cars parked in the front of each driveway. Fariq's house, a mixture of browns with a terra cotta roof, hides behind a brown ornate gate, two expensive cars in the driveway and two satellite TV aerials. It's extremely hot but no windows are open. There's no sign of life and no answer at the door. Opposite the house, young men building a stone wall outside a house look on curiously. An older couple come out of the house to anxiously observe the boys work. Fariq is gone but life goes on.

Three doors down is a kids' playcentre painted in gawdy red and yellow colours. A boy rides his motorbike by on the street, helmet-less, singing to himself.

The area is a touch schizophrenic; a strange mixture of immaculate houses with lovingly looked-after yards and dilapidated ageing residences with overgrown sections. It almost feels like a work in progress. There's construction going on at every corner. There's a rather desolate bare park a couple of hundred metres away. One of the park benches is broken but there's some children's play equipment. One wonders if Fariq and Nadira ever walked here. Vehicles come and go, all of them clean new models, driven almost exclusively by women in hajibs. Presumably their husbands are all at work in relatively high-paying jobs.

When he wasn't flying, Fariq was apparently a regular attender at the mosque. The mosque's Imam described Fariq as a "good boy, a good

Muslim, humble and quiet".

A shopping centre is just a short walk away, not 100m. Two large blocks of shops, including a chemist and a restaurant. Opposite, an upmarket Arabian restaurant is being built, Al Rawsha Restaurant. The taxi driver says he wouldn't go there, doesn't like Arabian food. We have a Nasi Goreng at a restaurant called Sri Gemilang with the taxi driver and wonder whether perhaps Fariq also took Nadira here. Two grey cats fight persistently under a table on the brown tiled floor. It's pleasant enough.

Zaharie's Shah Alam is a whole different pleasant - a step up. The difference between a junior and a senior pilot. As he drives, the taxi driver points to the Selangor Royal Club, most of which is hidden behind a hill from our eyes, and apparently very exclusive. The closer we get the more picturesque it is. We drive by the eye-catching and massive Blue Mosque, the state mosque and a big tourist attraction. It's so breathtakingly beautiful, it's enough to make one reconsider one's faith. Nearby are Shah Alam lake where one can go canoeing or cycling around and the national football stadium, Stadium Shah Alam.

The friendly taxi driver tells us that Zaharie's compound, Laman Seri, is mainly populated by people like pilots and engineers. We ask him how the public views pilots.

"Yes, we respect them because they are a very high class of people. The job is very important because it's a dangerous, responsible job. Pilots are disciplined people. They follow the procedures."

What does he think caused the disappearance of MH370?

"A political reason. Some sort of international conspiracy," he replies.

Laman Seri is spotless and inviting. Behind a gate with fountains and palms on both sides are lines of palatial large two-storey homes. It looks an attractive walk but security guards bar any access. We try to equate everything we've heard about Zaharie with what we see here. It's not hard. He was leading a privileged life and with enough time on his hands to indulge his hobbies. It seems comfortable, complacent and surely happy.

So what happened? How is it that Zaharie Ahmad Shah has become the major suspect in the biggest aviation murder/suicide in history?

Chapter 13

Zaharie, Prime Suspect

Soon after the disappearance of MH370 rumours of problems in Zaharie's personal life surfaced. Rumours about the state of his marriage and his disenchantment with the Government's treatment of opposition leader Anwar Ibrahim. Four months on from the disappearance of the flight, investigators still regard him as their chief suspect.

According to media reports, detectives carried out 170 interviews and profiled all of the 239 people on board the Boeing 777 and, if deliberate action is to blame, Zaharie is still seen as the most likely perpetrator. Investigators have previously refused to "clear" the captain's flight simulator of suspicious activity, and it now appears they found evidence of routes programmed to take a plane far out into the Indian Ocean and practising landing using a short runway on an island. The data from the simulated flights had been deleted, but computer experts were able to retrieve them, according to a widely reported story which first appeared in the Sunday Times.

The police probe has also apparently revealed that the 53-year-old captain was unique among those on board the flight for having no recorded commitments, either socially or for work, to take place after the date of the MH370 journey. This was not in keeping with Zaharie's usually outgoing and open nature, police said, and in contrast to the activities of his co-pilot, Fariq Hamid, and the rest of the crew. The inquiry also does not rule out the possibility that the jet crashed due to some form of mechanical failure or an act of terrorism. Zaharie's motives for such a crime cannot easily be nailed down, and everyone we interviewed dismissed their feasibility. Zaharie is a popular figure in Kuala Lumpur and many people don't want to see his reputation damaged. There was also considerable anger that Malaysia Airlines hadn't stood by their man and publicly backed him despite the suspicions about him. There was fierce loyalty but our impression was that we were being met by an endless supply of apologists prepared to vouch for Zaharie, regardless of how well they actually knew the man. Third-hand friends who'd never met Zaharie's family were being wheeled out to say what a great guy he was.

Soon after the plane's disappearance and the ensuing concerns about Zaharie's role in it, a sycophantic Facebook page was started by a former schoolmate Dr Mohd Ghouse. On the front it states: "A tribute page set up by Dr Ghouse to get more people to know who Capt Zaharie is, for those who believed that we should not judge a person in his absence." The page has 30,772 likes and there's not a word worth reading on it. We were beginning to get the impression that Zaharie Ahmad Shah was virtually untouchable.

Born in the Malaysian state of Penang in 1961, The Wall Street Journal described how Zaharie enjoyed a relatively comfortable childhood. Friends remember him as an above-average science student who enjoyed pickup soccer games and tinkering with a motorcycle. He preferred course work over Boy Scouts, intramural sports or other schoolwide events, according to Jalil Saad, a former schoolmate and now headmaster at Penang Free School, the colonial-era school Zaharie attended. Zaharie was a celebrated past pupil and since MH370's disappearance the school has held special assemblies in his honour.

As a teenager, Zaharie met and courted Faisa Khanum Mustafa Khan who lived just a few doors away from him. Faisa's brother Asuad Khan, who says Zaharie was two years ahead of him at Penang Free School, told us he remembers Zaharie courting Faisa.

"We lived about three houses away. My sister had a friend who lived just opposite his house. She would sometimes go to the house to meet friends and I think that's how it started. He was about 17 or 18 when they met. She was about 16 or 17."

Just like with Fariq, things came easy for Zaharie. Toward the end of his years in school, he decided to become a pilot. It was no surprise for friends who remember his passion for flying kites and the gasoline-powered model airplane he built himself. At around age 18, Zaharie was one of just 12 in his batch of 5000 applicants who was accepted to flight school, as a cadet for Malaysia Airlines.

At the time, Malaysia didn't have a flight school, so Zaharie headed to the Philippines for training, where he met another trainee pilot, Nik Huzlan. Outside the academy, cadets lived well, with much night life, says Huzlan.

"We were a poorer version of Tom Cruise," he told the Wall Street Journal, referring to the 1986 movie "Top Gun".

Asuad says Zaharie may have been having fun in the Philippines but he had his sights set firmly on Faisa, even getting his mother to do some of his spade work.

"He was making a lot of noise to his mother; 'better make sure when he came back he can marry my sister'. His mother came to the house and said 'please agree or he will never want to come back' and my father laughed at him. He would call her from Manila and say if you don't get that girl for me I will never come back to Malaysia."

Both men joined Malaysia Airlines in 1981 after graduation. Zaharie soon did get the girl and he and Faisa married. Zaharie did well with Malaysia Airlines, forming a reputation as a solid pilot with a good work ethic.

Huzlan eventually became chief pilot, a job that involved handling discipline problems. Most pilots, including Zaharie, were never a cause for concern, he said. "Zaharie is the ideal pilot, an invisible pilot," he told the Wall Street Journal. Nor, in the chatter among pilots, was there ever any suggestion of personal problems, Huzlan added.

Despite this, Zaharie seems to be something of an attention seeker. He went to enough trouble to make You Tube videos which he called community service, showing off his DIY and cooking skills.

In 2010, Zaharie attended a Penang Free School reunion. A former classmate Jason Lee said he didn't initially recognize the pilot.

"From being skinny, he'd become, what should I say, prosperous-looking, and his hair was gone," he said, but his jovial personality hadn't changed.

And Zaharie and Faisa were indeed prosperous. They moved out of their house in Subang and into the prestigious gated community in Shah Alam. They were doing well enough to be able to keep the old house so their youngest son could stay there, close to his friends.

Asuad appears to have had a reasonable relationship with Zaharie over the years. When Asuad lived in Kuala Lumpur for a while he and Zaharie used to go to play snooker together. Zaharie was often playing with his remote control plane and before that a remote control car, boats and helicopter.

"He was crazy about it."

Asuad says Zaharie also went through a stage of paragliding, but that all ended when he had an accident bad enough that Malaysia Airlines had to be informed. He can't remember what injuries Zaharie sustained.

Why would Zaharie commit this crime? Two main motives have been discussed.

There is no doubt he was disenchanted with the Government's treatment of the political leader he supported, Anwar Ibrahim and it is well documented that the day of the flight Ibrahim's acquittal on long-standing charges of sodomy were reversed. Zaharie, who had joined the People's Justice Party in January 2013, was a fervent supporter of Ibrahim. The political interest had been a relatively recent thing, something Asuad puts down to Zaharie having time on his hands.

Peter Chong, secretary to People's Justice Party MP Sivarasa Rasiah, recalls meeting Zaharie at a community event one afternoon.

"It was in a community programme where we invited people to come and talk about issues," says Chong who calls himself a friend of Zaharie. "He was there as a volunteer. At the end of the afternoon program there was this guy stacking up chairs. I never saw him before and people told me he worked for Malaysia Airlines. I approached him and he introduced himself. 'I'm Zaharie.' I looked at his business card - 'captain of a 777 and you are doing these things?' He just smiled. I remember when he joined the People's Justice Party. I remember when he handed over his form. I said 'are you sure about this?' He laughed."

It was a fair question from Chong because supporting Anwar Ibrahim is no walk in the park. The former Malaysian Deputy Prime Minister is a huge thorn in the side of the United Malays National Organisation (UMNO) that has ruled for 56 years. Ibrahim's ability to unite opposition has seen support rising steadily, and in 2008 opposition parties won more than a third of the seats in Malaysia's parliament. But Ibrahim has been a marked man and was acquitted in 2012 over charges of sodomy - a crime in Malaysia - after a two-year trial. Ibrahim and his supporters say the charges were politically motivated.

There are various accounts of Zaharie's political involvement but no one paints him as a fanatic. Yin Siao Loong, head of an opposition think tank, who met Zaharie as he volunteered as an absentee-vote monitor during Malaysia's 2013 general election, said Zaharie was patient and efficient, and far from a political fanatic as some media have suggested.

"Political fanatics don't have the patience to sit around as vote monitors," Mr. Yin said.

Soon after MH370 disappeared, an image emerged of the pilot of the missing Malaysia Airlines jet wearing a T-shirt with a 'Democracy is Dead' slogan, prompting suggestions he could have hijacked the plane in an anti-government protest. Chong laughs at this; it was he who tweeted the picture which went around the world and supposedly demonstrated Zaharie's motive for taking a plane down. He doesn't believe it. Chong doesn't buy the suggestion that Zaharie might have been infuriated by Ibrahim's fate. But then one senses part of Chong's reason for meeting us is to distance Zaharie from Ibrahim. Association with Zaharie is now a bad look for the politician, particularly in light of a Government that will use anything it can to take Ibrahim out.

It is well documented Zaharie is Ibrahim's daughter's great-uncle but the pair have barely met. Ibrahim has been careful to distance himself from Zaharie's actions and rubbishes any suggestion that Zaharie might have acted on his behalf.

But wasn't Zaharie angry about Ibrahim's court date?

"Every Malaysian in the country was angry with it because there was a by-election coming up four days after the court appearance. He was like many of us, pissed off. But Zaharie is an experienced pilot. Why is an experienced pilot interested in things like that?" asks Chong.

"Why not?"

"Based on a court decision like that you make a decision to take down a plane with 239 people?"

Chong says last time he met Zaharie, a week before the flight, he was his usual "fun, caring self".

"When he was with people he was the one who would try to introduce people. Fanatics tend to be loners. He didn't fit that profile."

Ibrahim, wary of Zaharie being used against him politically, admits Zaharie is a distant relative by marriage but emphasises he has barely ever met him. Contacted for an interview for this book, Ibrahim issued statements he has released publicly setting out his position and stating that Zaharie was no extremist.

"He supports our multiracial coalition. He supports democratic reform. He is against any form of extremism."

Ibrahim further admitted that Zaharie was a staunch opposition supporter and that he had met the pilot on a few occasions at party functions.

"I am not one to hide my associations with others. I have met him once or twice but I do not remember how many times," he said.

Ibrahim also corrected claims in some media that before his flight on March 8 Zaharie witnessed the three-man judiciary overturning his acquittal.

"He was not in the court. He may have been outside in the premises of the court. But from what I gather, from many of our colleagues, nobody actually saw him in the premises of the court."

This is backed up Asuad Khan who says Zaharie didn't even know of the decision until Faisa told him at home. Ibrahim also played down reading too much into Zaharie's reaction to the decision.

"I gathered later from many of his colleagues and from what is written about him that he was disturbed. Many others were disturbed. I mean, we were shocked and appalled by the speed of the process of the court of appeal. But I think that's quite normal. I don't think it's something that would trigger a person of his expertise, calibre, to do any unwanted activity. I am absolutely certain of that. I believe 90 per cent of taxi drivers support me and are not happy with the decision. But they did not hijack their taxi to Kajang," he said.

A more fundamental issue for Zaharie was the state of his marriage, his life and his mental health. Malaysian media appears to stay away from such speculation. It does not appear to be a place it feels it should dwell, but no such inhibition has applied to international media.

A week after the plane's disappearance on March 16 the Daily Mirror ran a story suggesting Zaharie's family had moved out of their house a day before the flight, based on the testimony of a maid.

On March 22 the Daily Mail in the UK ran a story claiming an analysis of Zaharie's phone record showed he had received a two-minute call shortly before take-off from a mystery woman using a mobile phone number obtained under a false identity. The newspaper said this was one of the last calls made to or from the mobile of Zaharie before the flight.

"Investigators are treating it as potentially significant because anyone buying a pay-as-you-go SIM card in Malaysia has to fill out a form giving their identity card or passport number… this ensures that every number is registered to a traceable person. But in this case police traced the number to a shop selling SIM cards in Kuala Lumpur. They found that it had been bought 'very recently' by someone who gave a woman's name - but was using a false identity."

The inference was of some sort of terror link as members of such groups routinely use untraceable SIM cards.

On March 26 came one of the most dramatic stories when a man purporting to be a close friend of Zaharie's came forward and talked to the New Zealand Herald, claiming that Zaharie had serious personal issues that may have distracted him from operating a plane at all.

"He's one of the finest pilots around and I'm no medical expert, but with all that was happening in his life Zaharie was probably in no state of mind to be flying," the man was reported as saying.

The friend, who is also a pilot, said that Zaharie had been going through many serious personal issues. He had separated from his wife and was having issues with a different woman he was seeing. His wife had ended the relationship leaving Zaharie "terribly upset," the confidant revealed, suggesting he may have used the 777 as one "last joyride" to see what he hadn't seen before. The friend said Zaharie, who he chatted to when they met several times a year through work, was a fanatic for "the three Fs" - food, family and flying. When he wasn't working he spent hours cooking or using his flight simulator for a variety of situations he wouldn't experience at the controls of a commercial airline, such as flying at the highest and lowest possible altitudes. The associate believed the co-pilot must have been incapacitated and the other flight crew kept out of the cockpit.

"It is very possible that neither the passengers nor the other crew on-board knew what was happening until it was too late."

Probably the coup de grace came when the Daily Mirror reported on March 30 what it claimed was leaked information relating to investigators' interviews with family of Zaharie in Kuala Lumpur. The Mirror's story concerned the fragility of Zaharie's state of mind. It suggested Zaharie was no longer in a relationship with Faisa but they still lived together for their children. Speaking about the mystery for the first time, the wife and daughter of Zaharie allegedly said the 53-year-old pilot had been distracted and withdrawn in the weeks before the aircraft's disappearance - and refused pleas to attend some marriage counselling sessions. According to the story, Faisa told investigators that he stopped speaking to her in the weeks before the fateful flight and spent time alone in his room on his flight simulator.

"He just retreated into a shell," the newspaper reported her saying.

Meanwhile, Aishah, Zaharie's daughter, allegedly said that in her last conversations with her father, she barely recognised the man who used to dote on her.

"He wasn't the father I knew. He seemed disturbed and lost in a world of his own," she said.

According to the story, the family were still convinced that he was not responsible for the plane's disappearance. Faisa broke down repeatedly during two lengthy interviews with police, the family source said. One of the interviews lasted more than four hours. She was initially reluctant to discuss the breakdown of her marriage, and refused to accept her husband might be involved in the flight's disappearance, protesting: "It's unfair to blame my husband." However, over the course of the interviews, she told police how her husband became increasingly distracted in the months leading up to the flight.

"I found him distant and difficult to understand," she said. She told investigators that although they continued to live in the same house, Zaharie spent his time alone. Faisa said her husband was so withdrawn he hardly spoke to his sons and was not close to them. When he wasn't working, Zaharie spent "more time with friends than with family members". She confirmed they had spoken of separating but had not taken any formal steps towards getting a divorce.

Aishah said her father spoke to her about his marital problems and told her he didn't think they could reconcile. In their conversations, he asked her how she would feel if her parents divorced. Aishah said she tried to persuade her father to seek the help of Islamic elders to try to mend the relationship but he refused. The daughter told investigators she did not know if there was another woman in her father's life. Although Aishah does not appear to have spoken to her father on the day the flight disappeared, she told investigators she knew from friends in Kuala Lumpur he was upset and felt 'utter frustration' over the jail sentence given to Anwar Ibrahim. Despite her father's personal problems, Aishah told investigators she did not believe he could be in any way responsible for the flight's disappearance.

"I don't believe he would ever intentionally endanger the lives of his crew and passengers," she insisted.

Investigators also spoke to the pilot's two sons - Ahmad Seth Zaharie, 26, a languages student, and Ahmad Idris Zaharie, 32. Ahmad Seth told them he had 'barely spoken' to his father in the weeks before the flight disappeared, even though they shared the same house.

The British tabloid's story infuriated Zaharie's family who accused it of fabricating the whole thing. Aishah immediately took to Facebook to slam the paper's report.

"Dear Dailymail (sic), You should consider making movies since you are so good at making up stories and scripts out of thin air," she posted. "May god have mercy on your souls. You can bet your ass I will not forgive you."

Ahmad Idris posted a message on Facebook thanking someone for a poem written in support of his father which he said had helped to counter the "wounds and sadness" from "baseless accusations made against my father".

He branded the story "rubbish". "I'm disgusted with this article ... they are really pushing the human patience to the limit ... how I wish its dat (sic) easy to get a lawyer n (sic) sue them. If I could I would sue them till the company needs to be closed down (which is very unlikely)," he posted on Facebook.

The issue of separation appears to be a grey area although, let's be frank, that may also have been the way it actually was, such is the nature of relationships.

Vengadesan concedes he understood that Zaharie and Faisa were separated.

"I don't know the specifics. I believe he was separated. It's not nice but I don't feel one man gets sent to jail and you're separated adds up to 'I want to go and kill myself.' Zaharie is extremely passionate about flying, very knowledgeable and very safety conscious. A lot of people are not happy. Maybe it's a Malaysian cultural thing. You are simply accusing someone who is not around to defend himself - that makes people angry. Most Malaysians aren't happy with that theory."

He acknowledges that some sort of mechanical problem with the 777 would be more palatable for Malaysian people.

Sadiq is also unconvinced and says Zaharie flew to Australia with a pilot friend of his at the end of February, during which time Zaharie saw his daughter in Melbourne.

"I think he might have asked for the flight to see his daughter in Australia. My friend is a very experienced guy; and he says he's a nice chap, speaks well, a DIY freak. He was completely all right, cracking jokes. Anwar (Ibrahim) gets sent to jail every few years so if you are a supporter of that party basically you are used to it. It's not that big of a deal. For someone to suddenly be suicidal over his 15th different conviction is not really plausible in my book.

"He wasn't distressed with his personal life. You spend 10 days with a pilot in Australia - you get to know a person very well. Muslims don't kill themselves as a rule. They don't kill themselves. Muslims - apart from weirdos in Middle East - don't commit suicide. I think most people don't reject it, they might readily accept he might have wanted to commit suicide. It doesn't make sense that you could lock up an entire plane and maybe kill your co-pilot."

Sadiq makes no doubt about his support of Zaharie.

"The airline didn't come out quickly enough to defend him. He's a most experienced guy. I don't think this chap would have done it. He's a true son of Malaysia Airlines from a cadet till now. Why would he take a plane into an ocean where there's no fuel?"

Chong rejects any suggestion that Zaharie and Faisa were separated.

"There's no truth in that at all," he says. "I've been in contact with the family subsequently. There's absolute no truth in it. They may have problems. What people don't have problems?"

He says he's not aware of Zaharie having a girlfriend.

"If he did, so what?"

But how well did Chong really know Zaharie? They had only known each other two years. Chong says they didn't talk that often but when they did, they spent hours together. But he also concedes their families never met up. There's a reason Chong's testimony feels third-hand. Because it is.

Any suggestion of a formal separation is rejected by Faisa's brother Asuad Khan who agreed to meet us in Penang. Asuad is a straight talker who makes a lot of jokes but also has an underlying aggression. He refuted any suggestion the family had moved out of the house in Laman Seri the day before Zaharie's final flight. It was simply the set-up whenever Zaharie flew. Asuad said Faisa would go back to the family's other house in Subang which they lived in before buying the house in Laman Seri. Asuad said their son, Ahmad Seth Zaharie, preferred to stay in the house in Subang because his friends were close and Faisa would stay there when Zaharie was away.

"Otherwise, she will be alone in that big house. That's been practiced since they bought the house."

Asuad says he doesn't believe Zaharie and Faisa were having serious problems.

"I would ask. I am a direct person, I would ask. She said no. Good enough. She got nothing to hide from me because I'm her right-hand man. Like husband and wife. No problems. I haven't argued with my wife for three days and I'm worried. Argument is normal. I asked my sister about (Zaharie having a) girlfriend. She said none she knows of. To us it's pretty simple. My sister is the type that if you want to get married go ahead. Let me be blunt. We are Muslim, we are allowed to have four wives. If you want to lose your head in two months' time go ahead. If you are talking about a girlfriend who is a friend, yes he had but if you are talking about a girlfriend he doesn't."

The story in which a former pilot friend said Zaharie was in no state to fly angers Asuad.

"We confronted that guy and he said he didn't say that. Daily Mail had a lot of shit. We thought of suing them but what's the point? Unless the guy is not brave enough to say he said it. If I say something like that I have to prove it."

But the New Zealand Herald, which first broke the story is no News of the World. It is a legitimate daily newspaper with a reputation for journalistic integrity. The story of an ex-colleague and friend worrying about Zaharie's sanity was not made up. It was based on a real interview and it was the impressions of a person who was in a position to have an informed view.

Asuad told us he was angry about people saying things without really knowing Zaharie.

"Someone is spreading something that isn't true in order to make him a scapegoat. I believe somebody is doing that."

He reacted sharply to a question about how Faisa is coping.

"If you've loved someone for 30 years and they suddenly disappear how do you feel? I told her yesterday. Just pray for him. If he ever comes back, it's a bonus. Right now this is what it is. He's not here, just pray for him."

What was Zaharie like?

"Funny, kind, nice to chat with, nice to argue with. Sometimes we disagree about something, then we argue, then we laugh about it, nobody wins. We argue about life. But I have no problem with him and he got no problem with me."

According to Ausad, Zaharie wasn't obsessed with politics.

"He joined politics because he has too much time on his hands and to make people know what he believes."

Although Zaharie was a life-long employee of Malaysia Airlines it was not all beer and skittles. In this Zaharie wasn't alone. Grumbles with any long-term employee at most organisations are normal.

"He would say the management are not treating people fairly on some things. The only thing I remember him saying is 'I will never recommend my kids work for Malaysia Airlines' - that's what he said, Asuad remembered.

"But Malaysia Airlines is his bread and butter. If he's angry definitely he would be working with Emirates or Qatar - they offered him a better salary six to seven years ago, both of them, but he declined."

Asuad indicates that Zaharie did have some disagreements with his children.

"We did have a moment long ago when the kids all liked me more than they liked him. So I told him you have to win them back. I'm good around kids, they like my jokes."

Asuad minimises his comment by adding that his own kids prefer Zaharie to him also. It's a standard thing for kids to prefer uncles to fathers. But later on in the conversation, when asked if he really knew what was going on in his brother-in-law's mind, Asuad admits he didn't.

"No, what's on his mind I wouldn't know. I'm sure he's not that stupid to do all those stupid things. His daughter, he loved the girls very much. She's the main issue last time we argue because the daughter likes me more than him. I said you have to win her back. She's always on my side each time they argue."

Zaharie's relationship with his children has also been mentioned by others. Although Zaharie and Asuad knew each other well, they weren't close. Asuad admitted he hadn't seen Zaharie and Faisa since October when Zaharie came to Penang, five months earlier. And Ausad was also unable to reproduce any photos of he and Zaharie together. Near the end of the conversation with Asuad in Penang he speculated about theories of what happened to MH370. Like many, Asuad appeared completely unable to accept Inmarsat's version of events. He was reluctant to admit MH370 even turned back from its flight path. At one point he echoed the theory MH370 was shot down. The Americans were the first suspect in his mind, and he talked of a documentary he had seen about the Americans having the capability to use a weapon that could "vaporise" an aircraft the size of a 777.

Ultimately Asuad did reveal a fact which had never been made public. We talked about the cockpit's voice tape that was released, and Asuad was critical that it was a tape of a tape and the quality was poor. However when we talked about who said "Goodnight Malaysian 370" Asuad was clear it wasn't Zaharie or Fariq.

"Too bass for Zaharie," he said. "Not his voice."

He added that whoever it was may well hold the answers to what happened to MH370. We talked more on it and he decided to call

Faisa. They had what appeared to be a relaxed conversation for two or three minutes, after which he ended the call.

"What did she say?"

Asuad admitted that Faisa told him it was Zaharie. Their eldest son Ahmad Idris Zaharie had listened to the tape and identified the voice as his father.

Ninety seconds before MH370 disappeared from radar, shut off communication and proceeded to dramatically change its course, Zaharie Ahamd Shah was at the helm.

Chapter 14

Humans and Technology

How could a modern aircraft such as a Malaysia Airlines 777 just disappear?

It has been a common question since it became clear a few days after March 8 that the aircraft would not be easy to find.

For a society like ours, it goes against the grain. We live in an era of instant communication and the common use of global positioning systems in our day-to-day lives to the point where when an airbag deploys in some modern cars a data message is sent to emergency services confirming its location and the need for assistance. We are told that we are surrounded by sophisticated satellites and sold the perception that virtually every inch of this earth is mapped in some shape or form and able to be zeroed in on by some eye in the sky. Some of this is exaggeration perpetrated by television and movie portrayals of high-tech crime and military surveillance operations. But with a state-of-the-art airliner with a well-deserved safety record, equipped with highly-sophisticated automation and multiple safety devices covering every possibility of another device's failure, we should be confident.

So one again has to ask the question: how could MH370 just disappear?

An essential component of unravelling the mystery of what happened to Malaysia Airlines Flight 370 and the lives of the 239 passengers and crew is understanding some of the technology used by the airlines, by air traffic control, and on board the 777 200ER aircraft itself.

Another essential component of investigating the loss of Flight MH370 is the science of 'Human Factors' and how both technology and the science of human factors intertwine. (Source: ATSB Human Factors Course Manual). It is said that human error is a natural part of life: a key principle is that human error, although undesirable, is nevertheless both frequent and widespread. The critical issue is whether the error is unintentional (the failure of planned actions to achieve a desired goal) or intentional - a violation (intentional deviation from safe operating procedures, standards or rules).

Transport incidents never occur in isolation, and frequently the causes are multi-factorial and, in the case of deliberate violation, are extremely difficult to eliminate through risk controls.

To ensure our investigation into the human factors aspects of the loss of MH370 were captured we used a well-respected investigation analysis model developed by the Australian Transport Safety Bureau. In simple terms we looked at organisational influences, risk controls, local conditions and individual actions. As the investigation unfolded we took a long hard look at how humans interact with technology and how humans can work around that technology if determined to do so.

The summary of the technology and systems used on the 777, in the airline industry and a brief look into the science of human factors for transport safety investigators below is non-exhaustive, but it will help in subsequent chapters to shed light on what likely happened on board Malaysia Flight 370. Furthermore, it will be critical in helping us eliminate a number of possible scenarios and will ultimately lead us to the devastating reality of what probably happened to all those on board.

An obvious place to start is with the aircraft itself.

The 777, first introduced by Boeing in 1995, was a game-changer. Any passionate aviator recognises that this aircraft is a technological marvel. It was an aircraft of many firsts. It was the first completely designed using a computer and Boeing's fly-by-wire technology which enabled pilots to feel they still had full control in the sense that they had the traditional stick and rubber on the surface rather than change to side-stick controllers as used in many fly-by-wire fighter aircraft and in many Airbus airliners.

The flight control system of the 777 aircraft is different from older Boeing airplane designs in that rather than having the aircraft rely on cables to move a flight control surface such as the elevator and rudder, wires carry the electronic signal from the pilot control column and pedals to a primary flight computer.

The 777 is the world's largest twin-jet and has a typical seating capacity of 314 to 451 passengers, with some models having a range of up to 9380 n/m.

It was designed to replace airliners such as the 747 and 767 and to increase the possible capacity.

A key to the 777's success is the range of redundancies; in other words back-up or cover for the computer system, electrical power, hydraulic power and communication. If a device fails, one or more other devices will cover it. For example, if a particular instrument is fed by a generator powered by the left engine then if the left engines fails, the right engine will take over that task. If that fails the auxiliary power unit will start up. There are numerous examples all the way down to what is known as the Ram Air Turbine (RAT).

If both engines have failed, as well as the auxiliary power and even the whole electrical system, a little propeller drops into the slip-stream from the plane and produces enough electrical power to drive the primary flight instruments and some hydraulics. The RAT will drive the flight instruments long enough to give a good flight crew an opportunity to try to glide the aircraft down to a safe landing.

The 777's level of redundancy, reliability and predictability makes it a pilot's best friend. Hence it is the world's top-selling twin-engine wide-body airplane flying today.

There is a range of 777s in service around the world today. The aircraft flying on the night of March 8 from Kuala Lumpur to Beijing was a 777 200ER, serial number 28420 registration 9M-MRO. According to Airfleet.Net it was the 404th Boeing 777 produced. It first flew on May 14, 2002, and was delivered new to Malaysia Airlines on May 31, 2002. The aircraft was powered by two Rolls Royce Trent 892 engines, and according to Malaysia Airlines' website had a seat configuration of 282 seats - 35 in business class and 247 in economy.

In the aviation sector an aircraft maintenance program and useful lifespan of a commercial aircraft is monitored by the number of hours flown and the number of cycles (a term referring to the number of takeoff and landings). According to Flightglobal.com 9M-MRO had an accumulated 53,460 hours and 7525 cycles, and underwent its last maintenance check on the February 23, 2014. The 777 was well used but the aircraft is designed to last 30 years and perform 40,000 cycles.

Since the first commercial 777 flight in 1995 the aircraft has enjoyed a near-spotless safety record. There have been three serious accidents but amazingly only three deaths. The first incident was British Airways Flight 38, which ironically originated from Beijing to London's Heathrow Airport. On final approach the aircraft suffered a twin-engine roll back (loss of power) which was subsequently determined to be a result of an unrecognised icing problem in the engines. The pilots were able to crash-land the airplane short of the runway. There were no deaths.

The second was a flight-deck fire in a parked Egyptair 777-200 at Cairo Airport Egypt in 2011 where there was no loss of life. And most recently, Asiana Airlines Flight 214 crashed in 2013 while on approach to San Francisco International Airport. The aircraft crashed short of the runway due to pilot error with the loss of three lives.

The 777's cockpit is equipped with an extensive range of communication devices including three VHF radios, two HF radios, two ADSB enabled transponders and one SATCOM unit. The VHF radios are self-explanatory and are used as the predominant means of communication from the aircraft while in range. HF and SATCOM are used predominantly for en route communication outside of the normal VHF range. Satellite communication (SATCOM) relies on satellites positioned in space, ground-based stations and a mobile terminal, in this case (the aircraft's) and its Satellite Data Unit (SDU) for voice and data telecommunications, interface with the aircraft's ACARS and the in-flight entertainment system (IFE).

The MH370 aircraft was equipped with an Aircraft Communication Addressing and Reporting system (ACARS), a digital text and datalink system which enables two-way transmission of messages between an aircraft and ground stations. The transmissions are via either radio (VHF or HF) or satellite. The system is set up to use the most cost-effective mode of communication first. For example, when the aircraft is flying within VHF radio range (usually 200n/m at altitude) the system will both transmit and receive using VHF radio. If out of radio range it will use SATCOM (satellite communication).

Airlines can purchase an array of packages that suits the airline's operational needs. In MH370's case the service provider was a company called SITA who in-turn used Inmarsat as the satellite network provider.

Like a lot of these modern systems, ACARS was introduced to reduce workload and improve efficiencies for both flight crew and air traffic control providers, and also airline operations centres by enabling a number of basic communications.

The best example of this is the two main types of ACARS messages:

1. Airline administrative / aeronautical operational control. This may include ACARS sending either real-time or at pre-programmed set times information about conditions of various aircraft systems. This normally includes engine conditions (to help with repair and maintenance planning) and fuel remaining on board, for example. One of the other key functions of ACARS is to automatically detect and report aircraft movements such as Out of gate, Off the ground, On ground, and Into gate times.

   ACARS enables airlines operation centres and the aircraft flight crew to send information to each other. It also interfaces with the Aircraft's Flight Management (FMC) system which enables flight plans and weather information to be sent from ground stations to the aircraft. This helps the crew to constantly evaluate and plan the best route to their destination. Other helpful information, such as connecting flight details for passengers on-board, is also sent to the aircraft.
2. Air Traffic Control, where the messages are used to request and provide clearances. This has significantly reduced the workload for the crew. In some aircraft this will also automatically update air traffic control when it arrives overhead a specific reporting point and then send the estimated flight arrival time to the next waypoint/ reporting point. This system is also used by the aircraft to send its own weather update to ground stations which then have a more accurate understanding of weather conditions in real time.

In the case of Malaysia Airlines Flight 370, ACARS either failed or was deliberately switched off. The latter is not a straightforward process but can be achieved in the cockpit. However, this does not stop the SATCOM system remaining on the satellite network. In MH370's case, if the ground base station (in this case in Western Australia) didn't hear from the aircraft's SATCOM at predetermined intervals (in MH370's case every hour) the ground station sent an automated message (a ping) via the satellite to the SATCOM on the aircraft and it in turn sent a ping back confirming that it was working. This process was called a handshake.

The aircraft was equipped with two transponders which ensure secondary ground radar (SSR) can pick up the aircraft to a range of about 200n/m. When the transponder receives an interrogation signal from the SSR it returns an encoded signal which contains the aircraft's position, altitude and its unique squawk code which will allow the SSR operator to identify the particular aircraft.

In MH370's case the transponders were ADSB enabled.

Automatic Dependent Surveillance Broadcast (ADSB) is the next generation of surveillance and is positioned to replace the highly expensive and limited range and accuracy of both primary and secondary radar. It is a real game-changer and will increase the range and accuracy of aircraft surveillance which will lead to safer, more efficient aircraft navigation and be more environmentally friendly when fully implemented by countries all over the world.

Aircraft are able to obtain their own GPS position in real time from orbiting GPS satellites. The information is then sent automatically from the aircraft to the ground stations, which can be land-based or on top of an oil rig in the ocean. The stations then relay the information to air traffic controllers and other parties such as airline operation centres and flight tracking website providers.

MH370 did have ADSB enabled transponders, and while the transponders were working they acted as a transmitter and the location of the aircraft could be followed. The information provided by ADSB includes location, speed, altitude and track. Unfortunately, the minute the transponder was switched off this information was no longer transmitted.

In the event of a depressurisation the aircraft has two independent oxygen systems - one for the flight crew and one for the passengers and cabin crew. Portable oxygen cylinders are located throughout the cabin for emergency use, and cabin crew have access to smoke hood masks in case of fire. There is also an oxygen mask if needed in all toilets and crew rest areas and galleys.

Oxygen masks drop automatically from the Passenger Service Unit (PSU) above passengers' heads when the cabin altitude exceeds parameters. The oxygen is supplied either by gaseous cylinders contained under the main cabin floor or through a chemical reaction generator contained in the PSU. Passenger oxygen can last up to 22 minutes. In every row of seats there's a spare oxygen mask for the cabin crew who may well be working in the cabin serving. Oxygen is also available next to their primary seats where the cabin crew sit for take-off and landing. The flight deck crew's oxygen masks are more sophisticated models which literally expand on depressing the release button and suck on to the face once the button is released, guaranteeing a better supply of oxygen.

How much fuel an aircraft will carry varies, and each airline will have a standing operating practice. Airlines try not to carry unnecessary fuel because the extra weight burns fuel faster. They will carry additional fuel, particularly if weather is a concern or if they know that fuel costs are high at a particular airport.

A general standard practice is to carry enough fuel needed for the flight time - in MH370's case, enough to arrive at Beijing, to complete a missed approach, and have enough fuel to divert to a listed alternate airport and still be left with about 45 minutes of fuel when the plane lands.

The most recent report from Bloomberg's news service stated MH370 was carrying 49.1 metric tonnes (54.1 tons) of fuel when it departed Kuala Lumpur. Based on rough calculations, this would give it about eight hours' total range for this aircraft's vintage, taking a predictable flight path and altitude. What fuel an aircraft burns is dependent on a multitude of factors, but a very rough calculation shows the 777-200ER will burn approximately 6,100kgs per hour.

MH370 was carrying a total cargo of 9,956kg or approximately 10 tonnes. Nearly half of that - 4500kg - was mangosteen fruit, a sweet and tangy, fibrous fruit. The only other item that has attracted significant attention was a consignment under waybill number 232-10677085, from NNR global logistics based in Penang, a shipment of a total weight of 2.4 tonnes. Highlighted on the waybill are the words "The package contains lithium ion batteries. Package must be handled with care and that a flammable hazard exists if the package is damaged. Special procedures must be followed in the event the package is damaged, to include inspection and repacking if necessary."

The waybill does not convey the actual weight of the lithium batteries. Subsequently Malaysia Airlines had to confirm the batteries weighed around the 200kg mark and the balance of the consignment were radio parts. No further details were given, other than an assurance that they were packed correctly and in accordance with International Air Transport Association processes when handling dangerous goods.

It is unusual that there was no requirement enforced to actually specify on the waybill how much of that 2.4 tonne cargo was lithium batteries. It should have been clearly itemised. This generalised reference leads people to assume that it was 2.4 tonnes of dangerous goods and we are then having to rely on a third party to confirm there was only 200kg. This indicates slack process - the waybill is an internationally-crafted document and it should have been clear. When the pilot, who is ultimately responsible for all freight on board, is given the cargo manifest he should have had this highlighted to him.

The best way to paint the picture of what happened to MH370 is to reiterate the route it took and where we believe the aircraft is now.

In all MH370 made eight changes of direction from its planned flight route from Kuala Lumpur to Beijing.

1. At 1:25am MH370 made its first deviation from its scheduled flight plan between waypoints IGARI and BITOD, making a turn north towards the top of the Gulf of Thailand. At the time of the turn the aircraft was about 110n/m from the southernmost tip of Vietnam.
2. The aircraft then turned west towards waypoint TIDAR and the east coast of the Thai and Malaysian peninsula. Then it continued its turn south-westerly, over the coastal city of Kota Bharu (the nearest airport with a runway length over 2400 metres - more than enough to land a 777-200ER if the aircraft was in trouble).
3. Near Kota Bharu the aircraft turned south-west and flew along the Thai and Malaysian border and across the peninsula, travelling from east to west towards the southern tip of the Malaysian island of Penang.

4. The aircraft then turned north-west and flew over Pulau Perak Island (we know from what little information was released by the Malaysian DCA that it was identified by primary radar flying over Pulau Perak Island at 2.02am some 89n/m from Butterworth base on a radial of 279 from Butterworth and along the Malacca Strait towards the Andaman Islands).
5. Near waypoint VAMPI the aircraft turned slightly more west and travelled towards waypoint MEKAR and the Nicobar Islands.
6. Near waypoint MEKAR the aircraft turned again slightly and tracked further north-west towards waypoint IGOGU. The last primary radar location conformation is at 2.22am on the 295 radial 200n/m from the Butterworth base.
   At 2.25am (The ATSB report MH370 - Definition of Underwater Search report states) that a log-on request was initiated by the aircraft. A log-on request in the middle of a flight is not common and can occur for only a few reasons. These include a power interruption to the aircraft's Satellite Data Unit (SDU), a software failure, loss of critical systems providing input to the SDU or a loss of the link due to the aircraft's altitude. An analysis indicated that the characteristics and timing of the log-on request were best matched to stem from a power interruption to the SDU. Approximately 90 seconds after the 2.25am log-on request, communication from the In Flight Entertainment (IFE) system on the aircraft was recorded in the SATCOM log. This may have been someone on the flight deck trying to deliberately shut off power to some of the aircraft's systems including the SDU, making it harder for ground-based radar to identify the aircraft, perhaps before making a radical direction change.
7. Most likely before reaching waypoint IGOGU the aircraft made a significant southerly course change and headed south towards the southern Indian Ocean. (There is considerable debate over when this turn occurred but the ATSB report says it happened before 3.12am.) After the turn south the aircraft passed close to Banda Aceh on the northern tip of the Indonesian island of Sumatra and out in to the southern Indian Ocean.

8. There is debate about subsequent direction changes, but Inmarsat analysis supports the view that there were no further course changes after 3.41am.

A key point is where the aircraft is suspected to be now and how that conclusion was arrived at.

The ATSB report MH370 - Definition of Underwater Search describes how an international group of experts have reconstructed the flight path based on data from a communications satellite system and aircraft performance data. The key was the aircraft's SATCOM system which used hourly communication pings between a satellite and MH370's SATCOM to try to determine where the aircraft was. The ATSB describes how, in order to connect to the SATCOM system, the aircraft transmits a 'log-on' request which is acknowledged by the ground station. Once connected, if the ground station has not heard from an aircraft within an hour it will check that the connection is still operational by transmitting a 'log-on interrogation' message. If the aircraft receives the message it returns a short 'hand-shake' message that it is still logged on to the network.

After the last recorded primary radar data, at 2.22am, the following were recorded at the ground station near Perth in Western Australia.

(Note: The first list shows timings of communication initiated by the aircraft. The second list is communication initiated by the ground station. All times are Malaysian local. The list does not include communication before the last primary radar contact.)

There was communication initiated between the aircraft and the ground station at 2.25am and 8.19am.

There was communication initiated between the ground station and MH370's SATCOM at 2.39am, 3.41am, 4.41am, 5.41am, 6.41am, 7.13am and 8.10am.

MH370 didn't respond to a last log-on interrogation from the ground station at 9.15am.

A complex analysis of Inmarsat's satellite data and the performance and operation of the aircraft has pinpointed a new search area for MH370's wreckage. The priority area of about 60,000 sq km with a width of 93km is further south and still about 1800km offshore from Western Australia.

With an understanding of the aircraft's technical capabilities, its communications systems, fuel load, cargo and the route it took and where it ended up we are now ready to look at the various scenarios as to what really happened to MH370.

Chapter 15

MH370 Wasn't Shot Down

Catastrophic structural failure is relatively easy to rule out as a cause of MH370's disappearance.

When an aircraft is at cruising level the outside atmospheric pressure is lower than inside the aircraft. In most commercial aircraft the cabin pressure is set at about 8000 feet. When there is a catastrophic failure under such pressure, caused by a structural failure where physically through fatigue or an explosion, part of the aircraft peels away, usually that is catastrophic. It creates a significant depressurisation which can lead to the aircraft no longer being structurally sound and falling from the sky.

MH370 quite simply did not fall from the sky as a result of catastrophic structural failure. Primary radar tracked it flying across the Gulf of Thailand and the Malaysian Peninsula and into the Straits of Malacca until 2.22am, 200n/m from the Malaysian Butterworth air base. From there, satellite data categorically shows the aircraft either initiating or acknowledging communication on the hour with a satellite for six more hours as it headed into the southern Indian Ocean. This is not some vague theory; Inmarsat's calculations have been peer reviewed, made public and are widely accepted.

The ATSB has followed up Inmarsat's initial work and produced a 58-page report around its analysis of radar data and satellite communication. To arrive at this conclusion the ATSB brought together satellite and aircraft specialists from the UK's Air Accidents Investigation Branch, Boeing, Australia's Defence Science and Technology Organisation, Malaysia's Department of Civil Aviation, Inmarsat, another international consultant Thales, and the US National Transportation Safety Board.

Shooting an aircraft down with a missile or an explosive device has a similar outcome to a catastrophic structural failure.

Tragically we've seen it all too recently with the shooting down of MH17 over Ukraine on July 17. A local described how "everything exploded in the air and fell to pieces - both bodies and the plane itself", adding that villagers thought they were being bombed.

We know from the Lockerbie tragedy on December 21, 1988, what happens when a bomb goes off under pressurisation and how devastating that is. According to the Air Accidents Investigations branch report into Lockerbie, the aircraft, Flight PA103 from London to New York, was cruising at 31,000 feet when the last secondary radar return was received.

"The radar then showed multiple primary returns fanning out downwind. Major portions of the wreckage of the aircraft fell on the town of Lockerbie, with other large parts landing in the countryside to the east of the town. Lighter debris from the aircraft was strewn along two trails, the longest of which extended some 130 kilometres to the east coast of England."

And we know from TWA (Trans World Airlines) Flight 800 near New York there are similar implications when a fuel tank explodes. On July 17, 1996, the Boeing 747-131 exploded in mid-air and then crashed into the Atlantic Ocean near East Moriches, New York, killing all 230 people aboard and destroying the aircraft. According to the National Transportation Safety Board Aircraft Accident Report many witnesses in the vicinity of the accident stated that they saw and/or heard explosions, accompanied by a large fireball over the ocean, and observed debris, some of which was burning, falling to the water. Pieces of the airplane wreckage were discovered floating on and beneath the surface of the Atlantic Ocean about eight miles south.

The one thing in common with these three tragedies is that every piece of that aircraft as it separates from other pieces, becomes a return for primary radar. Instead of seeing one blip you see multiple blips like a rain shower as each of these little pieces of aluminium sends back a primary radar return. We know that in MH370's case on March 8, primary radar did not pick that up. We know that primary radar instead picked up a plane that flew back across the Malaysian Peninsula. And we know that if MH370 had exploded in mid-air or fallen out of the sky, very quickly searchers would have found a significant debris field. A large debris field which is spread out is always an indication of a high altitude depressurisation situation caused by a bomb or a structural failure. And none of that debris was found. No debris at all relating to MH370 was found.

An explosion of this kind would certainly be another explanation as to why ACARS and the transponders suddenly went off and obviously, why radio contact was lost. But other than that it makes no sense whatsoever.

The shot-down theory appears to be popular in Malaysia where the possibility of some sort of conspiracy to cover it up whets conspiracy theorists' appetite. It also seems to be a far more palatable option than admitting some failure from Malaysia Airlines or one of its staff members and the shame that that brings. A book has fanned these ideas by claiming that the plane may have accidentally been shot down during joint United States-Thai military exercises in the South China Sea and that the search may have been led astray as part of a cover-up. Another popular theory is that MH370 was shot down in the southern Indian Ocean near a US Navy base at the atoll Diego Garcia.

The complete absence of a primary radar field or fall-out from an exploding aircraft and the fact that MH370 flew on for six hours till at least 8.19am - thousands of miles away from Diego Garcia - make a nonsense of this theory.

We can reject any suggestion that MH370's loss was caused by a structural failure, a missile or a bomb either in the Gulf of Thailand or further on in its journey in the southern Indian Ocean. There is no way this could have happened.

A complete electrical failure has also been mooted by some as a possible cause of MH370's disappearance, particularly as it might explain the complete loss of communication. It is entirely possible that the aircraft could have had an electrical failure but it doesn't stack up as a plausible theory. The logic of what occurred that morning doesn't support it.

A significant electrical failure could well have shut down ACARS, transponders and radio communication. It would make sense in this case to turn back away from the set flight plan. The next step would have been for MH370 to divert and land at the closest possible airport in line with protocol and Malaysia's AIP. This wasn't followed. Whoever was flying MH370 chose not to find the closest airport on which to land. It just kept on flying. Not only that, they changed direction a total of eight times, twice appearing to attempt to dodge primary radar as they did so.

It is also evident that the flight crew in the aircraft could have communicated if they had wanted to. The SATCOM was capable of working because we now know that the satellite and ground-based station in Perth was communicating with it right until the end of MH370's flight at around 8.19am. We also know that an aircraft flying to Japan felt that they did connect with an aircraft on the emergency frequency. As mentioned earlier, 777s are incredibly robust and there are multiple redundancies: in other words devices covering for each other. Even in the case of complete power loss and both engines failing, the auxiliary power unit will start up. If that fails the last step is the RAT, discussed earlier, which would give the pilot an opportunity to land the aircraft. But it is an emergency measure and the aircraft had no need of it. We know the aircraft flew on for seven hours after it first disappeared from secondary surveillance radar at 1.21am.

Fire has been widely suggested as a possible cause.

Fire and pressurised airplanes are not good friends and unfortunately history has shown that there have been a number of these incidents. This enables us when reviewing the series of events to better understand the survivability of an in-flight fire, the general time frame of how fires spread on an airplane and how quickly airplane systems can shut down. It also gives us a better understanding of how crew react and what actions they take.

At this point we need to draw a distinction between a fire occurring in cruise altitude and a fire occurring around take-off or landing, because in these latter situations the aircraft is not subject to the same cabin pressure and there is a reasonable opportunity to get back to the ground to seek help and evacuate the aircraft. The thing about fires in an airplane at cruise is that on average, they can overwhelm the airplane and the crew in about 20 minutes. Experience has shown that from the moment a fire is discovered to the fatal consequences there seems to be a magical period of about 20 minutes.

For MH370 the sudden turn-back to Malaysia would not be inconsistent with the crew discovering they have a fire, an emergency, and returning to an airfield. Where it doesn't make sense is when the sequence of other events is considered. We know that ACARS was switched off between 1.07am and 1.37am, and that the transponders suddenly went off, disabling the ADSB and marking the aircraft invisible to secondary radar at 1.21am. Nor was there any mayday call. Nor did the aircraft divert to the nearest airfield at Kota Bharu. All of these things don't stack up.

In two well known situations in which aircraft suffered fires, on neither occasion did ACARS or the transponders suddenly stop - or at least not until both aircraft were in their death throes. It occurred very much in the last phase of the emergency as the fire began to spread. It would be an unprecedented fire event that evolved so quickly that it eliminated ACARS, two transponders, three VHF radios, two HF radios and the SATCOM. In fact, we know it didn't disable the SATCOM because it kept on communicating with the ground station for seven hours until the plane's flight came to an end.

Let's use as an example, Swissair Flight 111 that left New York bound for Geneva on September 2, 1998.

According to a Transportation Safety Board of Canada report, about 53 minutes after departure, while cruising at flight level 33,000 feet, the flight crew smelled an abnormal odour in the cockpit. They initially found nothing visible but agreed it appeared to have come from the air conditioning system. When they assessed what they were seeing was definitely smoke, they decided to divert.

"They initially began a turn toward Boston; however, when air traffic services mentioned Halifax, Nova Scotia, as an alternative airport, they changed the destination to the Halifax International Airport", says the report. While the flight crew prepared to land in Halifax, they were unaware that a fire was spreading above the ceiling in the front area of the aircraft. About 13 minutes after the smell was detected, the aircraft's flight data recorder began to record a rapid succession of aircraft systems-related failures. The flight crew declared an emergency and indicated a need to land immediately. About one minute later, radio communications and secondary radar contact with the aircraft were lost, and the flight recorders stopped functioning. About 5½ minutes later, the aircraft crashed into the ocean about five n/m south-west of Peggy's Cove, Nova Scotia. The aircraft was destroyed and there were no survivors."

The fire started in the In-Flight-Entertainment wiring. That led to an electrical fire, there was a spark which eventually led to total loss of airplane.

In the case of a UPS (United Parcel Service Company) Boeing 747, a cargo of lithium batteries led to a disastrous fire on a flight near Dubai on September 3, 2010. Twenty-two minutes into the flight at an altitude of 32,000 feet the crew advised Bahrain Air Traffic Control of a fire on board. They declared an emergency and requested a return to Dubai International Airport. They said the cockpit was full of smoke and "they could not see the radios". One of the crew members became incapacitated through smoke inhalation and as they tried to land air traffic controllers told them they were approaching too high and too fast. The 747 over-flew the airport and tried to get to Sharjah International Airport 10n/m away. It never got there. The plane crashed and both crew members died.

In 2013, United Arab Emirates' General Civil Aviation Authority (GCAA) released a report on the crash. It found "with reasonable certainty" that the fire which caused the crash originated in a cargo container which held thousands of lithium batteries. The UAE GCAA's report states that the fire began in the section of the cargo that included "a significant number of lithium type batteries and other combustible materials" and added that "the fire escalated rapidly into a catastrophic uncontained fire".

A key understanding to take away from these two tragedies was how quickly the fires spread. Swissair 111 was gone in about 20 minutes, and UPS Flight 6 within about 27 minutes. The other crucial thing is that in both situations there was a great deal of communication between flight crew and air traffic controllers.

In MH370s case there was none.

In situations like this - despite the savage speed at which fire spreads -

the air traffic controllers are a pilot's best friend. It's sometimes said in the aviation world: "We aviate, we navigate and then we communicate."

But pilots are capable of multi-tasking and if there is an on-board fire, flight crew are going to want to make a mayday call immediately - no questions asked. Air traffic control is your best friend because their job is to keep every other bit of flying machinery out of your way. It's also their job to tell you where your nearest air strip is, and to ensure they are expecting you and see what emergency services you require. They are able to start putting in place search and rescue strategies. In most cases, they are also able to help you in the process of where you are going to dump some of your fuel, because often the challenge for an aircraft that has just recently got airborne is that it is too heavy to land. So with the Swiss Air 111 out of New York what we saw was constant communication with Canadian air traffic controllers. They discussed where the aircraft could land, although tragically they misjudged how quickly this fire was going to engulf them. They had a plan, they were in the midst of dumping fuel, when the fire just got on top of them and they all died.

Is there a way a fire could have damaged MH370's communications?

It's very unusual for a fire to go from being undiscovered to then suddenly having eliminated all of an aircraft's communications. It could only occur if it actually started in the electronics bay where most of this equipment is. Let's say a fire in the electronics bay overwhelmed the electronics equipment. The first thing you would see is the airplane commencing a descent and heading towards the nearest aerodrome. There will always be conjecture: should they fly all the way back to KL, should they fly to the long runway at Langkawi on the western side or should they fly the 89n/m to Kota Bharu that has a runway of 2400 feet where most people agree that in an emergency you could put a 777 down.

If MH370 had turned around, not communicated, descended and crashed and burnt on the way to Kota Bharu, a fire overwhelming the crew would be a strong possibility and we would all look for the flight data recorder (FDR) to confirm that. But the action of the crew was inconsistent with that. The plane flew back, it climbed, it descended and it continued on. Again, if crew were able to put out a fire that somehow disabled all of its communication equipment, you would measure the behaviour of the flight crew. If a plane loses communication there are protocols and procedures in their AIP that they are bound by law to follow. That would have involved diverting and landing at an airport nearby, not flying all the way to the southern Indian Ocean.

One of the theories advanced by those who have taken an interest in 370 is the nature of some of the cargo. One of them is the lithium batteries. Most of it, or at least half of it is a fruit - mangosteen. Could a lithium battery start a fire? Absolutely. Is lithium a danger? Without a doubt. Have there been fires caused where there's a high possibility they are caused by lithium batteries? Yes. UPS out of Dubai is an example already mentioned. So lithium is a known hazard. But the one thing the UPS flight showed us was that from the moment it started to the moment it ended was about 27 minutes.

These fires have devastating effects, but in both Swiss Air and UPS there was a sequence of time where there was communication and it was the decision of the crew in both cases to pick the optimum place to land which led to the plane being overwhelmed.

Even the most robust theorist would find that they run out of oxygen when trying to explain that this was a fire with overwhelming consequences when they have to acknowledge the plane flew on for seven hours. It is just inconsistent and impossible.

Chapter 16

Accidental Hypoxia Unlikely

With the ATSB report, MH370 - Definition of Underwater Search, the theory that MH370 was the victim of a depressurisation which led to passengers and crew suffering hypoxia and losing consciousness has gained currency.

The ATSB report admits that due to the imprecise nature of the SATCOM data, it had to make some assumptions regarding pilot control inputs to define a suitable search area. It emphasises that MH370 had multiple communication systems fitted to the aircraft - a point we have made earlier. But no radio contact was received from the aircraft from 1.19.29am, seven hours until the last SATCOM 'handshake' at 8.19am.

Analysis of the SATCOM data also showed that there were probably no significant changes to the aircraft's track after approximately 3.15am when it was on its route into the southern Indian Ocean, about five hours to the last SATCOM 'handshake'.

"Given these observations, the final stages of the unresponsive crew/hypoxia event type appeared to best fit the evidence for the final period of MH370's flight when it was heading in a generally southern direction," states the report. It also notes that MH370 had a long period without any route manoeuvring of the aircraft, a steadily maintained cruise altitude and appeared to end its flight by running out of fuel.

In fact as the report itself acknowledges, determining the actual factors involved in the loss of MH370 is the job of the accident investigation authority, and the ATSB's 'end of flight' scenario is made for the sole purpose of finding a search area. All the same, the ATSB's conclusion for the final period appears to have been misread or assumed by some to be the whole answer to what occurred on March 8.

We don't believe that to be the case.

Depressurisation can be broken into three clear parts - the first, an explosive depressurisation which we have covered. The second is a rapid depressurisation - a small hole suddenly erupts in the air frame as a result of structural fatigue, or perhaps an oxygen bottle explodes and punches a hole through the side of the airplane. These things have occurred. You are at altitude, you are flying along. An event occurs and the plane depressurises. It is a scary and dramatic occurrence. But not one that isn't planned for and trained for on a regular basis. It would be part of most pilots' renewal training in the simulator every six months. And there are some great examples when it has occurred and the outcome has been very little or no loss of life.

In the event of a rapid depressurisation there are technical and crew-initiated steps that can be taken to get out of trouble. When rapid depressurisation occurs, the flight crews' immediate priority is to get the aircraft down to a low enough altitude where the air the passengers are breathing holds enough oxygen content that they can survive. Otherwise hypoxia sets in. Hypoxia is lack of oxygen to the tissue sufficient to cause impairment of function. Partial pressure of oxygen decreases as altitude increases. For example, normal, oxygen saturation on the ground is 98 per cent. At an airliner cabin altitude (up to 8000ft) its saturation is 85 per cent. In other words, in normal flights as humans we are slightly behind the normal level of oxygen saturation. As the altitude increases oxygen levels fall even further behind and the impact will be felt faster.

Physical effects of hypoxia include loss of muscular coordination and tremors, vision and hearing loss, hot flushes, hyperventilation and skin turning blue. The psychological impacts are even more ominous. Hypoxic people can undergo personality change, loss of judgement and short-term memory. They can lose self-critical faculties and their reaction time can slow down. Worse, in a very short time one loses consciousness and dies within four to six minutes.

The severity and speed of a person's impairment depends on the altitude. It is defined in terms of time of useful consciousness (TUC); for flight crew, this is the amount of time an individual is able to perform flying duties efficiently, for a passenger or cabin crew member, it is the period of time before useful function is lost and the individual is no longer capable of taking proper corrective and protective action.

At 18,000 feet, TUC is about 20 to 30 minutes and at 25,000 feet it is just three to five minutes. It becomes progressively more alarming. At 30,000 feet one only has one to three minutes; at 35,000 feet it is 30 to 60 seconds. Once the altitude gets higher there is barely any time to get to oxygen before one is seriously affected. At 40,000 feet one has only 15 to 30 seconds to act and at 43,000 feet, just 9 to 12 seconds.

Flight crew and cabin crew are trained for these situations. Their job is to get oxygen to themselves and passengers, descend rapidly and then land as quickly as possible. Throttles back, nose down, the pilot would use full speed brake and a 777 can descend rapidly, probably 3500 to 6000 feet per minute. The aim is to head for that magical altitude of 14,000 feet. We know scientifically that 90 per cent of the population will be fine at this altitude. But those who are very young, very old, or sick will find that even at 14,000 feet their oxygen saturation levels are too low.

Back in the cabin, the minute the system realises the cabin has depressurised, it will drop oxygen marks down from above passengers' heads. They can expect to have up to 22 minutes of oxygen supply. On the 777 an automated message (in English) starts in the passenger cabin declaring an emergency and telling the passengers to put on their oxygen masks. The lights in the cabin will also come on. The cabin crew will also try to make announcements in different languages.

The flight deck crew would immediately put on their oxygen masks. In a situation where all that is required is a quick descent which might only take a few minutes, passengers have ample oxygen. But if a rapid depressurisation was to occur three hours away from land, 22 minutes of oxygen may not be enough even though the aircraft has descended to 14,000 feet. They need to ensure they have a buffer of oxygen in case some passengers, as indicated above, struggle to breathe at 14,000 feet. So before a flight takes off the flight crew undertake a vital calculation to ensure the pressure of the oxygen system is correct.

Rapid depressurisation is incredibly dramatic but it is nearly always survivable. On July 25, 2008, on a Qantas 747 carrying 346 passengers and 19 crew members, a passenger oxygen cylinder blew up, rupturing the fuselage and puncturing the cabin floor. The flight was cruising at 29,000 feet over the South China Sea on its way from Hong Kong to Melbourne. The aircraft was about 200 miles from Manila. Still it was able to descend rapidly to 10,000 feet and successfully land in the Philippines capital. None of the passengers or crew were injured, but they were certainly left with some tales to tell their families and friends.

A rapid depressurisation of an Aloha Airlines 737-200 over Hawaii on April 28, 1988, was even more dramatic. A weakness in the plane's structure caused an explosive decompression which blew a third of the aircraft's roof off in flight, sucking out and killing one of the cabin crew. The aircraft was able to land safely on the island of Maui just minutes after the decompression, but the incident had a chilling impact throughout the airline industry, prompting several changes to fuselage inspection and maintenance.

The other type of depressurisation that can occur is the opposite, the slow insidious nasty type which has more relevance for what is being suggested for MH370. Often this occurs through human error before the plane takes off. Someone in the flight crew pre-flight drill leaves the pressurisation knob on manual rather than auto and the plane never pressurises.

This is what occurred in the most famous occasion of slow depressurisation, Helios Airways Flight HCY522 on August 14, 2005. For Helios, a couple of events had occurred previously which led to the tragedy that killed 121 people. The aircraft, a 737-31S had a track record of once before having a depressurisation. On that occasion, the pilots did what they needed to do and descended to get the passengers on oxygen. A day or so later, without passengers, the plane flew unpressurised to an engineering base where they fixed the problem: one of the seals in the back door had given way. On a flight the day before the accident, as the plane was flying from London to Larnaca, one of the cabin crew said they heard a hissing sound from the back left galley door. So when the aircraft got on the ground, crew wrote up a snag in the technical log and engineers came to test it. They went through a whole series of pressurisation tests and decided there was no problem. As part of the test they had to switch the pressurisation system to manual to pressure-test the cabin. They signed the aircraft as having been fixed, leaving the knob switched to manual.

The plane was released for the next flight, leaving Larnaca at 6am on August 14 via Athens to Prague in the Czech Republic. Tragically, during the flight crew's pre-flight checks the knob was not turned back on to automatic pressurisation. It was still on manual - and that was all it took. The plane took off and at about 11,000 feet a warning horn, known as the configuration warning went off in the cock pit. The pilot contacted the company's operations centre and started consulting with an engineer about what might be wrong.

Meanwhile the plane continued to climb and the slow effect of hypoxia started to affect the crew, their cognitive functions began to deteriorate. The plane had simply never pressurised.

In the cabin, oxygen masks were deployed automatically for the passengers. They put the masks on but the plane didn't descend because the pilots had become incapacitated. From there on, the plane did exactly what the pilots had programmed it to do through the flight management computer (FMC) at the outset of the flight. It was to follow the route to Athens through a series of waypoints, conduct a missed approach at the airport at Athens and then go out to a holding point. With the pilots incapacitated, the plane flew on autopilot all the way to Athens. It got to Athens airport, started doing its own approach, did a missed approach as told to and then went out to a holding point and just held. Meanwhile the authorities, already concerned at not being able to contact HCY522, realised something was wrong and sent a pair of F16s up to investigate - just as Malaysia's authorities should have done with MH370.

The fighters flew alongside the 737 and reported the sight of passengers slumped in their seats with oxygen masks on, the cockpit was frosty, and there was no one in the pilot seat. They saw someone come into the cockpit who had somehow kept his consciousness despite the hypoxia. The flight attendant, who clearly was using crew portable oxygen, incredibly, was a trained commercial pilot. He wasn't trained on the 737 but gave them a positive signal. He was going to try to fly the plane and the F16 pilots gave him instructions. But he didn't seem to respond to the instructions and almost immediately the F16 pilots saw both engines flame out. HCY522 had run out of fuel. Just as the young flight attendant was trying to save the aircraft, it descended and smashed into a hill, killing everyone on board.

Examination of the passengers and crew found that they were killed by the impact of the crash. They all had some heart function beforehand, although due to the results of prolonged hypoxia they were in a deep non-reversible coma.

How can we distinguish the Helios flight from MH370?

Helios never pressurised, and by the time it got to 26,000 feet they were in trouble. MH370 had been flying for 41 minutes and had got to its cruise altitude of 35,000 feet within 20 minutes. Ground contact personnel would know if the plane had never pressurised. They would never have heard the subsequent radio calls, because flight personnel would have been affected. Air traffic controllers are quick to pick up on any voice cues which suggest flight crew are suffering hypoxia. There have been situations when an air traffic controller has noticed a pilot slur his words and immediately directed the pilot to descend.

The minute MH370 transitioned past 13,500 feet pilot and co-pilot would have started to get into big trouble. Yet Zaharie's and Fariq's voices were alert.

There is still the prospect that they were fully pressurised and there was a gradual loss of pressure during the flight. That's why we cannot absolutely disregard a slow insidious depressurisation, other than to say this:

If there had been such an event, MH370 would surely have flown on to Beijing. Just as the flight crew programmed HCY522's FMC before taxiing, so had Zaharie and Fariq. And at 35,000 feet it was flying on autopilot based on the flight plan loaded into the FMC, and there is no doubt that that flight plan was taking them to Beijing. If the crew had become incapacitated like Helios the plane would have continued to fly all the way to Beijing and gone into a holding pattern over the airport just as HCY522 did.

Could Zaharie or someone else flying the plane have been hypoxic and made strange illogical decisions? Yes, it would be highly unlikely but hard to rule out. But unlikely because it doesn't explain why they would turn ACARS and the transponders off. And suddenly there was no more communication from MH370 on the radio whatsoever. All of these things occurred conveniently at a blind spot between Malaysian and Vietnamese airspace.

Yet after the radio contact stopped, MH370 flew on, and over the course of the next few hours made eight changes to its route.

If a pilot suspects hypoxia, his first step is to descend. Thirty years as a pilot would have ingrained that into Zaharie. He didn't. Instead he not only turned the aircraft back towards Malaysia but also increased his altitude. Let's say he was in a hypoxic state and there was no malice in his actions. He disengages the autopilot, decides to fly up, then go down across Malaysia at low altitude as if he's trying to avoid primary radar and skims along the Malaysian and Thai border quite neatly, seems to take a relatively well-calculated series of turns to the north-west along a series of waypoints, appears to take what looks like a cynical attempt to avoid Indonesian radar, then turns to go south. And all the time he never bothers to communicate via the radio.

You do stupid things when you're hypoxic but these don't appear to be stupid things. They appear reasonably calculated. The theory of an unresponsive crew for the last hours of the flight is not inconsistent with the scenario we believe brought about the end of MH370 on March 8. The two are not mutually exclusive at all.

We consider that it is quite possible that for the last five hours of the flight the person in the cockpit of MH370 could have been hypoxic and unresponsive or else content to leave the aircraft on autopilot.

It is what happened in the earlier hours of the flight where the real key lies. We don't believe depressurisation of MH370 led to its demise. We cannot rule it out altogether but we will shortly propose two other scenarios which we believe are far more likely to have occurred.

But first there is one more highly unlikely scenario we must address - the possibility of hijacking by a passenger. This is impossible to rule out completely, simply because there is so much evidence that the loss of MH370 stemmed from a deliberate action. The question is not so much, was it deliberate? It is who did it?

For a start we know from our own experience that there's a robust series of checks of passengers' clothes and bags before leaving on a flight at KL International Airport. Passengers first are checked to ensure their boarding pass matches their passport. Immediately afterwards the first thorough security check of carry-on baggage occurs in which liquids, laptops, cellphones and every human goes through a scanner X-ray.

And because KL airport does not have inbound-outbound passenger segregation, there is an additional security check before entering the boarding gate. Documents are checked again, carry-on baggage is again X-rayed and every passenger X-rayed. Check in baggage also goes through X-rays looking for explosives.

It's worth noting that there is also a thorough system to ensure that a passenger who has checked in a piece of baggage but then subsequently doesn't board the airplane creates an alert. The bag has to be removed before the flight can proceed.

We watched the crew go through the same process. We also know there's a robust process for other airport staff, ground handlers, baggage handlers, engineering, food caterers, all of whom have their own entrances and their own series of multiple processes. History has shown that those totally intent on doing harm could get on the aircraft anyway. It is highly unlikely they would carry any sort of menacing weapons, but there's still a possibility.

The problem with hijacking these days is that the perpetrators of 9/11 have done the terrorists who came after them no favours at all. Post 9/11 the cockpit on an international passenger liner is impenetrable - it is a fortress, blast-resistant, bullet-proof and smash-proof.

Cabin crew can only get access to the cockpit using a code which is entered into a digital door entry pad. Crew are given a code of the day and must tap it into the pad to enter the cockpit. But that doesn't open the door, it simply triggers a sound in the cockpit and then the flight crew process is that they have to identify the face on the video camera at the cockpit door. They turn a knob which permits the door to open and if they don't want to open it they turn the knob to deny. If a flight attendant suspects the pilots are incapacitated and there is no response in the cockpit once they have entered the daily code, they can put in an emergency code. But it won't open until it has given anyone in the cockpit enough time to decide if they want the visitor to enter. Someone on the flight deck can still turn the knob to deny them entry. If there is a period of inaction, clearly indicating the pilots are incapacitated, the door to the cockpit will finally open.

It is a highly secure cockpit these days. In fact one airline, Israel's EL AL Airline goes even further and has a double security door into the cockpit. The first door has to be closed before the second will open and only one person can get into the middle area at once. There is also a video camera trained on the area between these double doors.

In MH370's case, if someone did somehow try to bust in, while that's occurring, the flight crew could easily send a message with a transponder code. There is a specific code to say 'I'm being hijacked' and for that matter there is a code that says 'I have lost all radio communication'.

But the only real way hijackers can enter a cockpit these days is by threatening cabin crew or passengers. Flight crew have training for such situations. It's not a scenario they would ever want to encounter, but even if a hijacker has a knife to the throat of a flight attendant the flight crew must not open the door. The cabin crew member has to be sacrificed. If a hijacker gets into the cockpit, potentially everyone on board is dead. 9/11 has taught us that people on the ground are also under threat.

There has been the odd suggestion that Fariq could be a potential weak link, given his propensity for young attractive women. But his silly behaviour in allowing two South African women into the cockpit two years ago hardly seems relevant. One occasion on a daylight one-hour flight on a 737 flight from Phuket, Thailand, to Kuala Lumpur is a vastly different setting from a 777 international red-eye service from Kuala Lumpur to Beijing, particularly when he is on his first flight as a full 777 co-pilot.

Lastly, if it was an attempted hijacking, where was the terror, where were the demands? The SATCOM was still working; a hijacker had seven to eight hours to make their demands. Hijackers want to incite terror, they want publicity and fear all around. All that occurred was silence. It is possible any demands issued by a hijacker were not made public and were kept secret by the Malaysian Government or whoever else the extortion was aimed at. But nor were there any demands or attempts to claim responsibility by any organisation either during or in the wake of the aircraft's disappearance.

It is surely also significant that no Governments which appraised the passenger list, or Interpol which investigated the false passport episode, have any concerns, nor have they identified any hijacking candidates among the passengers or cabin crew.

Chapter 17

Pilot Suicide

For all we have heard about and know of Zaharie Ahmad Shah we actually don't know much about the real man. Zaharie appears to us an enigma. Acquaintances and people calling themselves friends, would say nice things about him. He was jovial, he was funny, he liked to indulge in a good argument, he was extremely thorough and methodical, he helped out at community open days and sometimes brought food. We know from watching them that he made You Tube videos as part of what he called a community service showing off DIY skills such as optimising air conditioners to minimise electricity consumption and also displaying his cooking skills.

Despite all the media comment and our own interviews, we couldn't find evidence that any of those talking about him - with the exception of his brother-in-law Asuad Khan - really knew him well at all. Even Asuad hadn't seen Zaharie in the flesh for six months and acknowledged he had no idea what was really going on in the man's mind.

Zaharie did not seem to be a man who was especially close to anyone except perhaps his daughter Aishah. The rest of her family's comments about him appear more dutiful than loving and warm. His youngest son, Ahmed Seth, a Japanese language student who preferred to stay in Zaharie and Faisa's other home instead of moving with them to the luxurious Laman Seri compound, gave an interesting insight when he defended his father publicly to the New Straits Times, early after the aircraft's disappearance.

"I've read everything online. But I've ignored all the speculation. I know my father better," the 26-year-old was quoted as saying. "We may not be close as he travels so much. But I understand him."

There are repeated comments from Asuad about Zaharie getting frustrated that his children were more likely to side with others, which suggests he was strict on them or perhaps liked to dominate.

Zaharie's obsession with aviation does make one wonder how much time he actually spent with his family. He was away from home continually flying, and yet he indulged his passion relentlessly at home, even to the extent of building an expensive flight simulator.

There seems little doubt that Zaharie and his wife Faisa were having serious problems. They may have stopped short of a formal separation. They may have been in turmoil, they may have gone as far as agreeing to continue to live together for the sake of the family, they may have been at a crossroads. Some say they were separated, some say they weren't. Either way, there are strong indicators that the pair were locked in a loveless marriage. They wouldn't be the first couple by any stretch to be living unhappily ever after, and Zaharie wouldn't be the first man to spin out of control as a result. Zaharie was a man with plenty of time on his hands and his brother- in- law suggests that was part of his reason for getting involved in politics. Zaharie went as far as joining the People's Justice Party in 2013, and the photo of him in a tee-shirt saying "Democracy is dead" suggests a man with strong views on Malaysia's political situation. There is no doubt he was a strong supporter of Anwar Ibrahim, and various people have described Zaharie's fury at a court's decision to quash Ibrahim's acquittal on sodomy charges, a cynical move, days before a by-election. Zaharie was furious at his Government, the Government which owns a large part of Malaysia Airlines.

Both Asuad and Jahabar Sadiq, whose friend is a Malaysia Airlines pilot, referred to a flight Zaharie made to Australia shortly before the March 8 flight. While there he went to see Aishah. Was this a final good bye?

But there is evidence we haven't seen. Evidence that is locked up by Malaysian authorities. They do know more, and earlier we discussed how a source told the media that after carrying out 170 interviews and profiling all of the 239 people on board the 777 that night, Malaysian police believe that if human action was behind MH370's loss, Zaharie is the most likely perpetrator.

While we acknowledge there is an element of doubt, there is compelling circumstantial evidence from what occurred on the night that Zaharie was involved. Let's quickly refresh what it is. In a vulnerable communication area between Malaysian and Vietnamese airspace - widely acknowledged as a perfect spot to make a plane disappear - Zaharie was the last man to be heard 90 seconds before radio contact was cut, ACARS and the transponders were turned off. The plane turned around, made eight changes of direction, some of them obviously to avoid radar contact, before sailing off into the vast southern Indian Ocean where detection of the aircraft would be hardest. There was an attempt to shut-down critical systems - possibly to avoid ground-based radar - prior to significant direction change into the Indian Ocean at 2.25am. No radio contact was made the entire time, despite the fact that we know the SATCOM system was working.

In preceding chapters we have ruled out any chance MH370's loss was caused by catastrophic structural failure, fire and electrical failure. We have shown why hijacking by a passenger or accidental depressurisation are highly unlikely scenarios. By a process of elimination, this leaves pilot suicide as the only other serious option in our analysis of what occurred on March 8. Such an act is by no means without precedent. Our research indicates there have been five previous incidents of murder/suicide in commercial flights over the last three decades or so, accounting for 422 lives. The sad addition of MH370 would bring that number to 661.

Our research indicates that the number of lives lost through pilot murder/suicide in commercial airlines over this period far exceeds similar statistics related to lives lost through accidents caused by flight crew drug or alcohol use. Disturbingly, there is a pattern of pilots' unions, airlines and Government agencies in Muslim countries such as Egypt, Indonesia and Morocco refusing to accept conclusions of pilot suicide.

One murder/suicide that has hauntingly familiar parallels with what occurred on March 8, 2014, was on October 31, 1999 when Egypt Air Flight 990 with 217 people on board crashed off Nantucket Island, US, on a flight from New York to Cairo. Twenty minutes into the Boeing 767-366ER's flight, the first officer Gameel Al-Batouti suggested that he relieve another officer at the controls, who then left the flight deck. Eight minutes later the captain decided to go to the toilet and 21 seconds later the flight data recorder picked up the first officer stating quietly "I rely on God."

The first officer soon pitched the aircraft into a steep dive and before it crashed into the ocean four minutes later he repeated the phrase "I rely on God" 10 more times.

The Egyptian Civil Aviation Authority "investigation" tried to blame mechanical issues. But the US National Transportation Safety Board, involved because the accident was in international waters, determined the probable cause was the first officer's actions, the reasons for which "were not determined". Its primary theory was that Gameel Al-Batouti committed suicide.

It was later revealed Gameel Al-Batouti had been reprimanded for sexual misconduct and the executive who told him he would not be allowed to fly US routes again was on board the plane. Sources close to the investigation revealed his career was in ruins after a series of allegations of sexual misconduct.

The key similarity with MH370 was the staunch refusal - this time by Egyptian authorities - to entertain any possibility of suicide. At least two Egyptian newspapers, A Gomhuria and Al-Musawar, put up theories that the US accidentally shot the plane out of the sky. A surgeon at Cairo's Anglo-American Hospital summed up the attitude: "It is inconceivable that a pilot would kill himself by crashing a jet with 217 people aboard. It is not possible that anyone who would commit suicide would also kill so many innocent people alongside him."

Another disturbing murder/suicide occurred on December 19, 1997, when SilkAir Flight 185 en route from Indonesia to Singapore crashed, killing 104 people. Twenty-eight minutes into the Boeing 737-36N flight the cockpit voice recorder ceased recording and six minutes later the Flight Data Recorder also stopped recording. A minute later the aircraft started a rapid descent and it crashed into the Musi River Delta in southern Sumatra.

The NTSB concluded the captain Tsu Wai Ming may have committed suicide by switching off both flight recorders and intentionally putting the plane into a dive, possibly when the first officer had left the flight deck. The NTSB concluded the accident was a result of "deliberate flight control inputs, most likely by the captain". Earlier in the year Tsu Wai Ming had experienced problems at work and financial difficulties due to his propensity for gambling. Coincidentally, the accident happened on the exact anniversary of the date in 1979 when the captain was forced to withdraw from an Air Force jet training mission because of a mechanical problem with his aircraft. The other three aircraft continued with the mission and all crashed into mountains in bad weather, killing all aboard.

The Indonesian National Transport Safety Committee (NTSC) said it could not determine the cause of the accident. Bizarrely and tellingly, the strong Muslim beliefs of chief investigator for the NTSC, Professor Oetargo Diran hopelessly prejudiced the investigation. Media reports said Professor Diran admitted he did not want relatives of the victims receiving insurance monies from an event that was the will of Allah. "Professor Diran does not want his investigation involved in litigation," one highly placed source said. "He says if today is your day to die, so be it. He said it is not proper to claim for God's will." The American NTSB's accident report was hugely controversial, resulting in lengthy legal action and a US court decision by a jury not allowed to hear the NTSB's conclusions that the accident was caused by a defective valve in the plane's rudder.

On November 29, 2013, captain Herminio Dos Santos Fernandes, in charge of Mozambican Flight TM 470, crashed his Embraer ERJ-190AR on a flight from Mozambique to Luanda in the Bwabwata National Park, killing himself and 32 others. Investigations revealed the crash was intentional. Preliminary investigations showed that minutes before the crash the co-pilot left the cockpit to go to the toilet. The captain then manually changed the flight altitude from 38,000 feet to 592 feet and retarded the throttles to idle, amongst other measures, to ensure the plane crashed. The cockpit voice recorder revealed the sound of someone pounding on the cockpit door. Further investigations indicated the pilot was suffering from depression due to marital problems.

A failed love affair was blamed for a tragedy on August 21, 1994 in which Younes Khayati on a Royal Air Maroc flight bound for Casablanca directed an ATR-42-312 aircraft into a steep dive, killing himself and 43 others. The co-pilot sent out a distress signal but she was unable to stop the pilot killing everyone as he flew the plane downward into the Atlas Mountains 10 minutes after take off. The dead included a Kuwaiti

Prince. The co-pilot was heard on the flight recorder screaming "Help, help! The captain is..." at which point she was cut off. Airline group, the Moroccan Association of Navigators, said it was "stupefied" by the conclusions and demanded more proof.

In 1982 a mentally disturbed pilot, Deiji Katagiri, captaining a JAL Flight350 on a Japanese domestic flight, threw two of the DC-8-61's engines into reverse on descent before landing in Tokyo, crashing the plane into water before the runway and killing 24 passengers. The pilot wasn't indicted on grounds of insanity.

These are not pleasant cases to review, but they do reinforce two very important facts: Pilot suicide is not new. Pilots are human and susceptible to the same problems as anyone else. They perform a stressful job and are under significant pressure to maintain their expertise and professional standing. As we will soon discuss, the personality profile of pilots can also contribute to significant psychological issues. Secondly, there is resistance from authorities, particularly in Muslim countries, to accept any suggestion of pilot suicide. It is an area of taboo and thus not confronted with the scrutiny it deserves.

Before we discuss how Zaharie might have gone about it, let's ask ourselves why? What would have make a man do such a thing?

One would have to surmise that Zaharie had either some sort of personality disorder or had undergone some sort of emotional breakdown. It may have been to do with his marriage situation as speculated, it may have been his anger with the Malaysian Government, it may have been neither, it may have been a mixture of both.

Renata Bellve-Wack, a clinical and forensic psychologist who specialises in risk assessments and in the management and treatment of people with histories of violence, said she couldn't comment on Zaharie in particular because she had not assessed him. But Dr Bellve-Wack, who has practiced in the US and New Zealand, said if the disappearance of MH370 was planned, pilot suicide was only half the issue - the other being mass murder.

"While suicide is usually a private event, suicide-mass murder scenarios are usually intended to make a powerful public statement and gain notoriety." She said studies of people who have committed mass murders have found a number of common denominators.

"The perpetrators had accumulated a list of grievances and perceived injustices, they felt alienated from the world and became increasingly socially isolated prior to the murders," she said.

"They felt depressed or hurt to a degree that they thought they had nothing to lose and were willing to die, and they were angry or paranoid to such a degree that they blamed others for their situation and felt justified punishing them by taking their lives. However, rather than directing their retributive violence against specific others they targeted groups of people who they regarded as representatives of what ailed them.

"For example, (they must target) a group of students because they had been bullied by students in the past; employees of a company against which they held grievances; people of a particular persuasion, religious or political affiliation, that they felt had harmed them or had posed a threat to their values or lifestyle. In effect they displaced the rage or paranoia they held against specific people or an organisation onto a group of anonymous, supposedly representative people and punished those instead."

Dr Bellve-Wack said the profile of the alienated, aggrieved individual doesn't seem to fit very well with pilots who, as a group, are highly regarded as leaders of their team who hold responsible jobs with great technical expertise. Studies of pilot characteristics show that as a group they score low on anxiety, anger, hostility and depression and score high on characteristics such as conscientiousness, competence, self discipline and assertiveness. Yet she points out that since the late 1970s, more than a dozen instances of "suicide by plane" have been recorded that killed many people.

"Could it be that there is a downside to the selection criteria for pilots?" she asks. "Obviously the job requires people who have high standards for their performance, are logical, analytical and decisive, who like to be in charge and who exemplify leadership, quick decision-making and technical expertise. However, there might be a downside to these characteristics. It seems that people who score very high on these qualities and are selected for their ability to be logical and analytical under stress and to 'keep emotions out of the cockpit', are more likely to be relatively unskilled in dealing with emotional stress.

"In fact an article that examined adaption and stress-related disorders in pilots found tendencies to be emotionally avoidant, having a low tolerance for personal imperfections and not handling failure well; tendency to avoid introspection and to attribute feelings to external circumstances, and emphasis on modifying the environment rather than changing their own behaviour. They also found it difficult to cope when confronted with emotional or ambiguous situations."

Dr Bellve-Wack said while feelings of sadness and helplessness are hard for anyone to handle, they are particularly difficult to tolerate for people whose self-image and identity come from their ability to problem-solve, take charge and "save the day". "So when they encounter emotional problems or depression, the first line of defence tends to be denial - they do not even let themselves know how they feel. They are unlikely to say, "Oh, I need to see a psychologist and talk about my problems.'"

A vicious cycle may start in which the person lacks energy, sleeps poorly and performance falls away and irritation with others grows, and exacerbates the situation.

"Trying to keep up appearances he continues to work even harder, but becomes socially more isolated. The gap between his inner reality and outward activities widens and reinforces feelings of hollowness and depression that makes functioning increasingly difficult." But Dr Bellve-Wack says this doesn't explain the distinction between depression and suicide and suicide/homicide.

"Is there a special ingredient that makes the perpetrator feel justified to take the lives of many others along with his own? It has been found that many mass murderers have strong narcissistic personality traits. They are excessively preoccupied with personal adequacy, power and prestige, being quite self-centred and vain and often going out of their way to assure that they gain admiration or even fame. To others they tend to be non-empathetic, discrediting, even exploitative, but tend to be unable to see or care about the damage they cause in relationships. Yet, while insensitive towards others they tend to be hypersensitive to any criticism directed at them, indicating a fragile sense of self-esteem. They tend to hold on to perceived slights or negativity and collected grievances or grudges."

Said Dr Bellve-Wack: "The focus on an external target alleviates feelings of shame and generating a plan for retribution counteracts feelings of powerlessness and helplessness."

Dr Bellve-Wack's last comment is fascinating and possibly significant.

"The planning process itself, which in some cases has taken years, may be an exercise in self-affirmation, especially if technical skills and expertise are being brought into play. The goal, to 'go down in a blaze of glory' while taking along many others is perceived not only as just but also as the only sort of solution.

"A sort of post-mortem triumph".

Chapter 18

Our Scenario

Fariq Hamid had taxied, taken off and climbed to cruise at 35,000 feet and now, about 40 minutes into the flight, Zaharie suggested he take a break. Fariq should pop out, stretch his legs and go to the toilet if he needed to. Fariq agreed and left the cockpit.

Most airlines have a protocol that the minute there is only one pilot left on the flight deck at cruise altitude the remaining pilot should don their oxygen mask in case of a depressurisation. Listening to the radio exchange between the aircraft and the controller it is clear that Zaharie did not at that time have his mask on.

Kuala Lumpur Air Traffic control passed MH370 over to Vietnamese Air Traffic control and instructed the cockpit to change frequency and make contact.

"Goodnight, Malaysian 370," was Zaharie's response at 1.19am.

Zaharie then put on the oxygen mask he was obliged to wear if in the cockpit alone.

At 1.21am, alone at the controls, Zaharie turned off the transponders and ACARS. At 1.25am, about 100n/m from the southern-most tip of Vietnam, he commenced a slow climbing turn in the direction of waypoint TIDAR, towards the top of the Gulf of Thailand by simply putting a heading and altitude into the Mode Control Panel (MCP). The MCP can be used to instruct the autopilot to hold a specific altitude, to change altitudes at a specific rate, to hold a specific heading or to turn to a new heading if required. MH370 quickly ascended to 39,000 feet at which point Zaharie depressurised the aircraft by opening the out-flow valves, turning off the bleed air and air-conditioning packs to stop air flowing into the cabin. There has been a lot of conjecture about the aircraft climbing to 45,000 feet, including suggestions that the aircraft isn't capable of achieving that altitude. The reality is that the aircraft is certified to 43,100 feet and we have no doubt that it could achieve 45,000 feet.

However, even if he kept the aircraft at 35,000 or 39,000 feet, Zaharie had depressurized the plane and the lack of oxygen had a near-immediate impact on passengers and cabin crew - and Fariq who was now locked outside the cockpit and couldn't get back in. Regardless of the altitude, the reality is that TUC is extremely limited even at 35,000 feet. At 35,000 feet TUC is between 30-60 seconds. At 40,000 feet it is between 15-30 seconds and at 43,000 feet it is 9-12 seconds.

The cabin crew and Fariq, locked out in the cabin, had minimal time to get themselves to an oxygen mask. If the altitude was close to 40,000 feet they had about 15 to 30 seconds before they were in trouble.

The system on the 777-200 is designed to automatically release the passenger oxygen masks when cabin altitude exceeds 13,500 feet (normal cabin pressure is 8500 feet). Zaharie couldn't have stopped the oxygen masks from dropping down as soon as he depressurized. MH370 was a night flight and most passengers at 1.25 in the morning were either asleep or close to it. It was warm in the cabin and the lights were off when oxygen masks suddenly dropped from above the passengers and an automated announcement (in English and for most of the 227 passengers English was not their first language) told them it was an emergency and they must put oxygen masks on. The lights in the cabin automatically came on. Cabin crew would have tried to yell out to warn passengers but also needed to put their own oxygen masks on. Once he had his oxygen mask on, chief steward Andrew Nari would try to make announcements telling passengers to put on their mask.

It would be a frightening and confusing time throughout the cabin, with some passengers on oxygen, looking around and wondering what was occurring while others remained asleep. By the time some of the passengers had woken up groggy, heard the commotion and looked around in confusion it would have been too late for them. Those passengers who did not react in time would lapse into unconsciousness and death would follow within four to six minutes.

MH370 flew back across the Malaysian Peninsula towards Kota Bharu and then descended to about 23,000 feet across Malaysia. By the time he began a slow descent over Malaysia, MH370 had been at altitude for more than 25 minutes. Passengers who were able to put their oxygen mask had between 12 and 22 minutes and many of those were now unconscious. When an aircraft is at 40,000 feet there are serious questions about the quality of the oxygen passengers are getting, given their oxygen masks are far inferior to those used by flight-deck crews and don't force the oxygen into the mouth. The crew's portable oxygen can last up to 70 minutes on high flow - longer on low flow - and it's quite possible most of the cabin crew survived the initial depressurisation. The aircraft descended possibly as low as 12,000 feet near the island of Penang which may explain Fariq's cell phone connecting to the cell tower there. He either tried to make a call for help or had simply left it on and it connected itself.

At first the cabin crew may have suspected there was some technical problem and Zaharie was flying them somewhere to land. But the length of time they flew without looking for an airport and the fact that Fariq was locked out of the cockpit would have alerted the cabin crew to the fact that something was very badly wrong.

Zaharie started increasing altitude again as he took the aircraft out into the Straits of Malacca before turning north-west to avoid Indonesian primary radar. He made an attempt to shut off critical systems which we mentioned earlier, leading the SDU to reboot and commence a log-on sequence, after which he swung south into the Indian Ocean.

As MH370 increased altitude again the remaining cabin crew would once again be needing their portable oxygen. Many would have survived the initial depressurisation but now that the aircraft was at a high altitude again and with their oxygen running out, they would lose consciousness.

Zaharie took the aircraft back to cruising altitude for the remainder of the flight. Inmarsat calculations show MH370 needed to be at a cruising altitude for most of its flight if it was to travel the distance before running out of fuel that their calculations show. As MH370 returned to cruising altitude any passengers who survived the initial depressurisation would have perished.

For the time being Zaharie had plenty of oxygen to keep himself going. Flight-deck crew oxygen is designed to be used for the emergency descent then during a diversion if required. In general it could have provided up to three hours for each pilot. Around this time as he got back into cruise altitude Zaharie had a decision to make. He probably had about a good few hours of oxygen left.

There are two scenarios for what happened next.

One is that Zaharie chose not to repressurise the airplane and so when his oxygen finally ran out he then suffered the same fate as his passengers and fellow crew.

He simply entered latitude/longitude coordinates into the FMC, selected lateral navigation steering (LNAV) push button on the mode control select panel and at some stage between 3.12am and 3.41am, the aircraft took its last turn, a left turn south heading into the vast Indian Ocean. MH370 became a true zombie or ghost flight, cruising on in silence until its engines finally ran out of fuel and it crashed into the southern Indian Ocean.

We have a major question about this scenario because a 777 hitting the ocean in this fashion would inevitably break up on impact, leaving significant debris. Yet at the time of publication of this book none had been found. But with the isolation and ocean currents it may explain why no debris has been found thus far. It's been well documented how vast a search area is involved and we acknowledge that a cyclone did pass through the search area soon after the search began.

According to a 777 pilot on a popular pilot thread who tried to recreate in a simulator what the plane may have done, there is no scenario where the plane would not break up; no way it sank intact.

"As a 777 pilot I, like many others, have wondered how the 777 would perform in the scenario where the pilots were incapacitated and the aircraft ran out of fuel. I had my ideas but there is nothing like seeing it for 'real' so we tried this in a 777-2 full motion zero flight time approved simulator," said the pilot.

"We used a zero fuel weight of 175 tonnes. We let it run out of fuel at FL250 (25,000 feet altitude) in track hold and alt capture (holding a specific speed and altitude). However, it would not make any difference what mode it was in as everything would drop out. In real life one engine uses fractionally more fuel per hour than the other and there is typically a difference between main tanks of a few hundred kilos, so we had a 300kg difference between the contents of the left and right tank.

"When the first engine failed TAC (Thrust asymmetry compensation) automatically applied rudder. The speed reduced from 320 knots indicated to 245 knots indicated. It was able to maintain 245 knots and FL250 (25,000 feet altitude). When the second engine failed the rudder trim applied by TAC was taken out and the trim went to zero. The autopilot dropped out and the flight controls reverted to direct mode. The speed initially came back to 230 knots but then the nose started to lower. The nose continued to lower and the rate of descent increased to 4000 feet per minute. The nose kept lowering and the descent rate increased to 7500 feet per minute with a bank angle that increased to 25 degrees. The speed at this point had increased to 340 knots indicated, above VMO (maximum operating limit speed) but there was no horn as it was on limited electrics. About this point the RAT (Ram air turbine) chipped in and the CDUs and co-pilot's PFD (Primary flight display) came alive. The flight controls stayed in direct mode. Then with a max descent rate of almost 8000 feet per minute the nose started to slowly rise and keep rising. We had dropped to about FL170 (17,000 feet) but the nose slowly rose up to 6 degrees pitch up and we started climbing at about 3000 feet per minute and the bank angle reduced to only 5 degrees. It climbed back up to FL210 (21,000 feet altitude) at which point the speed had come back to 220 knots and then the nose dropped down again and we were soon back to descending at 8000 feet per minute.

He described how the aircraft's nose dropped and the aircraft descended rapidly up to 8000 feet per minute, gaining airspeed, followed by the nose of the aircraft rising and then climbing between 3000 and 4000 feet losing airspeed, nose pitching down again; this process repeating itself again and again in what is called a series of phugoid oscillations. "We didn't watch it all the way down due to time constraints and stopped the experiment at 10,000 feet but it was consistent all the way down. Having watched it I can say with certainty that if the pilots were incapacitated and it ran out of fuel there is no way it could have landed on the water with anything like a survivable impact."

There is a second scenario that we consider should be looked at when determining the search area for MH370 and one which is more suited to the side of Zaharie's character which would want to make the puzzle incredibly hard to solve and the aircraft as difficult to find as possible for searchers. In other words, against all odds, he was able to just make the aircraft disappear.

We believe Zaharie could well have chosen to repressurise the aircraft once he had flown through the Straits of Malacca and made his turns south. By then all the passengers were either dead or comatose, and it is highly unlikely any of the cabin crew would still be alive either. He would have had ample time to programme the FMC with a series of way points or by longitude and latitude into the southern Indian Ocean, and the auto pilot would quite happily fly him there while he enjoyed the ride. Why fly it manually when the aircraft can do it for you?

The path to the southern Indian Ocean set, MH370 took a final excruciating journey south for four, perhaps five hours. As the fuel of both engines started to run out the auxiliary power unit started which might explain the last partial handshake received by satellite at the ground station near Perth at 8.19am. Finally, both engines flamed out and the auxiliary power unit too, and finally the auto pilot failed and the RAT deployed. Zaharie took control of the aircraft and flew on. There is precedent for what we are about to suggest happened next - the most famous being the Gimli glider incident on July 23, 1983. On this occasion an Air Canada 767 was incorrectly fuelled and ran out of fuel while cruising at 41,000 feet half way on its trip from Montreal to Edmonton. The RAT deployed and Captain Robert Pearson, an experienced glider pilot, at the suggestion of his co-pilot Maurice Quintall, a former Canadian Royal Air Force pilot, landed the aircraft at a former air force base which had been converted into a motorsports park. There was a minor fire on landing but none of the 61 passengers was seriously hurt.

We believe Zaharie may have taken control as the small propeller in the slip stream, the RAT, gave the aircraft enough electrical power to keep a limited number of cockpit instruments going and hydraulics to power the flight surfaces.

Non-aviators will find this hard to believe but all aircraft glide - even helicopters. Some fixed wing aircraft's glide ratio (performance) are better than others. It is said that as a general rule, the more fuel-efficient the aircraft the better it will glide. Lots of things, including wind, affect how long an aircraft will glide for. But the point we are making is that just because the engines stop, this does not mean that the aircraft falls out of the sky.

With the remaining power possessed by the ailing 777, Zaharie glided the aircraft for perhaps 100n/m until it would go no further. The aircraft glided closer and closer to the ocean, sacrificing altitude for speed and distance. Finally, Zaharie used his skills as a commercial pilot, honed over 30 years, to try a controlled ditching of the plane intact and it sunk beneath the surface to the ocean floor. The engines are designed to tear off and would sink, as would the balance of the aircraft very quickly. We saw that this ditching scenario was possible with the likes of US Airways Flight 1549 which, after encountering a dual engine failure due to bird strike, successfully completed a controlled ditching in the Hudson River in 2009 (although we're the first to accept that the Hudson River is considerably more manageable than the Indian Ocean). In MH370's case, there would be no huge fuel slick as there was very little fuel left, other than a small unusable amount in the bottom of the fuel tanks. As the aircraft sank it may well implode (which in simple terms is the opposite to explosion) due to the hydrostatic pressure.

So what would this mean? The wreckage of Malaysia Airlines Flight 370 could be nearly 100n/m in any direction outside the current search area.

In a sick way Zaharie would have joined the same club as the Gimli Glider pilot Robert Pearson and Flight 1549's pilot, Captain Chesley D. Sullenberger, but with a psychopathic cruelty and a complete absence of humanity and honour.

For more than four months afterwards, while the search went on, and with the prospect of many more harrowing months ahead for relatives, it would be what clinical psychologist Renate Bellve-Wack described as the ultimate "postmortem triumph". Zaharie was a man known for his methodical, thorough nature, for his love of the technical and probably for his ego too. It would have been Zaharie Ahmad Shah's final sad statement to his family, to Malaysia Airlines, to the Malaysian Government and to the world.

Find this one.

Chapter 19

Conclusion

What lessons can be learnt from the tragic events that led to the disappearance of Malaysia Airlines Flight 370 and the devastating loss of all 239 people on board? And are there recommendations that could be implemented around the world by both government regulators and airlines to ensure there is no repeat?

And given the fear and shockwaves caused by the shooting down of MH17, what lessons do we take from this? Will the world of commercial airlines ever be the same?

The answer is no, on both counts.

These two events within 131 days may well have changed the face of commercial aviation travel forever.

The loss of MH370 has shown us that there are some obvious and immediately available steps that could be taken to lessen the likelihood of the incident reoccurring and if it did, helping us understand far more quickly what happened, why and where the aircraft is.

The technology to prevent it is available. In fact, some of the basic steps we could take are incredibly affordable. It simply requires an acceptance by some and the mandatory introduction of rules by others.

A first logical step should be a review of each nation's policies and procedures when an aircraft suddenly disappears off either primary or secondary radar for a prolonged period. What we saw in the case of Flight 370 was a systemic failure across both Malaysia Airlines, several countries' departments of civil aviation and the Malaysian military. It is hard to find a better example of when so many did so little.

The obvious problem is that inherently, governments act in what they believe is in the best interest of their own national sovereignty and security. In other words, sometimes they can't afford to tell the truth. They are scared of revealing the weaknesses in their national defence systems or the incompetence either in their own Government departments or in the private companies contracting for them, thus opening themselves up to expensive litigation.

These secretive self-preservation strategies are not the sole domain of the third world or developing countries. One does not have to look far to see examples in the developed world. The aftermath of tragic air accidents tends to aggravate such behaviour. Our own country of New Zealand is recognised around the world as one of the least corrupt nations with a well-respected government and corporate regulatory structure. Yet the tragic crash of an Air New Zealand flight into Mount Erebus in Antarctica on November 29, 1979 led a high court judge to describe the ensuing cover up by Air New Zealand as "an orchestrated litany of lies". It was a scandal and a perfect example of the type of concealment and evasion that occurs when the stakes are high.

The 777 which departed Kuala Lumpur for Beijing at 12.41am on March 8, 2014, was well-equipped with both communication and navigational technology. If the transponder with its enhanced Automatic Dependencies Surveillance Broadcast (ADSB) capability could not have been switched off the aircraft would not have been invisible to secondary radar for critical parts of its journey. This simple step alone could be actioned nearly immediately by removing the ability of the transponder to be turned off. We can already hear the screams of protest from pilots, airlines and engineers all on the basis that pilots must be able to access and turn these components off in case of fire or an electrical problem. The reality is these components have become so reliable we believe the likelihood of such an emergency is minuscule and the immediate safety benefits to the travelling public are obvious and substantial.

Tragic events often generate a human desire to understand what and why something happened in the pursuit of ensuring that the tragedy is never repeated. The sole purpose of air accident investigation organisations such as the ATSB, AAB and NTSB is prevention. They are not focused on placing blame or culpability, they leave the task of pursuing intentional violations to others.

The most important development in understanding how and why

an air accident occurred was developed by an Australian by the name of David Warren after his father was tragically killed in a plane crash. In 1953 he was working as an aeronautical engineering researcher and developed the premise of a flight data recorder, more commonly known as the black box. There is some conjecture about whether the term black box was in reference to the fact that the integral workings of the box are of less interest than the value of its output or that they were essentially photograph-based since the record was made on a scrolling photographic film and the inside of the recorder was pitch black.

Either way the black boxes (as there are always two - a flight data recorder and a cockpit voice recorder) - which are in fact, a bright orange colour with fluorescent tape that makes them easier to find, have helped explain what happened and why commercial airliners have crashed for well over 50 years. As technology has improved all the data is now recorded on digital chips and includes a wide variety of critical aircraft parameters such as most of the aircraft's primary flight display including aircraft altitude, VSI, engine power settings and flight control surfaces to mention but a few. These rugged, reinforced water-proofed containers have helped unravel numerous air accidents and left a lasting impact on the very few who get to hear the cockpit voice recordings and the often tragic, desperate and heart-wrenching last words of the pilots as they fight to keep the aircraft airborne.

In the last 30 years, to improve the usefulness of black boxes in aircraft crashes into water, underwater locator beacons (ULB) have also been fitted. The significant weaknesses are two-fold; the current requirement is that batteries last only 30 days once immersed in water, and the normal signal strength in comparison to the vastness of the ocean is incredibly weak. Unfortunately, as Air France Flight 447 and subsequently Malaysia Airlines Flight 370 have shown, the remoteness of the location and the depths of the ocean can make these black boxes very hard to find. Clearly an immediate requirement is to increase the lifespan of the underwater locator beacon batteries to at least 120 days, and serious thought must be given to increasing frequency band-width and hopefully the range of the signal itself.

But are we not missing the real point? Hasn't the paradigm shifted? In an age when we no longer talk about saving data to our home desktop but to a second party via the cloud, can we not have a dynamic and real-time upload of these critical flight parameters? The answer is yes of course we can. It is called the glass box (one assumes it's a descriptive meaning to imply transparency) and it is available now - it's simply a matter of cost. An innovative Canadian company called Star Navigation Systems has patented a system called Star -ISMS, an in-flight safety monitoring system that transmits data continuously and in real-time to a ground-based recording station.

The inherent problem, however, is the reluctance of the regulators to force aircraft manufacturers to adopt this technology, and an even greater reluctance on the part of the airlines to pay the cost. But this will change as satellite communication and data costs reduce and the travelling public start to demand improved safety features. Governments, aircraft manufacturers and airlines will have to succumb to public pressure.

Like all of these technological innovations such as ADSB and real-time flight data information uploads, manufacturers will have to take into account the most unpalatable scenario - the rogue pilot. Human factor training has taught us that whenever there is a human interface there is a likelihood of human error or deliberate human violation.

Some time ago there was a requirement for the flight data recorders to increase the duration of recording to reflect the nature of some of the long-haul flying that now occurs. However, there is an absurd inconsistency where, depending on the age of the aircraft, the cockpit voice recorder is only required to record between the last 30 to the last 180 minutes of a flight.

Surely the very minimum should be the duration of the flight, and if that happens to be a 17-hour long-haul flight then that should be the length of the cockpit recording. Pilots and their unions have protested loudly at the suggestion of increasing the length of cockpit recordings, arguing that it is an invasion of their privacy. Surely, the safety of the travelling public outstrips such concerns about revealing the contents of prolonged cockpit conversations. After all, if nothing happens then no one gets to hear the recordings.

The MH370 tragedy also exposed the risk of light flight crews if there is a rogue element among the crew. With a two-person flight crew, the cockpit is exposed; with three, at least there is an element of cover should one of the flight crew be unbalanced. The events of March 8 should prompt a rethink about whether it is good enough for 200 to 300 passengers to trust their lives to a situation in which on a whim, one person can relatively easily have the power and opportunity to commit mass murder. MH370 is surely an argument for considering the extra investment required to ensure safety in numbers. In other words, a team of more than two in the flight deck.

Surely, if Zaharie did commit the unfathomable, unforgiveable act we suggest, it must prompt another look at mental health in the cockpits of the thousands of aircraft in the world's skies. The number of commercial air accidents that can be contributed to alcohol or drug addiction is incredibly low at 1.5 per cent over the last 32 years. This reflects government regulations and a number of processes that airlines have implemented to weed out or help those with addiction problems. The regularity of commercial pilots' medical and modern testing procedures has played a critical role in achieving this. Meanwhile, our research shows that there have been five pilot suicides on commercial flights over the very same time period, killing 422 people. If MH370 was indeed as murder/suicide that would bring the death toll 661.

Mental health is tricky territory. Testing for such illnesses is incredibly difficult. It is particularly difficult trying to pick up such problems simply from a pilot's regular medical checks and it probably relies on someone saying something or the pilot acknowledging they have a problem. In general, a pilot who acknowledges they are going through a difficult time, whether it is through a mental illness or related to a relationship breakdown or financial pressures or whatever, is not exactly warmly embraced. In fact, such an admission would be widely regarded as a career-limiting move. Mental health is one of the highest causes for pilot loss of license in the United States.

The stigma is such that society still finds the thought of a pilot in control of an aircraft who has any association with mental illness unacceptable. There is a fair point here. Air travel is statistically safe but still a potentially dangerous form of mass public transport. The pilot's health should be beyond doubt. Then again, if pilots and airlines are not open about such things, they will continue to get nasty, tragic surprises.

Surely they are doing passengers more of a service by confronting issues early.

There is a real argument to say that airlines and regulators must proactively encourage pilots who are feeling mentally unwell to seek assistance, and that acknowledging the problem doesn't necessarily mean the end of their flying career. The alternative is that problems get ignored until it is too late. The United States Federal Aviation Authority has been one regulator which has taken a proactive approach and has recently approved four different types of antidepressants that can be taken by commercial airline pilots in the USA. Clinical psychologist Renate Bellve-Wack indicates that rather than playing up the issue of mental illness, major focus needs to go on the issue of pilot stress. She suggests better screening for stress could be an effective tool for airline companies.

"If there were a way of integrating a screening, if you will, for stress it could have a number of different aspects. You could look from an HR point of view: has this person had more sick days, has this person had more complaints against them by the flight crew? Are they currently going through major personal issues which we know about? Have there been more reports of them drinking more?

"So there are some objective things which might come to the attention of the employers at some point. (Screening for stress) would be a more objective screening to see if there is something changing. Then, of course, there is the more subjective screening from the person themselves. How are they sleeping, how are they feeling, what's going on in their lives? Even the way people are able to talk about that, or not talk about that, tells you something."

Dr Bellve-Wack says much of the problem comes down to corporate culture needing to change its values.

"You can't expect people to be open if they get punished for it. I think there's a huge case for corporate culture to become more psychologically-minded."

She says that in the US most corporates in the 1980s were under the impression that they were good organisations to work for. Increasing incidents of workplace violence led to more openness and HR staff trained to look for early warning signs. Dr Bellve-Wack says organisations should focus on risk-management rather than risk-assessment.

"Risk-assessment is predicting if someone is going to be a problem and what kind of problem it may be. Flagging it, and then everyone is like 'no more flying!' That's counter-productive on many levels. What people should try to look at is early warning signs that indicate that somebody's function may be affected and then to put risk-management into place, counselling or support, whatever the person needs, with the express goal of helping the person to function better rather than being eliminated. I think that kind of mindset is really really important and that needs to come from the top down."

What is particularly concerning is the attitude of some Asian and Middle Eastern countries to the issue of pilot suicide and pilots' mental health in general. In case studies of pilot suicides we looked at earlier, authorities in Egypt, Morocco and Indonesia were all reluctant to admit pilot actions caused horrific tragedies. The same brick wall we discovered in Malaysia appears to exist in other mainly Muslim countries. The mantra we were greeted with was "Muslims don't commit suicide". The clear inference was that "if they do, we won't acknowledge it". This profound cultural difference will take time to work around, if it can ever be addressed. Surely the travelling public deserves better than the cases of denial we have illustrated in which investigations in some countries preferred to look for mechanical causes of accidents when pilot behaviour as the cause was staring them in the face. We can only hope some pressure can be applied to encourage more engagement on such issues with airlines in these parts of the world.

Otherwise, the only other possible remedy is for the travelling public, where possible, to make choices based on what they know to be safe airlines, with the players prepared to open their scrutiny of flight crew's mental health to international standards. Does it need to get to a stage where certain airlines which refuse to engage on such issues are put on some sort of blacklist? This would scarcely be practical given the geographic nature in which airlines operate. Perhaps MH370 will help put the spotlight on airlines' management of pilot stress and mental health, but we are not hopeful of significant change.

Meanwhile, the brutal and unforgivable shooting down of MH17 by pro-Russian Ukrainian separatists under the watchful gaze and helping hand of Russian President Vladamir Putin will forever change the use of air corridors by airlines over conflict zones. Not only does the horrendous and unthinkable mass murder highlight the short-comings of both regulatory and industry associations like ICAO, IATA and the individual states that provide and bank the profits of the management of the airways corridors, it also re-focuses the decision-making processes an airline goes through in determining what air routes it will use. Clearly, being motivated by choosing the shortest distance between two points that leads to fuel economy should not be the paramount concern. The MH17 tragedy shows how very different one airline's approach can be over a number of others. Most airlines continued to use the routes over Eastern Ukraine despite the cautionary note issued by the FAA. Qantas was one of the world leading airlines to say two months ago they were not going to over fly a known conflict zone. This unpalatable lesson with its unfathomable cost will lead to airlines avoiding these conflict zones and inevitably a small increase in cost of air travel. If Malaysia Airlines had chosen to avoid Eastern Ukraine airspace it would have cost the airline between 10 and 20 minutes more of flying time - between $1500 and $3000 dollars. When balanced with 298 lives that is a small price to pay.

For the airline concerned, the events of March 8 have no doubt been profound. It is now regarded as bad luck. Who would book a ticket on the airline right now?

As we mentioned in earlier chapters, before the second tragedy, Malaysia Airlines was already suffering at the stock exchange and its market share had shrivelled. Media recently reported how the airline posted its worst quarterly loss in more than two years, after passengers kept away from the company. The aviation firm's losses reached US$138 million in the quarter ending March, 31, 2014, its worst loss since the quarter ending December, 31, 2011. Passengers in Asia have taken their custom elsewhere and passenger numbers were down by 60 per cent.

Past experience shows the travelling public are relatively quick to forget, and in most cases, driven by price. Malaysia Airlines' problem is its customers tend to be low-yield. It is the high-yield passengers which most airlines strive for, but these are usually the most discerning.

All the same, the Malaysian Government wants a national carrier.

The national pride that airlines generate and the overall importance to the Malaysian economy has been a more important argument for keeping the airline going than the short-term viability. One could say the most valuable asset the airline has is its landing slots at some of the world's busiest airports.

But two tragic occurrences in four months is surely one too many. Malaysia Airlines was already on the mat. Now it has received what feels like the coup de grace and the brand is so damaged there is little hope for recovery. One just needs to look at history and the tragic consequences for the likes of Pan Am after the Lockerbie disaster and TWA (Transworld World Airlines) after the loss of a 747 off the coast of New York. These airlines are now distant memories. Two occurrences is likely to mean that even those attracted and motivated by cheap fares are not so quick to forget. If Malaysia Airlines was a private airline its financial demise would be inevitable. However, given the public ownership, the Malaysian Government is faced with a huge dilemma. Perhaps the only way forward is winding up of the brand we know as Malaysia Airlines and the rebirth of a new Asian carrier. Malaysia is in an interesting situation because unlike other countries with no alternatives, with AirAsia, the country does appear to have a successful and profitable private airline alongside the national carrier. One wonders whether the Malaysian Government would ever consider allowing Air Asia to step in and fill the void. Before MH17 it seemed unlikely, but now the airline may be just too much of a noose around the Government's neck. It wouldn't be the first time a country finally says enough is enough. Switzerland did it with Swissair and the Belgian Government did it with Sabena.

An interesting recent development is news that the Malaysian state investor Khazanah Nasional has been looking to privatise Malaysia Airlines. A Reuters' report suggests the state-owned group was mulling over selling the airline to private companies. The news went down well with investors and on hearing these reports on July 3, Malaysia Airlines' shares soared by nearly 17 per cent. Reuters' sources suggested that by privatising the airline, investors would be able to cut head count, focus on installing a new management team and sell off some of its lucrative engineering capabilities. Prime Minister Razak was about to enter talks on the prospect of a sale. This deal was being mooted before the tragedy on July 18 which further rocked the airline. Is the deal still on the table? If not, you would have to say the future of Malaysia Airlines in its current form is probably over.

Lastly, and with all of our hearts we, as authors of an account of this sad and tragic event, convey our deep condolences to the relatives and friends of those lost on Malaysia Airlines Flight 370.

In a small way we have tried to touch on some of the human stories of March 8, 2014, but in doing so we acknowledge from the start we did not know these people. They were not our family members or friends. What little we knew of them we presented as best we could to tell the story of that awful day. Our debt to these people is not to pretend to know their lives in intimate detail but more to pursue the truth of what happened as best we can. That is what we have done.

To the family and friends of those lost on MH370 - and those lost on MH17 - no one can stand in your shoes and feel your pain and no one should pretend to.

We don't.

But may you find some peace, somehow, in the years ahead.

APPENDICES

I MH370 Passenger Seating Plan

II Malaysian Preliminary Report

III Pilot - ATC Radiotelephony Transcript

IV MH370 Action Taken Report

V Australian Transportation Safety Bureau (ATSB) Definition of Search Area

Also, visit www.wilsonaviation.co.nz for copies of the following reports:

MH370 Cargo Manifest

Dr Richard E Cole, University College London - Analysis of the Inmarsat Data

Swiss Air flight 111 Investigation Report

UPS Flight 6 Air Accident Investigation Interim Report

Qantas Flight 30 - Oxygen cylinder ruptures on QF30

Helios Flight 522 Aircraft Accident Report

EgyptAir Flight 990

Air Canada Flight AC143 - Gimli Glider

Silk Air 185 - National Transportation Safety Board

Aloha Flight 243 - National Transportation Safety Board

MH 370
08 March 2014
KUL - BJS

NAME	NATIONALITY	Age	Gender	Class	Seat No
TAN/CHONGLING	MYS	48	M	GCCL	1C
GAN/FUXIANG	CHN	49	M	GCCL	2A
CHNG/MEI LING	MYS	33	F	GCCL	2D
WEEKS/PAULMR	NZL	39	M	GCCL	2K
YUE/GUIJUMS	CHN	51	F	GCCL	3A
BRODSKII/NIKOLAI	RU	43	M	GCCL	3K
BAI/XIAOMO	CAN	37	F	GCCL	4A
MUKHERJEE/MUKTESH	CAN	42	M	GCCL	4C
MOHAMADSOFUAN/IBRAHIMMR	MYS	33	M	GCCL	4J
XING/QIAO	CHN	27	F	GCCL	4K
TIAN/QINGJUN	CHN	51	M	EYCL	11A
WOOD/PHILIP	USA	51	M	EYCL	11C
LIN/ANNANMR	CHN	27	M	EYCL	11D
XIE/LIPING	CHN	51	F	EYCL	11E
ZHANG/XUEWENMR	CHN	61	M	EYCL	11H
HUE/PUIHENGMR	MYS	66	M	EYCL	11J
LI/LE	CHN	36	M	EYCL	11K
BIBYNAZLI/MOHDHASSIM	MYS	62	F	EYCL	12A
DINA/MOHAMEDYUNUSRAMLI	MYS	30	F	EYCL	12C
MARIA/MOHAMEDYUNUSRAMLI	MYS	52	F	EYCL	12D
HASHIM/NOORIDA	MYS	57	F	EYCL	12E
WANG/SHOUXIAN	CHN	69	M	EYCL	12G
KOH/TIONGMENG	MYS	40	M	EYCL	12H
MUHAMMADRAZAHAN/ZAMANIMR	MYS	24	M	EYCL	12J
NORLIAKMAR/HAMIDMDM	MYS	33	M	EYCL	12K
ZHANG/SHAOHUA	CHN	32	F	EYCL	14A
ZHANG/HUALIAN	CHN	42	F	EYCL	14C
LI/YUCHEN	CHN	27	M	EYCL	14D
LI/YUAN	AUS	33	M	EYCL	14E
LI/JIE	CHN	27	F	EYCL	14F
KANG/XU	CHN	34	M	EYCL	14G
GU/NAIJUN	AUS	31	F	EYCL	14H
SHARMA/CHANDRIKAMS	IND	51	F	EYCL	14J
CHAN/HUANPEENMR	MYS	46	M	EYCL	14K
LEE/SEWCHUMDM	MYS	55	F	EYCL	15A
NG/MAYLIMS	MYS	37	F	EYCL	15C
YANG/LI	CHN	35	F	EYCL	15D
LU/JIANHUA	CHN	57	M	EYCL	15E
MA/WENZHI	CHN	57	F	EYCL	15F
SIM/KENGWEI	MYS	53	M	EYCL	15G
ZHANG/CHI	CHN	58	F	EYCL	15H
WAN/HOCKKHOONMR	MYS	42	M	EYCL	15J
TEE/LINKEONGMR	MYS	50	M	EYCL	15K
LI/ZHIJIN	CHN	30	M	EYCL	16A
YAP/CHEEMENGMR	MYS	39	M	EYCL	16C
SUGIANTO/LOMR	IDN	47	M	EYCL	16D
VINNY/CHYNTHYATIOMRS	IDN	47	F	EYCL	16E
ZHANG/QIMS	CHN	31	F	EYCL	16G

Malaysia Airlines System Confidential 24/07/14 Page 1

MH 370
08 March 2014
KUL - BJS

NAME	NATIONALITY	Age	Gender	Class	Seat No
BIAN/LIANGJING	CHN	27	M	EYCL	16H
MATRAHIM/NORFADZILLAHMISS	MYS	39	F	EYCL	16J
TONG/SOONLEEMR	MYS	31	M	EYCL	16K
WENG/MEI	CHN	39	F	EYCL	17A
ZHANG/NAMS	CHN	34	F	EYCL	17D
HU/XIAONINGMR	CHN	34	M	EYCL	17E
HU/SIWANCHD	CHN	3	F	EYCL	17F
SIREGAR/FIRMAN CHANDRA	IDN	25	M	EYCL	17G
SHIRSATH/KRANTI	IND	44	F	EYCL	17H
MUSTAFA/SUHAILIMISS	MYS	31	F	EYCL	17J
LEE/KAHKINMR	MYS	32	M	EYCL	17K
GAN/TAO	CHN	44	M	EYCL	18A
LU/XIANCHU	CHN	33	M	EYCL	18C
ZHAO/QIWEIMR	CHN	37	M	EYCL	18D
ZHANG/XIAOLEIMS	CHN	32	F	EYCL	18E
ZHAO/YINGXINCHD	CHN	3	F	EYCL	18F
LIU/QIANG	CHN	40	M	EYCL	18H
RAMLAN/SAFUANMR	MYS	32	M	EYCL	18J
YUSOP/MUZIMR	MYS	50	M	EYCL	18K
JU/KUN	CHN	32	M	EYCL	19A
WANG/XIMIN	NZL	50	M	EYCL	19C
SUADAYA/FERRYINDRAMR	IDN	42	M	EYCL	19D
SUADAYA/HERRYINDRAMR	IDN	35	M	EYCL	19E
TANURISAM/INDRASURIAMR	IDN	57	M	EYCL	19F
WANG/WILLYSURIJANTOMR	IDN	53	M	EYCL	19G
YANG/AILINGMS	CHN	60	F	EYCL	19H
GUAN/HUAJINMS	MYS	34	F	EYCL	19J
JIA/PING	CHN	32	F	EYCL	19K
BURROWS/RODNEYMR	AUS	59	M	EYCL	20A
BURROWS/MARYMRS	AUS	54	F	EYCL	20C
CHEN/JIAN	CHN	58	M	EYCL	20D
FENG/JIXIN	CHN	70	M	EYCL	20F
WANG/YONGGANGMR	CHN	27	M	EYCL	20G
ZHANG/JIANWU	CHN	31	M	EYCL	20H
MENG/GAOSHENG	CHN	64	M	EYCL	20J
DING/LIJUN	CHN	43	M	EYCL	20K
LAWTON/CATHERINEMRS	AUS	54	F	EYCL	21A
LAWTON/ROBERTMR	AUS	58	M	EYCL	21C
XING/FENGTAO	CHN	36	M	EYCL	21D
CHEW/KARMOOIMS	MYS	31	F	EYCL	21E
WONG/SAISANGMR	MYS	53	M	EYCL	21F
LIM/POWCHUAMS	MYS	43	M	EYCL	21G
TAN/AHMENGMR	MYS	46	M	EYCL	21H
TAN/WEICHEWMR	MYS	19	M	EYCL	21J
CHUANG/HSIULINGMS	TWN	45	F	EYCL	21K
GUAN/WENJIEMR	CHN	35	M	EYCL	22A
LIU/JINPENGMR	CHN	33	M	EYCL	22C
WANG/CHUNHUAMR	CHN	34	M	EYCL	22D

Malaysia Airlines System Confidential 24/07/14 Page 2

MH 370
08 March 2014
KUL - BJS

NAME	NATIONALITY	Age	Gender	Class	Seat No
ZHANG/SIMING	CHN	71	F	EYCL	22H
DOU/YUNSHANMR	CHN	61	M	EYCL	22J
ZHANG/LIJUANMS	CHN	61	F	EYCL	22K
XIN/XIXIMS	CHN	32	F	EYCL	23A
HUANG/YIMS	CHN	30	F	EYCL	23C
LIU/ZHONGFU	CHN	72	M	EYCL	23D
MAIMAITIJIANG/A	CHN	35	M	EYCL	23E
MAO/TUGUI	CHN	72	M	EYCL	23F
ZHAO/GANGMR	CHN	46	M	EYCL	23H
WEN/HAO DONG	CHN	32	M	EYCL	23J
YAN/XIAO DAN	CHN	27	F	EYCL	23K
OUYANG/XIN	CHN	38	F	EYCL	24A
YIN/BOYAN	CHN	33	M	EYCL	24C
ZHANG/YANHUI	CHN	44	F	EYCL	24D
YANG/JIABAO	CHN	26	F	EYCL	24E
WANG/DAN	CHN	54	F	EYCL	24F
LI/HONGJING	CHN	20	F	EYCL	24G
LI/GUOHUI	CHN	56	M	EYCL	24H
HUANG/TIANHUI	CHN	43	M	EYCL	24J
JIANG/CUIYUN	CHN	62	F	EYCL	24K
LIU/SHUNCHAO	CHN	46	M	EYCL	25A
DI/JIABIN	CHN	36	M	EYCL	25C
WATTRELOS/AMBRE	FRA	14	F	EYCL	25D
WATTRELOS/HADRIEN	FRA	17	M	EYCL	25E
WATTRELOS/LAURENCE	FRA	52	F	EYCL	25F
ZHAO/YAN	FRA	18	F	EYCL	25G
TANG/XUDONG	CHN	31	M	EYCL	25H
YAN/LINGMR	CHN	29	M	EYCL	25J
CHEN/CHANGJUNMR	CHN	35	M	EYCL	25K
ZHAO/PENG	CHN	25	M	EYCL	26A
TIAN/JUNWEI	CHN	29	M	EYCL	26C
LUI/CHING	CHN	45	F	EYCL	26D
WANG/SHU MIN	CHN	61	F	EYCL	26E
WANG/XIANJUN	CHN	61	M	EYCL	26F
LI/ZHIXIN	CHN	35	M	EYCL	26H
TAN/SIOH PENG	MYS	42	F	EYCL	26J
CHEN/WEI HOING	MYS	43	M	EYCL	26K
DEINEKA/SERGII	UKR	45	M	EYCL	27D
CHUSTRAK/OLEG	UKR	45	M	EYCL	27E
ZANG/LINGDI	CHN	58	F	EYCL	27G
LIANG/LUYANGMR	CHN	60	M	EYCL	27H
MOHDKHAIRULAMRI/SELAMATMR	MYS	29	M	EYCL	29A
PUSPANATHAN/SUBRAMANIAN	MYS	34	M	EYCL	29C
JIANG/XUEREN	CHN	62	M	EYCL	29J
LI/YANLIN	CHN	29	M	EYCL	29K
JIANG/YINGMS	CHN	27	F	EYCL	30A
KOZEL/CHRISTIAN	AUT	30	M	EYCL	30C
XU/CHUANE	CHN	57	M	EYCL	30D

Malaysia Airlines System Confidential 24/07/14 Page 3

MH 370
08 March 2014
KUL - BJS

NAME	NATIONALITY	Age	Gender	Class	Seat No
ZHANG/YAN	CHN	36	F	EYCL	30E
MENG/BING	CHN	40	M	EYCL	30F
MENG/FANQUAN	CHN	70	M	EYCL	30G
MENG/NICOLECHD	USA	4	F	EYCL	30H
ZHANG/MENG	CHN	29	F	EYCL	30J
YAN/PENG	CHN	29	M	EYCL	30K
ZHOU/JINLING	CHN	61	M	EYCL	31A
ZHOU/FENG	CHN	56	F	EYCL	31C
ZHAO/ZHAOFANG	CHN	73	F	EYCL	31D
XIONG/DEMING	CHN	63	F	EYCL	31E
WANG/LINSHI	CHN	59	M	EYCL	31F
LOU/BAOTANG	CHN	79	M	EYCL	31G
LIU/RUSHENG	CHN	76	M	EYCL	31H
DONG/GUOWEI	CHN	48	M	EYCL	31J
BAO/YUANHUA	CHN	63	F	EYCL	31K
CHEN/YUNMS	CHN	57	F	EYCL	32A
DING/YINGMS	CHN	62	F	EYCL	32C
HOU/AIQINMS	CHN	45	F	EYCL	32D
SONG/CHUNLINGMS	CHN	60	F	EYCL	32E
TANG/XUEZHUMS	CHN	57	F	EYCL	32F
YANG/QINGYUANMR	CHN	57	M	EYCL	32G
YANG/XIAOMINGMS	CHN	59	F	EYCL	32H
SURTIDAHLIA/MRS	NLD	50	F	EYCL	32J
FENG/DONG	CHN	21	M	EYCL	32K
CAO/RUI	CHN	32	F	EYCL	33A
MA/JUNMR	CHN	33	M	EYCL	33C
SONG/FEIFEIMR	CHN	32	M	EYCL	33D
ZHANG/HUAMR	CHN	43	M	EYCL	33E
TEOH/KIMLUNMR	MYS	36	M	EYCL	33G
YAO/LIFEI	CHN	31	M	EYCL	33H
YA/NA	CHN	26	F	EYCL	33J
HAN/JING	CHN	53	F	EYCL	33K
FU/BAOFENG	CHN	28	M	EYCL	34A
MARALDI/LUIGI	ITA	37	M	EYCL	34C
YUE/WENCHAO	CHN	26	M	EYCL	34D
ZHANG/YAN	CHN	45	F	EYCL	34G
WANG/YONGQIANG	CHN	30	M	EYCL	34H
SU/QIANGGUO	CHN	71	M	EYCL	34J
SONG/KUN	CHN	25	M	EYCL	34K
KOLEKAR/VINOD	IND	59	M	EYCL	35A
KOLEKAR/CHETANA	IND	55	F	EYCL	35C
KOLEKAR/SWANAND	IND	23	M	EYCL	35D
WANG/HAITAO	CHN	26	M	EYCL	35G
LUO/WEI	CHN	29	M	EYCL	35H
LI/YAN	CHN	31	F	EYCL	35J
GAO/GE	CHN	27	F	EYCL	35K
HOU/BO	CHN	35	M	EYCL	36A
WEN/YONGSHENG	CHN	34	M	EYCL	36B

Malaysia Airlines System Confidential 24/07/14 Page 4

MH 370
08 March 2014
KUL - BJS

NAME	NATIONALITY	Age	Gender	Class	Seat No
WANG/CHUNYONG	CHN	43	M	EYCL	36C
LI/ZHI	CHN	41	M	EYCL	36G
TAN/TEIKHINMR	MYS	32	M	EYCL	36H
DU/WENZHONG	CHN	50	M	EYCL	36J
LIN/MINGFENG	CHN	34	M	EYCL	36K
SHI/XIANWEN	CHN	26	M	EYCL	37A
WANG/LIJUN	CHN	49	M	EYCL	37C
WANG/RUI	CHN	35	M	EYCL	37D
JIAO/WEIWEI	CHN	32	F	EYCL	37H
ZHOU/SHIJIE	CHN	64	M	EYCL	37J
YIN/YUEWANG	CHN	21	M	EYCL	37K
LI/WENBO	CHN	29	F	EYCL	38A
ZHENG/RUIXIAN	CHN	42	F	EYCL	38C
JIAO/WENXUE	CHN	58	M	EYCL	38D
JINGHANG/JEE	MYS	41	M	EYCL	38G
DAI/SHULING	CHN	58	F	EYCL	38H
BIAN/MAOQIN	CHN	67	F	EYCL	38J
WANG/YONGHUI	CHN	33	M	EYCL	38K
LI/MINGZHONG	CHN	69	M	EYCL	39A
LIU/FENGYING	CHN	65	F	EYCL	39D
YUAN/JIN	CHN	63	F	EYCL	39G
ZHANG/LIQIN	CHN	43	F	EYCL	39J
WANG/HOUBIN	CHN	28	M	EYCL	39K
ZHU/JUNYAN	CHN	41	F	EYCL	40A
ZHANG/ZHONGHAI	CHN	43	M	EYCL	40C
ZHANG/JINQUAN	CHN	72	M	EYCL	40D
YAO/JIANFENG	CHN	70	M	EYCL	40E
YANG/MEIHUA	CHN	65	F	EYCL	40F
DAISY/ANNE	MYS	56	F	EYCL	40G
AN/WENLAN	CHN	65	F	EYCL	40K
LIANG/XUYANG	CHN	30	M	EYCL	41D
DING/YING	CHN	28	F	EYCL	41G
CHE/JUNZHANG	CHN	68	F	EYCL	4J
WANG/MOHENG	CHN	2	M	EYCL	
ZHANG/YAN	USA	2	M	EYCL	

OFFICE OF THE
CHIEF INSPECTOR OF AIR ACCIDENTS
MINISTRY OF TRANSPORT
MALAYSIA

MH 370 PRELIMINARY REPORT — *SERIAL 03/2014*

Aircraft Type & Registration:	Boeing 777-2H6ER, 9M-MRO
Year of Manufacture:	29th May 2002
State of Registration:	Malaysian
No & Type of Engines:	2 Rolls Royce RB211 Trent 892B17
Location:	Unknown (Last known Secondary Surveillance Radar (SSR) return, Waypoint IGARI)
Date & Time (Local Time)	8 March 2014 & Unknown (last known SSR return at 01:21:13 hours)
Operator:	Malaysian Airlines (MAS)
Call-sign:	MH 370
Type of Flight	Scheduled (Commercial Air Transport), IFR
Persons on Board	227 passengers + 12 crew

The investigation

At 01:38 hours Malaysian Time[1] (MYT) on 8 March 2014 (Saturday), a Boeing 777-2H6ER, registration 9M-MRO,and call-sign MH 370 with 227 passengers and 12 crew on board, was reported missing after passing waypoint IGARI[2] while en-route from Kuala Lumpur, Malaysia to Beijing, China.

---

[1]Malaysian time (MYT) is Universal Coordinated Time (UTC) + 8 hours.
[2]Waypoint IGARI is located at N6°56.87' E103°34.63' (Latitude/Longitude).

The Department of Civil Aviation (DCA) Malaysia was informed that flight MH370 was missing and an investigation was launched.

In accordance with International Civil Aviation Organisation (ICAO) Annex 13 *Aircraft Accident and Incident Investigation*, and Malaysian Civil Aviation Regulation 1996 Part XII *Investigation of Accidents* and with established international arrangements, the National Transportation Safety Board (NTSB) of the USA, representing the State of Design and Manufacture of the aircraft, has appointed an Accredited Representative to participate fully in the investigation. The Air Accidents Investigation Branch (AAIB) of the United Kingdom, representing the State of Design and Manufacture for the engines, has also appointed an Accredited Representative.

The NTSB Accredited Representative is supported by a team of technical advisers from the US Federal Aviation Administration (FAA) and Boeing.

The AAIB Accredited Representative is supported by technical advisers from Rolls-Royce and Inmarsat the operator of a Satellite which was in communication contact with the aircraft during the flight.

The Australian and Chinese Governments have also appointed Accredited Representatives in accordance with ICAO Annex 13, Para 5.23.

Malaysian Airlines (MAS) the operator, is cooperating with the investigation and providing expertise as required and the DCA Malaysia are being kept informed of developments.

History of the flight

At 00:41:43 MYT on 8 March 2014 (Saturday), MH 370 took off from Runway 32R at Kuala Lumpur International Airport (KLIA) on a scheduled flight to Beijing, China.

At 00:42:07 MYT, MH 370 was cleared to climb to Flight Level (FL) 180[3] and was issued a direct track by LUMPUR APPROACH at Kuala Lumpur Air Traffic Control Centre (KLATCC) to waypoint IGARI. MH 370 was transferred to LUMPUR RADAR at KLATCC at 00:42:52 MYT. The flight was then cleared to climb to FL 250 at 00:46:51 MYT and subsequently to FL 350 at 00:50:06 MYT. MH 370 reported maintaining FL 350 at 01:01:16 MYT and reported maintaining FL 350 again at 01:07:55 MYT.

At 01:19:24 MYT LUMPUR RADAR at KLATCC instructed MH370 to contact HO CHI MINH Air Traffic Control Centre (HCMATCC) on radio frequency 120.9 MHz. MH 370 acknowledged with "*good night Malaysian Three Seven Zero*".

At 01:21:04 MYT, MH370 was observed on the radar screen at KLATCC as it passed over waypoint IGARI. At 01:21:13 MYT the radar label for MH 370 disappeared from the radar screen at LUMPUR RADAR KLATCC.

At 01:38 MYT HCMATCC made a query to KLATCC on the whereabouts of MH 370. Thereafter KLATCC initiated efforts involving MAS OPS Center, Singapore ACC, Hong Kong ACC and Phnom Penh ACC to establish the location of MH 370. No contact had been established by any ATC units and thus the Rescue Coordination Centre (RCC) was activated at 05:30 MYT.

It was later established that the transmissions from the Aircraft Communication and Reporting System (ACARS) through satellite communication system occurred at regular intervals starting before MH 370 departed Kuala Lumpur, Malaysia at time 12:56:08 MYT and with the last communication occurred at 01:07:49 MYT.

Search and Rescue (SAR)

Kuala Lumpur Rescue Coordination Centre (KL RCC) was activated at 05:30 LT after all effort to communicate and locate the aircraft failed. Search and Rescue

[3]At altitude above 11,000 feet in Malaysia, an aircraft altitude above sea level is referred to as a Flight Level (FL).FL 180 equals to 18,000 feet.

(SAR) operations were conducted in the South China Sea where the aircraft position was last known.

A playback of a recording from military primary radar revealed that an aircraft with a possibility of MH 370 had made an air-turn back onto a Westerly heading crossing Peninsular Malaysia. The search area was then extended to the Straits of Malacca.

After ACARS stopped transmitting the satellite communication system automatically transmitted seven messages that confirmed that the system was still logged onto the network. The last message was received by the satellite ground station at 08:19 MYT. With the primary radar data, analysis of the satellite data and aircraft performance data, the Investigation established that flight MH 370 flew along either a Northern or Southern Corridor. The last transmission occurred when the aircraft was on an arc of 40 degrees from the satellite. Based on this new development the search area was moved from the South China Sea and the Straits of Malacca to the Northern and Southern Corridors.

On 24 March 2014 further analysis of the Inmarsat satellite data, using the changes in the satellites communication signal frequency (signal using the Doppler Effect), indicated that MH 370 flew the southern corridor and ended its flight in the southern part of the Indian Ocean. The investigation continues to analyse the satellite data and aircraft performance in order to further refine the area where the flight ended.

To date, a total of 26 countries have participated in the search for MH 370 comprising of 82 aircraft and 84 vessels.

SAR operations are on-going.

Safety recommendations

While the aircraft had the necessary communication equipment to provide information on its location, the last ACARS message occurred at 1:07:29 MYT, the last secondary radar detection at 1:21:13 MYT and the last satellite communication at 08:19 MYT on March 8th. Over a month after the aircraft departed Kuala Lumpur International Airport, its location is still unknown.

While commercial air transport aircraft spend considerable amounts of time operating over remote areas, there is currently no requirement for real time tracking of these aircraft. There have now been two occasions during the last five years when large commercial air transport aircraft have gone missing and their last position was not accurately known. This uncertainty resulted in significant difficulty in locating the aircraft in a timely manner. Therefore, the Malaysian Air Accident Investigation Bureau makes the following safety recommendation to ICAO:

It is recommended that the International Civil Aviation Organisation examine the safety benefits of introducing a standard for real time tracking of commercial air transport aircraft.

Note

The information contained in this preliminary report is correct at the time of issue and is intended to inform the aviation industry and the public of the general circumstances of the event. Readers are cautioned that there is the possibility that new information may become available that alters this Preliminary Report.

This report has been written in accordance with the ICAO Doc 9756 AN/965 Manual of Aircraft Accident and Incident Investigation – Part IV Reporting.

The Chief Inspector of Air Accidents
Ministry of Transport
Malaysia

9 April 2014

MAS 370 (Kuala Lumpur to Beijing)

PILOT-ATC RADIOTELEPHONY TRANSCRIPT

Departure from KLIA: 8 March 2014

	ATC DELIVERY	
12:25:53	MAS 370	Delivery MAS 370 Good Morning
12:26:02	ATC	MAS 370 Standby and Malaysia Six is cleared to Frankfurt via AGOSA Alpha Departure six thousand feet squawk two one zero six
12:26:19	ATC	... MAS 370 request level
12:26:21	MAS 370	MAS 370 we are ready requesting flight level three five zero to Beijing
12:26:39	ATC	MAS 370 is cleared to Beijing via PIBOS A Departure Six Thousand Feet squawk two one five seven
12:26:45	MAS 370	Beijing PIBOS A Six Thousand Squawk two one five seven, MAS 370 Thank You
12:26:53	ATC	MAS 370 Welcome over to ground
12:26:55	MAS 370	Good Day
	LUMPUR GROUND	
12:27:27	MAS 370	Ground MAS370 Good morning Charlie One Requesting push and start
12:27:34	ATC	MAS370 Lumpur Ground Morning Push back and start approved Runway 32 Right Exit via Sierra 4.
12:27:40	MAS 370	Push back and start approved 32 Right Exit via Sierra 4 POB 239 Mike Romeo Oscar
12:27:45	ATC	Copied
12:32:13	MAS 370	MAS377 request taxi.
12:32:26	ATC	MAS37..... (garbled) ... standard route. Hold short Bravo
12:32:30	MAS 370	Ground, MAS370. You are unreadable. Say again.
12:32:38	ATC	MAS370 taxi to holding point Alfa 11 Runway 32 Right via standard route. Hold short of Bravo.
12:32:42	MAS 370	Alfa 11 Standard route Hold short Bravo MAS370.
12:35:53	ATC	MAS 370 Tower
12:36:19	ATC	(garbled) ... Tower ... (garbled)
	MAS 370	1188 MAS370 Thank you

LUMPUR TOWER		
12:36:30	MAS 370	Tower MAS370 Morning
12:36:38	ATC	MAS370 good morning. Lumpur Tower. Holding point.. [garbled]..10 32 Right
12:36:50	MAS 370	Alfa 10 MAS370
12:38:43	ATC	370 line up 32 Right Alfa 10.
	MAS 370	Line up 32 Right Alfa 10 MAS370.
12:40:38	ATC	370 32 Right Cleared for take-off. Good night.
	MAS 370	32 Right Cleared for take-off MAS370. Thank you Bye.
LUMPUR APPROACH		
12:42:05	MAS 370	Departure Malaysian Three Seven Zero
12:42:10	ATC	Malaysian Three Seven Zero selamat pagi identified. Climb flight level one eight zero cancel SID turn right direct to IGARI
12:42:48	MAS 370	Okay level one eight zero direct IGARI Malaysian one err Three Seven Zero
12:42:52	ATC	Malaysian Three Seven Zero contact Lumpur Radar One Three Two Six good night
	MAS 370	Night One Three Two Six Malaysian Three Seven Zero
LUMPUR RADAR (AREA)		
12:46:51	MAS 370	Lumpur Control Malaysian Three Seven Zero
12:46:51	ATC	Malaysian Three Seven Zero Lumpur radar Good Morning climb flight level two five zero
12:46:54	MAS370	Morning level two five zero Malaysian Three Seven Zero
12:50:06	ATC	Malaysian Three Seven Zero climb flight level three five zero
12:50:09	MAS370	Flight level three five zero Malaysian Three Seven Zero
01:01:14	MAS370	Malaysian Three Seven Zero maintaining level three five zero
01:01:19	ATC	Malaysian Three Seven Zero
01:07:55	MAS370	Malaysian...Three Seven Zero maintaining level three five zero
01:08:00	ATC	Malaysian Three Seven Zero
01:19:24	ATC	Malaysian Three Seven Zero contact Ho Chi Minh 120 decimal 9 Good Night
01:19:29	MAS370	Good Night Malaysian Three Seven Zero

 # end of file/BIT 30 March #

ACTIONS TAKEN BETWEEN 01:38 AND 06:14 ON SATURDAY 8 MARCH

The following table is based on recorded communications on direct lines, summarising the events associated to MH370 after the radar blip disappeared until activation of the Rescue Coordination Centre.

No	MYT	Event
1	01:38:19	Ho Chi Minh first enquired about MH370, informed KL-ATCC that verbal contact was not established with MH370 and radar target was last seen at BITOD.
2	01:41:21	KL-ATCC informed HCM that after IGARI, MH370 did not return to Lumpur frequency.
3	01:46:46	HCM queried about MH370 again, stating that radar contact was established over IGARI but there was no verbal contact. Ho Chi Minh advised that the observed radar blip disappeared at waypoint BITOD.
4	01:50:28	KL-ATCC queried HCM if any contact with MH370. HCM's reply was 'negative'.
5	01:57:02	HCM informed KL-ATCC that there was officially no contact with MH370 until this time. Attempts on many frequencies and aircraft in the vicinity received no response from MH370.
6	02:03:48	KL-ATCC queried HCM on status MH370. HCM confirmed there was no radar contact at this time and no verbal communications was established. KL-ATCC relayed the information received from Malaysia Airlines OPS that aircraft was in Cambodian airspace.
7	02:07:00	HCM queried for confirmation that MH370 was in Phnom Penh FIR. KL-ATCC requested to check further with the supervisor.
8	02:11:37	HCM queried on status but KL-ATCC has no update.
9	[02:15] [no voice recording]	(extracted from Watch Supervisor's Log Book) KL-ATCC Watch Supervisor queried Malaysia Airlines OPS who informed that MH370 was able to exchange signals with the flight and flying in Cambodian airspace.
10	02:18:53	KL-ATCC queried if flight planned routing of MH370 was supposed to enter Cambodian airspace. HCM confirmed that planned route was only through Vietnamese airspace. HCM had checked and Cambodia advised that it had no information or contact with MH370. HCM confirmed earlier information that radar contact was lost after BITOD and radio contact was never established. KL-ATCC queried if HCM was taking Radio Failure action but the query didn't seem to be understood by the personnel. HCM suggested KL-ATCC to call MAS OPS and was advised that it had already been done.
11	02:34:01	Watch Supervisor KL-ATCC enquired with MAS OPS Centre about communication status with MH370 but the personnel was unsure if the

		message went through successfully or not.
12	02:35:03	HCM queried about status of MH370 and was informed that the Watch Supervisor was talking to the company at this time.
13	02:35:54	MAS OPS Centre informed KL-ATCC MH370 in normal condition based on signal download giving coordinate N14.90000 E109 15 00 at time 1833 UTC.
14	02:37:36	KL-ATCC relayed to HCM the latitude and longitude as advised by Malaysian Airlines Operations.
15	02:53:51	MH386 was requested by HCM to try to establish contact with MH370 on Lumpur radar frequency. KL-ATCC then requested MH386 to try on emergency frequencies as well.
16	[03:30] (no voice recording)	(extract from Watch Supervisor's Log Book) MAS OPS Centre informed KL-ATCC that the flight tracker information was based on flight projection and not reliable for aircraft positioning.
17	03:30:01	KL-ATCC queried if HCM had checked with next FIR Hainan.
18	03:56:19	KL-ATCC queried Malaysia Airlines OPS for any latest information or contact with MH370.
19	04:25:23	HCM queried KL-ATCC on last position that MH370 was in contact with ATC. KL-ATCC queried if any information had been received from Hong Kong or Beijing.
20	05:09:18	Singapore queried for information on MH370.
21	05:20:17	Capt [name redacted] requested for information on MH370. He opined that based on known information, "MH370 never left Malaysian airspace".
22	05:30	The Watch Supervisor activated the Kuala Lumpur ARCC.
23	05:41:21	HCM query for any updates.
24	06:14:14	KL-ATCC queried HCM if SAR was activated.

MH370 - Definition of Underwater Search Areas

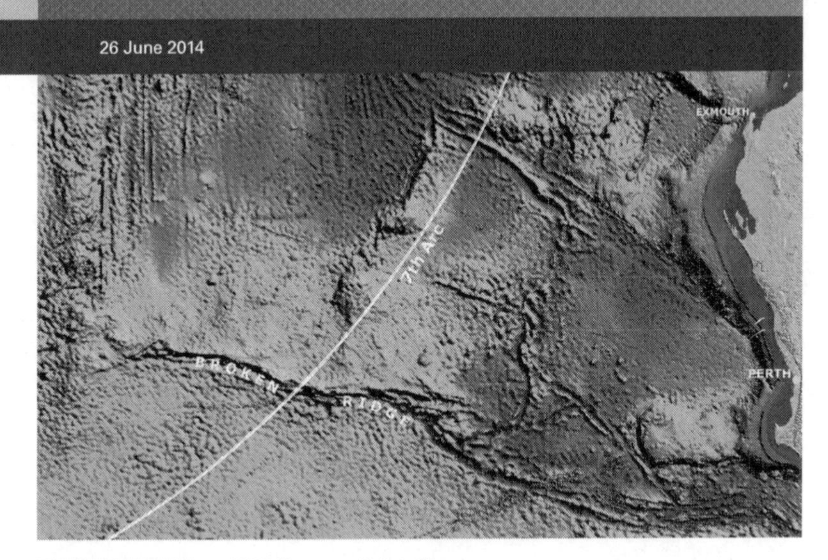

Investigation

ATSB Transport Safety Report
External Aviation Investigation
AE-2014-054
26 June 2014

Publishing information

Published by:	Australian Transport Safety Bureau
Postal address:	PO Box 967, Civic Square ACT 2608
Office:	62 Northbourne Avenue Canberra, Australian Capital Territory 2601
Telephone:	1800 020 616, from overseas +61 2 6257 4150 (24 hours) Accident and incident notification: 1800 011 034 (24 hours)
Facsimile:	02 6247 3117, from overseas +61 2 6247 3117
Email:	atsbinfo@atsb.gov.au
Internet:	www.atsb.gov.au

Addendum

Page	Change	Date

Executive summary

On 08 March 2014, flight MH370, a Boeing 777-200ER registered 9M-MRO, lost contact with Air Traffic Control during a transition of airspace between Malaysia and Vietnam. An analysis of radar data and subsequent satellite communication (SATCOM) system signalling messages placed the aircraft in the Australian search and rescue zone on an arc in the southern part of the Indian Ocean. This arc was considered to be the location where the aircraft's fuel was exhausted.

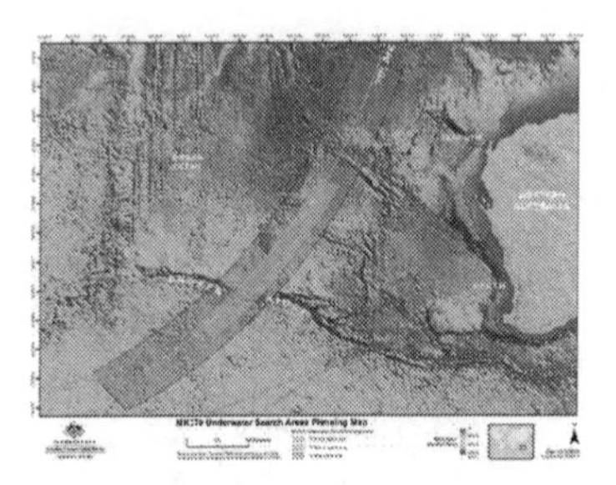

A surface search of probable impact areas along this arc, coordinated by the Australian Maritime Safety Authority, was carried out from 18 March – 28 April 2014. This search effort was undertaken by an international fleet of aircraft and ships with the search areas over this time progressing generally from an initial southwest location along the arc in a north-easterly direction. The location of the search areas was guided by continuing and innovative analysis by a Joint Investigation Team of the flight and satellite-communications data. This analysis was supplemented by other information provided to ATSB during this period. This included possible underwater locator beacon and hydrophone acoustic detections.

No debris associated with 9M-MRO was identified either from the surface search, acoustic search or from the ocean floor search in the vicinity of the acoustic detections. The ocean floor search was completed on 28 May 2014.

Refinements to the analysis of both the flight and satellite data have been continuous since the loss of MH370. The analysis has been undertaken by an international team of specialists from the UK, US and Australia working both independently and collaboratively. Other information regarding the performance and operation of the aircraft has also been taken into consideration in the analysis.

Using current analyses, the team has been able to reach a consensus in identifying a priority underwater search area for the next phase of the search.

The priority area of approximately 60,000 km^2 extends along the arc for 650 km in a northeast direction from Broken Ridge. The width of the priority search area is 93 km. This area was the subject of the surface search from Day 21-26.

Work is continuing with refinements in the analysis of the satellite communications data. Small frequency variations can significantly affect the derived flight path. This ongoing work may result in changes to the prioritisation and locale of search activity.

Table of contents

Introduction

On 7 March 2014 at 1722 UTC[1] (8 March 0022 local time Malaysia), flight MH370, a Boeing 777-200ER registered 9M-MRO, lost contact with ATC during a transition of airspace between Malaysia and Vietnam. An analysis of radar data and subsequent satellite communication (SATCOM) system signalling messages placed the aircraft in the Australian search and rescue zone in the southern part of the Indian Ocean.

On 17 March 2014, Australia took charge of the coordination of the search and rescue operation. Over the next 6 weeks from 18 March, an intensive aerial and surface search was conducted by assets from Australia, Malaysia, China, Japan, Korea, UK and the USA.

During this period, the Australian Maritime Safety Authority (AMSA) and the ATSB jointly determined a search area strategy correlating information from a Joint Investigation Team (JIT[2]) located in Malaysia and other government and academic sources.

On 28 April 2014, the aerial search concluded and the search moved to an underwater phase. More details of the search effort can be found on the Joint Agency Coordination Centre website www.jacc.gov.au/.

The ATSB is responsible for defining a search area. Since May 2014, a search strategy group, coordinated by the ATSB, has been working towards defining the most probable position of the aircraft at the time of the last satellite communications at 0019. The group brought together satellite and aircraft specialists from the following organisations:

- Air Accidents Investigation Branch (UK)
- Boeing (US)
- Defence Science and Technology Organisation (Australia)
- Department of Civil Aviation (Malaysia)
- Inmarsat (UK)
- National Transportation Safety Board (US)
- Thales (UK)

The group was faced with the challenge of using data from a communications satellite system and aircraft performance data to reconstruct the flight path of MH370. This was in effect using a satellite communications system as a navigation tracking system. Two pieces of information recorded by a satellite ground station at the time of a transmission with MH370 were used to estimate the track of the aircraft. These transmissions occurred only 7 times after loss of radar contact.

This report presents the results of analysis conducted by this group and the ATSB's determination of a priority 60,000 km^2 search area.

On 4 June 2014, the ATSB released a request for tender to acquire the services of a specialist company capable of conducting a deep-water search for 9M-MRO under ATSB direction. Bathymetry of the ocean floor in areas of the search zone commenced in mid-May using an ATSB contracted vessel and a Chinese military vessel.

---

[1] All times used in this report are referenced to Coordinated Universal Time (UTC) using the format hhmm.ss

[2] The Joint Investigation Team comprised specialists from Malaysia, China, US, UK and France

Figure 1: B777 9M-MRO

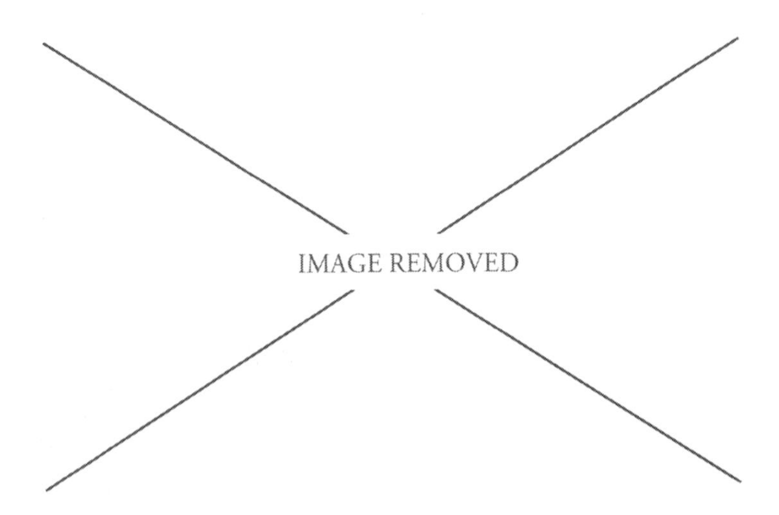

Background on over-water searches

Over-water aircraft accident locations are usually found by conducting a broad-area aerial search. The search area is generally determined by a combination of:

- Position information from ground-based radar systems (maximum range is generally 250 NM)
- Position information automatically transmitted from the aircraft at regular intervals
- Position reports from the crew
- Re-tracing the flight-planned route
- Eye-witness reports (possibly located on the shore, on other aircraft or on ships)

Uncertainty in the position of an accident location increases with time from the aircraft's last known position (fix) so the search area will expand accordingly as the position data becomes 'stale'.

Once floating wreckage is observed, reverse-drift techniques can be used to determine the aircraft impact location. Only a small-area underwater search is then required to locate the wreckage and map the wreckage field. This underwater search can be aided by the underwater locator beacons fitted to the flight recorders. As they have a limited operational duration of nominally 30 days, and to minimise the inaccuracies of the reverse-drift calculations, it is important that an aerial search is commenced as soon as possible and the floating debris is found quickly.

In the case of MH370:

- The aircraft departed Kuala Lumpur on 7 March 2014 at 1641
- The final automatically transmitted position from the aircraft occurred at 1707
- No radio notification of a problem was received from the crew
- No radio communications were received from the crew after 1719
- The final ATC (secondary) radar fix occurred at 1722
- At 1725 the aircraft deviated from the flight-planned route

- The final primary radar fix occurred at 1822 (Figure 2)
- The satellite communications log indicated the aircraft continued to fly for another 6 hours until 8 March 0019
- No confirmed eye-witness reports were received
- No Emergency Locator Transmissions were received
- The search in the Australian search and rescue zone commenced on 18 March (10 days after the aircraft went missing)

Figure 2: MH370 flight path derived from primary and secondary radar data

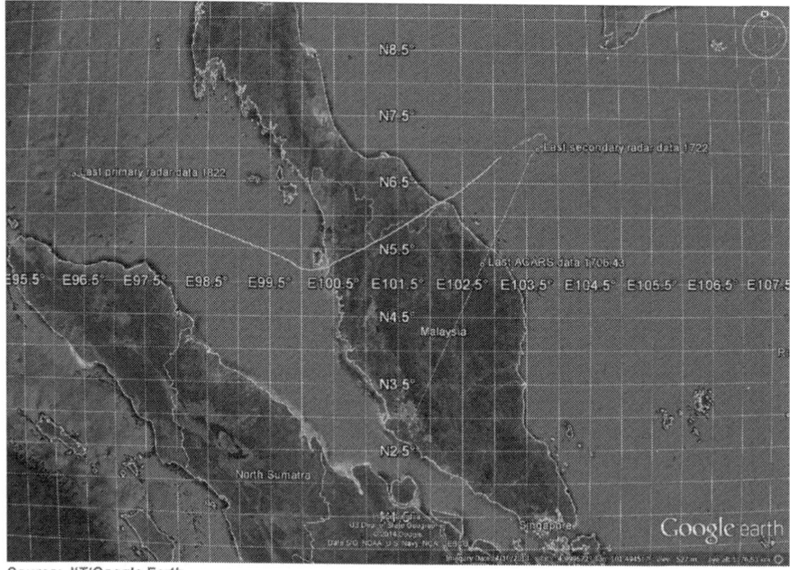

Source: JIT/Google Earth

These factors have meant that the search area for MH370 has remained very large.

A comparison with the search for Air France flight 447, which crashed in the Atlantic Ocean on 1 June 2009, is useful. The search for the aircraft began on 1 June 2009 and the first wreckage was discovered on 6 June 2009, 5 days after the accident.

Air France 447 (AF447) accident search area definition[3]

The ACARS system, is used to transmit non-voice messages between an aircraft and the ground by VHF radio or satellite communication. The AF447 aircraft was programmed to automatically transmit its position approximately every 10 minutes.

On 1 June 2009, the last position report occurred at 0210 and 24 maintenance messages were received between 0210 and 0215. These messages were all transmitted via the same satellite (Atlantic Ocean West, operated by the Inmarsat Company) and SITA's ACARS network.

The maximum distance the aircraft could have feasibly travelled was computed from the time of its last reported position to the time when a scheduled response from the ACARS system was not received. The impact time was estimated based on the time of the last ACARS message received

[3] BEA Report 18 March 2011: Triggered Transmission of Flight Data Working Group, page 27.

and the expectation (unfulfilled) of a subsequent message in the next 60 seconds. This analysis indicated that the end of the flight occurred between 0214.26 and 0215.14, which makes a flight time since the last reported position of about 5 minutes. Considering a maximum ground speed of 480 kt (or 8 NM/min), this makes a search area in the shape of a circle of radius 40 NM centred at the last known position. This area extended over more than 17,000 km² and was situated more than 500 NM from any coastline. After a search effort involving five separate phases, the aircraft wreckage was located on 3 April 2011.

MH370 search area definition

As none of the conventional sources of data was able to be used to locate the aircraft wreckage from MH370, novel sources of data and analysis techniques were required. This has led to a larger than typical search area and changes in its location as refinements occur to the analysis after validation and calibration checks have been performed.

Surface search for MH370

On 17 March 2014 (Day 10[4]), Australia assumed responsibility for coordinating the search and rescue effort in the southern Indian Ocean. AMSA as Australia's search and rescue authority was responsible for this activity. More details of the surface search effort can be found on the AMSA website www.amsa.gov.au/media/mh370-timeline.

Possible impact areas

On 17 March 2014 (D10) the initial search area was determined by a Joint Investigation Team (JIT)[5] to be a 600,000 km^2 area approximately 2,500 km from Perth, WA. The initial search area was determined following analysis of satellite communications data to and from MH370 during the accident flight that was recorded at a ground station in Perth, WA. The data indicated the aircraft flew an additional 6 hours after the last radar contact with a track south to the Indian Ocean. The area was determined using only limited radar, satellite and performance data and assumed a southern turn of MH370 at the north-west tip of Sumatra, Indonesia.

Areas in the Southern Indian Ocean designated S1 –S3[6] were defined from the aircraft's predicted performance and endurance (Figure 3). Two speeds resulted in the longest, straightest tracks to the 6th arc[7] and were used to define possible impact locations within areas S1 and S2.

Figure 3: Possible southern final positions S1-S3 based on MH370 max range and time

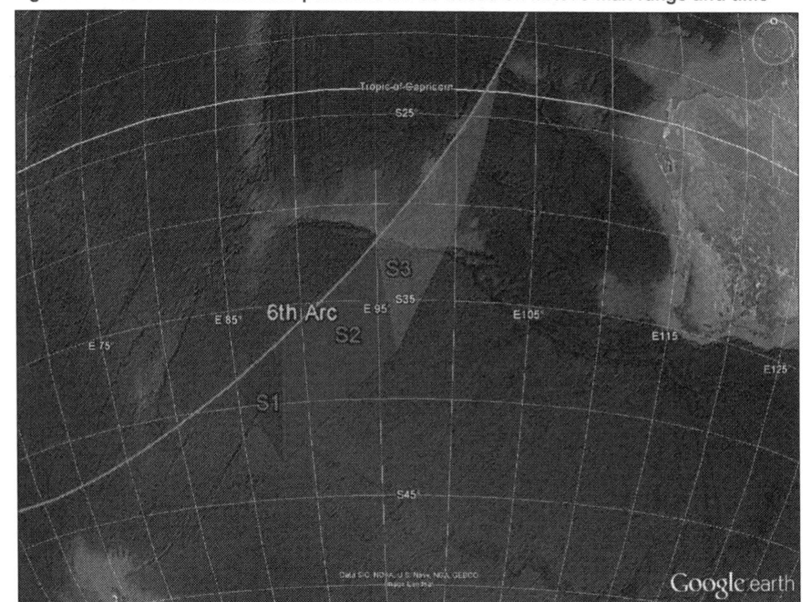

Source: JIT/Google Earth

---

4 8 March 2014 is considered to be Day1 (D1), the date In Malaysia when MH370 departed Kuala Lumpur, Malaysia.

5 US and UK investigation agencies and their technical advisers with representatives from Malaysia, China and France.

6 JIT designation of areas – Note Malaysian designation of areas was in opposite direction.

7 Refer to Burst Timing Offset (BTO) section in Defining the Search Area section of this report

Over the following days regions of S1 and S2 were drifted[8] and provided surface search areas. Some possible satellite debris sightings were also incorporated to produce additional search areas.

On 27 March (D20), the JIT advised they now had more confidence in the increased speeds provided by primary radar near Malaysia. This increased the aircraft fuel burn and the most probable track moved north to the S3 area. The JIT additionally had more confidence that a 7th arc was a fuel exhaustion point. Two new search areas designated S4 and S5 were defined. The most probable impact location was moved to the bottom of the S4 area on the 7th arc within the S3 area. On 28 March (D21) a surface search of a drifted S3/S4 area (Shape A in Figure 6) was commenced.

Figure 4: Possible final positions S4-S5 with 7th arc and max range cruise line

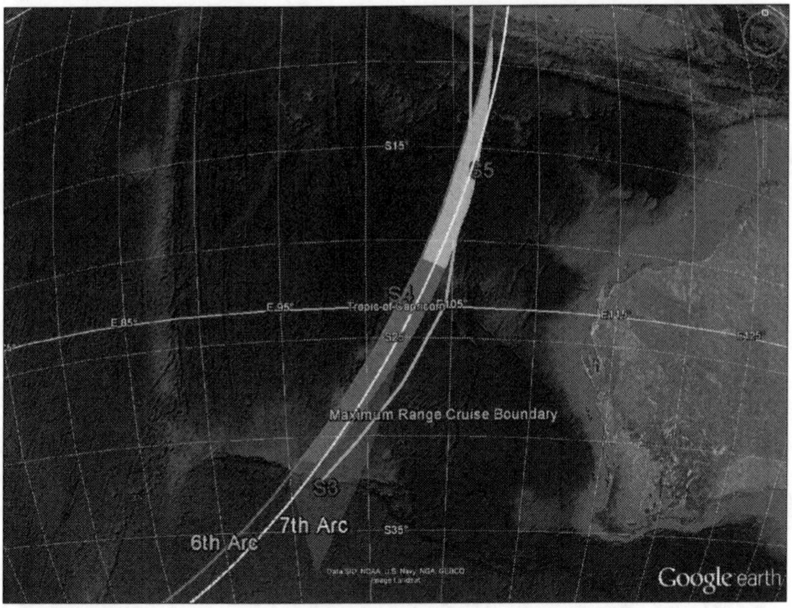

Source: JIT/Google Earth

On 1 April (D25) the JIT advised AMSA/ ATSB of further aircraft performance and path analysis starting at a distance further NW of Sumatra that had the effect of shifting the most probable area NE within S4 and into S5. Probable impact areas red, yellow and green were defined within S4/S5 (Figure 5).

[8] A drifted area is the computer modelled movement of a body of water over the period of time since 8 March to the search day. This modelling incorporated wind and current effects on a variety of debris characteristics.

Figure 5: Red, yellow and green boxes within S4-S5 and M641 route

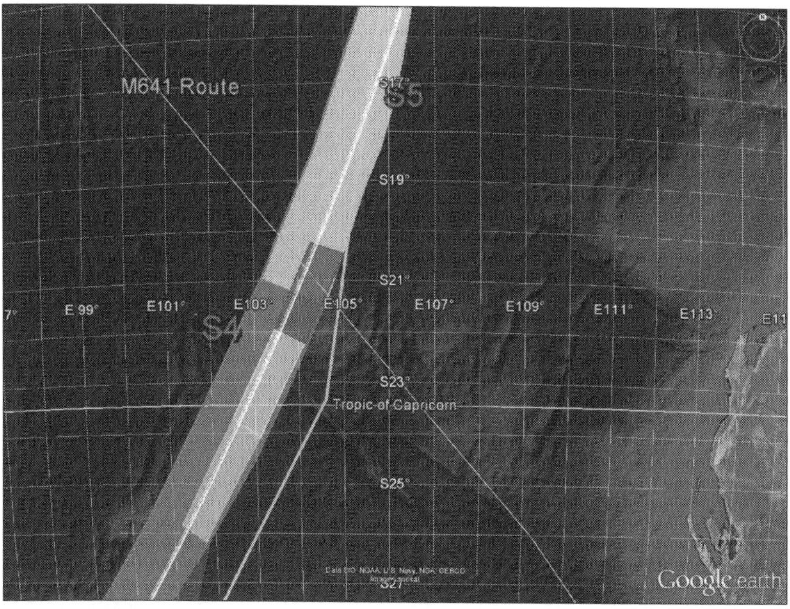

Source: JIT/Google Earth

The S4/S5 boundary on the 7th arc was considered the best starting location due to convergence of a number of candidate paths using independent techniques and because airways route M641 passed through that location. By this stage drifted area B in Figure 6 was being searched. On 2-3 April (D26/ D27) a surface search of a drifted red area was commenced.

A summary of data used in planning search area refinements is shown at Appendix A: Information used in determining and refining search areas.

Drifted search areas

For one month from 28 March (D21), areas along the 7th arc in the S3, S4 and S5 areas were drifted to guide the conduct of the surface search. The original and drifted areas are shown in Figure 6, comparison to other regions shown in Figure 7 - Figure 10.

Figure 6: Original and drifted search areas 28 Mar- 29 Apr (D21-D52)

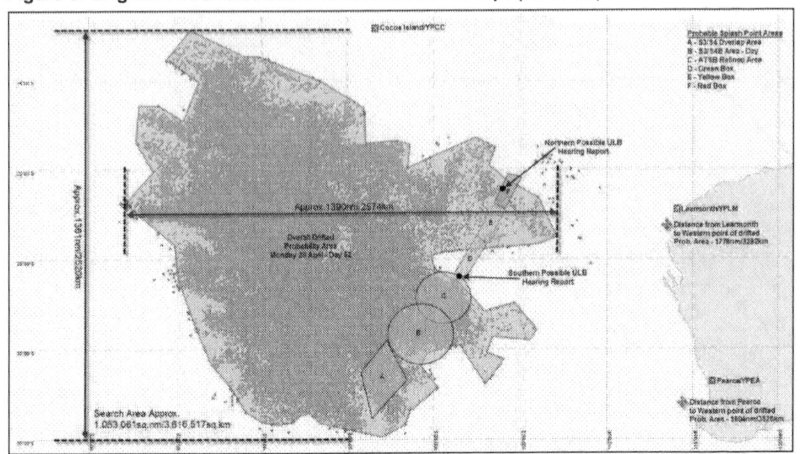

Source: AMSA

Figure 7: D21-52 drifted area comparison – East Coast Australia

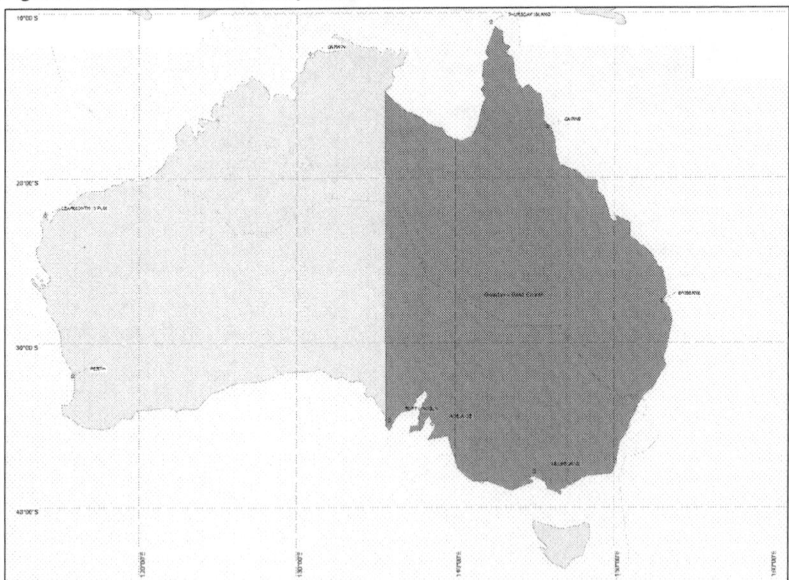

Source: AMSA

Figure 8: D21-52 drifted area comparison – Europe

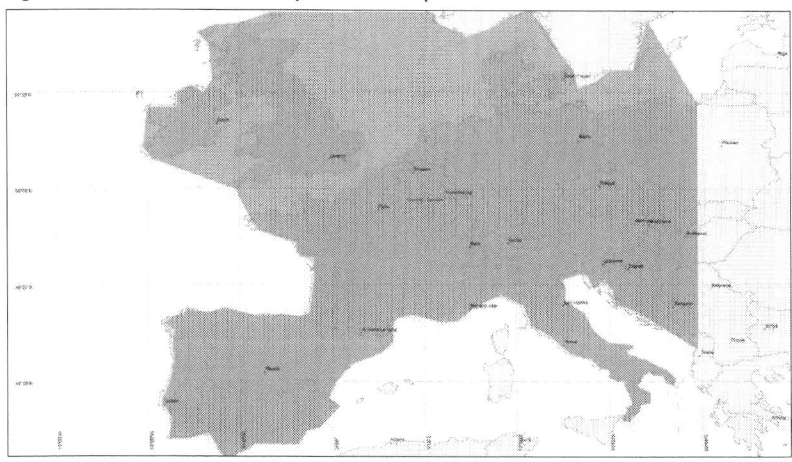

Source: AMSA

Figure 9: D21-52 drifted area comparison – North America

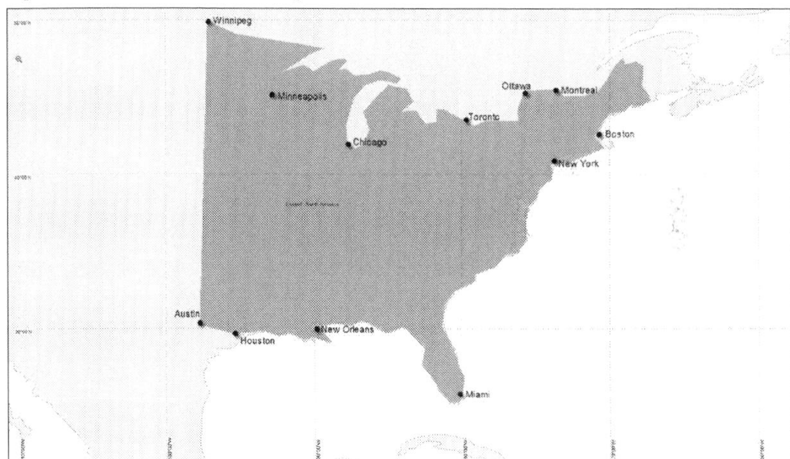

Source: AMSA

Figure 10: D21-52 drifted area comparison – China

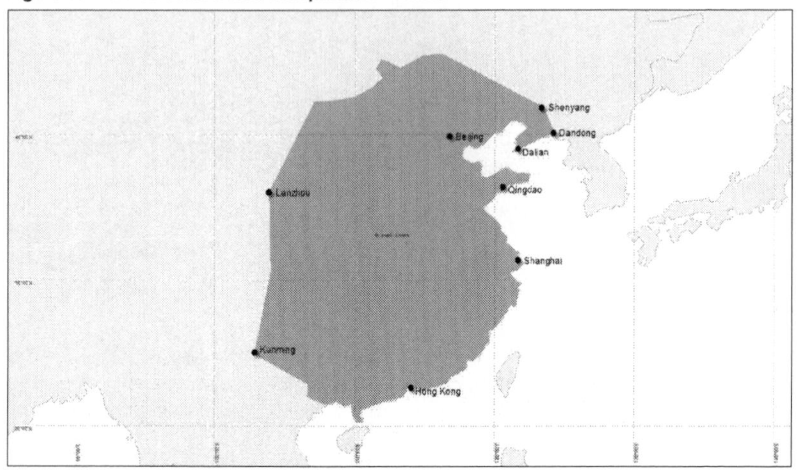

Source: AMSA

Debris sightings

A number of items were sighted by aircraft especially from Area A, though most of the sightings were unable to be relocated by surface assets and no debris considered to be from MH370 was recovered.

Acoustic search

Underwater locator beacons

The flight recorders fitted to 9M-MRO were equipped with Dukane DK100 underwater acoustic beacons that activate on immersion in salt or fresh water. The beacons had the following characteristics:

- Operating frequency: 37.5 ± 1 kHz
- Pulse Length: 10 ms
- Repetition rate: 1 pulse per second
- Operating life following immersion: minimum 30 days[9]

The nominal distance at which an underwater locator beacon (ULB) may be detected is considered to be between 2,000 m to 3,000 m[10]. However, the detection may be made at greater range, about 4,500 m, under more favourable conditions. Many conditions influence the actual detection range, environmental noise, the ability of the water to conduct the acoustic signal, and the sensitivity of the equipment used to make the detection. In reality for a robust search a maximum range to target area of approximately 1 km is used.

Acoustic search area definition

Search vessels with equipment capable of acoustic detections were en route to or near the 7th arc on 2 April. The most probable arc crossings current on 2 April 2014 were the red/ yellow/ green areas in Figure 6. The areas had been sized so that the primary TPL system embarked on Australian Defence Vessel (ADV) *Ocean Shield* could cover the red area prior to the predicted expiry of the flight recorder ULB batteries. ULB detection resources were deployed to commence operations at the S4/S5 boundary within the red box and on the 7th arc.

Acoustic detections

HMS Echo

On 2 April 2014, the UK defence vessel HMS *Echo*, using a hull-mounted acoustic system reported a possible ULB detection close to the 7th arc and S4/S5 boundary. The hull mounted system was designed to provide high accuracy deep water positioning by monitoring the location of subsea transponders operating between 27 kHz and 30.5 kHz. The acoustic system was retuned to 37.5 kHz, by the crew of HMS *Echo*, to enable detection of the flight recorder ULB. On 3 April, following tests, this detection was discounted as being an artefact of the ship's sonar equipment.

MV Haixun 01

On the 4 April 2014, the crew of the Chinese Maritime Safety Administration vessel, MV *Haixun 01*, were operating Benthos pinger detector equipment from a rescue boat at the Southern end of the green zone in ocean depths of about 4,500m. The crew detected a pulsed signal with a frequency of 37.5 kHz, repeating at once per second. A second detection on the same frequency was made the next day, at a position about 3 km west of the first detection. The second detection was reported to be a much weaker strength signal than the previous day.

---

9 The manufacturer predicted maximum life of the ULB batteries was 40 days.

10 Underwater Communications Specialist, Visiting Fellow, Australian Defence Force Academy, Canberra

The Benthos pinger locator specifications include:

- Detectable frequency range: 5 kHz to 80 kHz
- Practical ULB detection range: 2,000m

ADV Ocean Shield

The Australian Defence Vessel *Ocean Shield* (ADV-OS) was deployed from Perth, Western Australia to the search area on 31 March 2014, equipped with a Phoenix International towed pinger locator (TPL) system. The system included two towfish (Figure 11) with the following specifications:

- Detectable frequency range: 3.5 kHz – 50 kHz
- Maximum operating depth: 6,000 m

Figure 11: TPL towfish

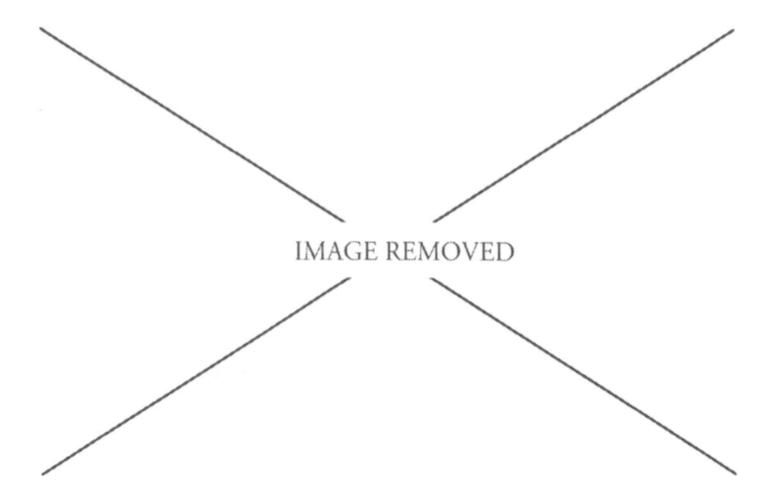

The ADV-OS deployed the first towfish on 4 April 2014. The first towfish exhibited acoustic noise and was required to be changed out with the second towfish. The second towfish was deployed on 5 April 2014 and shortly after, whilst descending, detected an acoustic signal at a frequency of approximately 33 kHz. Further detections were made on 5 April 2014 and on 8 April; however, none were able to be repeated when following an opposing track. The first towfish was redeployed with no detections.

Figure 12: Ocean Shield TPL search coverage 04-14 April

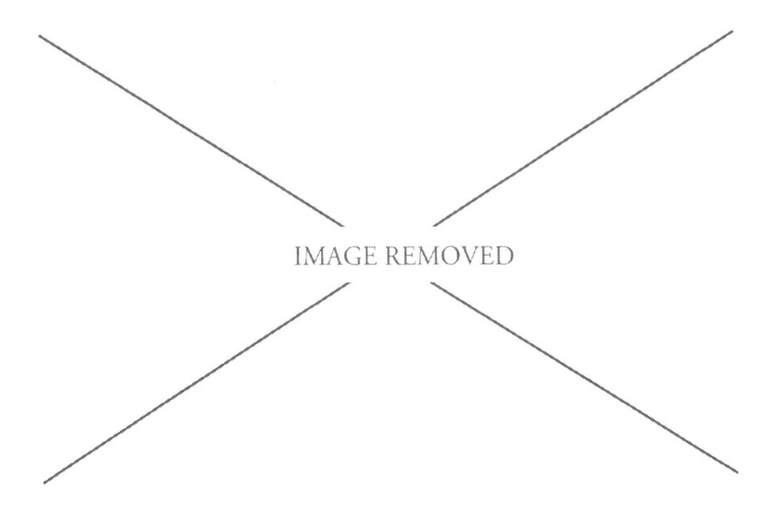

Source: Phoenix International

Analysis of acoustic detections

HMS *Echo* was tasked to the area of the MV *Haixun 01* detections. HMS *Echo* reported that the detections were unlikely due to the depth to the seafloor, surface noise and the equipment utilised. A submarine tasked to the area was unable to get any detections.

A review of the *Ocean Shield* acoustic signals was undertaken independently by various specialists. The analyses determined that the signals recorded were not consistent with the nominal performance standards of the Dukane DK100 underwater acoustic beacon. The analyses also noted that whilst unlikely, the acoustic signals could be consistent with a damaged ULB. However, it was decided that that an ocean floor sonar search should be performed to fully investigate the detections.

AP-3C sonobuoy acoustic search capability

When Australia joined the international effort to locate flight MH-370, the Australian Defence Force and Australian Defence Industry worked together to enhance the search capabilities available to the coordinating authorities. They provided an ability to detect a ULB signal at a range of up to 4,000 m water depth. This capability from an AP-3C aircraft was achieved by deploying sonobuoys at a depth of 300m beneath the ocean surface. One sortie was capable of searching an area of approximately 3,000 km^2. Sonobuoy drops were undertaken from 6-16 April (D30-D40). These sonobuoy drops were in the region of the 7th arc where depths were favourable and specifically in the location of the *Ocean Shield* and Curtin University hydrophone bearing (see later section) acoustic detections. No acoustic detections considered to be related to ULB transmissions were detected using sonobuoys.

Ocean floor sonar survey in area of Ocean Shield acoustic detections

Based on the analysis of the acoustic detections on ADV-OS, an underwater sonar survey using an autonomous underwater vehicle (AUV) commenced on 14 April 2014. 30 missions to depths between 3,800 - 5,000 m were completed. The side scan sonar tasking comprising a 10 km radius area around the most promising detection and a 3 km radius area around the other three detections was completed on 28 May. The total area searched during this time was 860 km^2 with nil debris or wreckage detected. The ATSB considers that the search in the vicinity of the ADV-OS acoustic detections is complete and the area can now be discounted as the final resting place of MH370.

Figure 13: Ocean Shield AUV

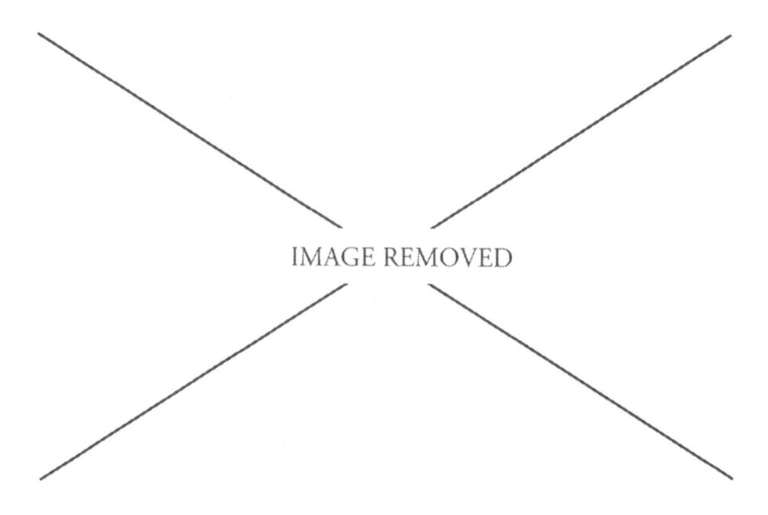

Further work is being carried out in an attempt to determine the likely source of the ADV-OS acoustic detections.

Defining the search area

Search area introduction

Three factors were important in defining the search area along the 7th arc:

- The position of the turn to the South from the previous North-West heading along the Malacca Strait
- Aircraft performance limitations
- Analysis of the satellite-communications data

There was uncertainty associated with each of these factors.

Position of the turn to the South

The last primary radar return related to MH370 was at 1822 – this was the final positive fix for the aircraft. At this time the aircraft was tracking north-west along the Malacca Strait. BFO data associated with the satellite arc at 1825 indicated that it was likely that the aircraft was still tracking north-west at this time. However, by the time of the 1941 arc, the BFO data indicated that the aircraft was tracking in a south/south-easterly direction.

As no evidence was available to conclusively determine where the turn(s) to the south occurred, two approaches were taken:

- the satellite data analysis was performed using a range of assumed locations for the turn.
- analyse the satellite data independently without assuming where the turn occurred. In this case the better matching solutions should be checked for realistic times and distances between their starting point and the position of the last primary radar point.

Aircraft performance limitations

Altitude, airspeed (Mach number at normal cruising altitudes) and wind are important parameters in determining aircraft range and performance. At 1707, the last ACARS transmission from the aircraft provided the total weight of the fuel remaining on board. Between that time and 1822, while the aircraft was being tracked by primary radar, the aircraft's speed and consequently fuel burn could be estimated.

During the period of the aircraft tracking to the south, there was no altitude or speed data available. While there was wind information available, it varied as a function of time, altitude and location. As a consequence, a variety of speeds and altitudes had to be assumed when calculating possible flight-paths using the satellite data.

The aircraft satellite transmission associated with the 7th arc is assumed to have been triggered by power interruptions on board the aircraft caused by fuel exhaustion. The time of this transmission is consistent with the maximum flight times expected for MH370.

Satellite data analysis

The satellite communications system comprises the on board equipment, satellite and ground earth station. It is a reliable and high-performance communications system. In the case of MH370, and in the absence of other data, it was necessary to use monitoring and maintenance data and, in effect, convert a communications system into a positioning system. Without this data, it would not have been possible to define a restricted search area at all but it should be appreciated that by using the satellite data it was necessary to model and analyse tiny variations in otherwise very stable signals. The satellite carrier frequencies are measured in GHz or 1 billion (1,000,000,000) cycles per second. To put the numbers into perspective, a tolerance of ± 5 Hz in these signals corresponds to a variation of ±0.0000005%.

Satellite system Information

Satellite communication (SATCOM) relies on transmissions between a ground station, a satellite and a mobile terminal (the aircraft in this case) (Figure 15). The Boeing 777 uses a satellite link for the following functions:

- Audio communication
- Interface with Aircraft Communication Addressing and Reporting System (ACARS)
- In-Flight Entertainment equipment (IFE)

The system used during flight MH370 consisted of the Inmarsat Classic Aero ground station located at Perth, Western Australia and the Inmarsat Indian Ocean Region (IOR) I-3 satellite. The Classic Aero service uses a single global communication beam per satellite, and contains no explicit information relating to the mobile terminal location being available.

Figure 15: Schematic of basic satellite communications

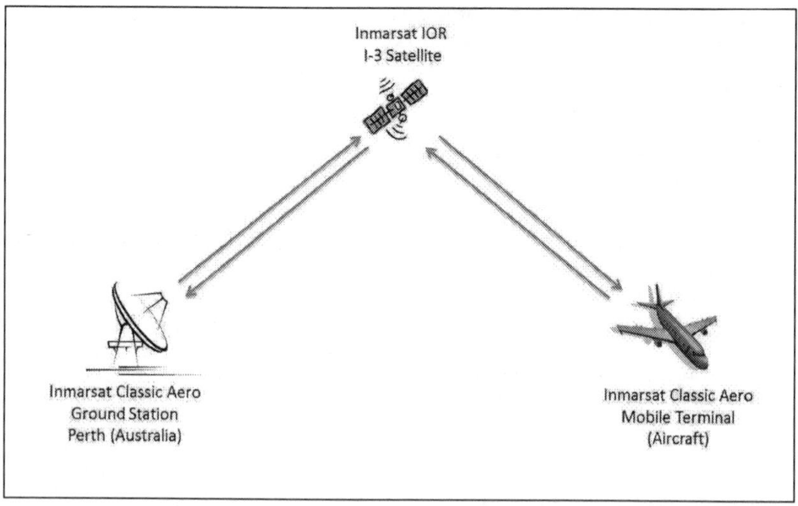

Source: Satellite Comms Working Group

The aircraft satellite communication system operates on L band[11], transmits at 1.6 GHz and receives at 1.5 GHz for the satellite to/from aircraft RF links. The ground station to satellite RF links use C band[12], transmitting at 6 GHz and receiving at 4 GHz.

There are a number of channels within those bands available for messages to be sent between the satellite and earth station. One of the channels is called the P-Channel which the aircraft continually listens to and is used for signalling and data transmissions from the ground to the aircraft. The R-Channel is used for short signalling and data transmissions from the aircraft to the ground.

In order to connect to the SATCOM system, the aircraft transmits a 'log-on' request on the R-Channel which is acknowledged by the ground station. Once connected, if the ground station has

---

[11] L band refers to a part of the electromagnetic spectrum.

[12] C band refers to a part of the electromagnetic spectrum.

not heard from an aircraft within an hour[13], it will check that the connection is still operational by transmitting a 'Log-on Interrogation' message on the P-Channel using the aircraft's unique identifier. If the aircraft receives its 'unique identifier', it returns a short message on the R-Channel that it is still logged onto the network. These processes have been described as handshakes.

After the last recorded primary radar data, at 1822, the following were recorded at the ground station:

	hhmm.ss
• 1st handshake initiated by the aircraft	1825.27
• Unanswered ground to air telephone call	1839.52
• 2nd handshake initiated by the ground station	1941.00
• 3rd handshake initiated by the ground station	2041.02
• 4th handshake initiated by the ground station	2141.24
• 5th handshake initiated by the ground station	2241.19
• Unanswered ground to air telephone call	2313.58
• 6th handshake initiated by the ground station	0010.58
• 7th handshake initiated by the aircraft	0019.29
• Aircraft did not respond to log-on interrogation from the satellite earth ground station (failed handshake).	0115.56

For each R-Channel transmission, information is logged at the ground station including the burst timing offset (BTO) and the burst frequency offset (BFO).

The recorded BTO and BFO at each transmission were used to estimate the track of the aircraft. The BTO was used to estimate the distance of the aircraft from the satellite while the BFO was used to estimate the speed and direction the aircraft was travelling relative to the satellite. By combining these three parameters with aircraft performance constraints, a range of candidate paths matching the BTO/BFO data can be found.

Two basic analysis techniques were used across the group:

- Data-driven – attempting to match the BTO/BFO data exactly to a flight path with speed/ heading tolerances then filtering results for a reasonable aircraft flight path with respect to aircraft performance.
- Aircraft flight path/ mode driven – scoring a set of reasonable aircraft flight paths by their statistical consistency with the BTO/BFO data[14].

Burst Timing Offset (BTO)[15]

For system efficiency and for the satellite communication to remain reliable, aircraft R-Channel transmissions are in time slots referenced to the P-Channel as received by the aircraft. The BTO is a measure of how long from the start of that time slot the transmission is received. This is essentially the delay between when the transmission was expected (given a nominal position of the aircraft) and when it actually arrives and is caused by the distance of the aircraft from the satellite (Figure 16).

---

13 This time is determined by the expiration of an inactivity timer. At the time of the loss of 9M-MRO, the inactivity timer was set to one hour.

14 The set of likelihood-weighted trajectories represents the Bayesian posterior distribution of aircraft flight path

15 Some additional information regarding BTO analysis is provided at Appendix G: Explanatory notes on BTO and BFO analysis.

The BTO was only a relatively recent addition to the ground stations data set. It was added at the suggestion of the satellite operator following the AF447 accident to assist in geo-locating an aircraft.

Figure 16: Difference in time delays between nominal and actual locations

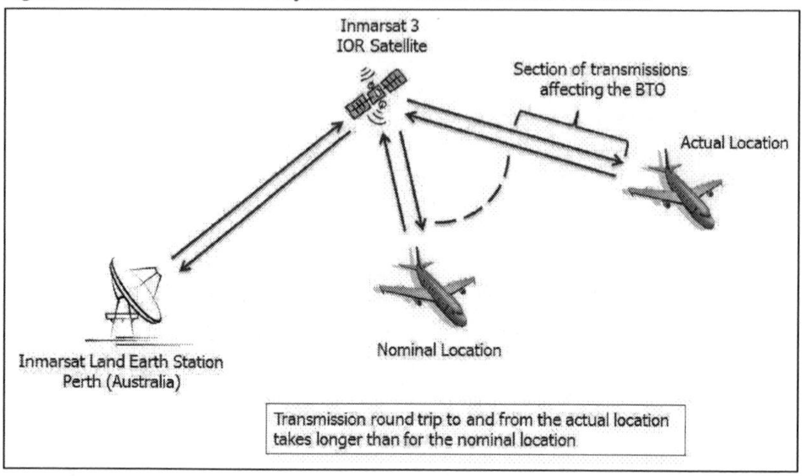

Source: Satellite Comms Working Group

A set of locations can be plotted on the surface of the earth at the calculated distance from the satellite. The result is a ring of locations equidistant from the satellite (Figure 17).

Figure 17: Position ring defined by BTO measurement

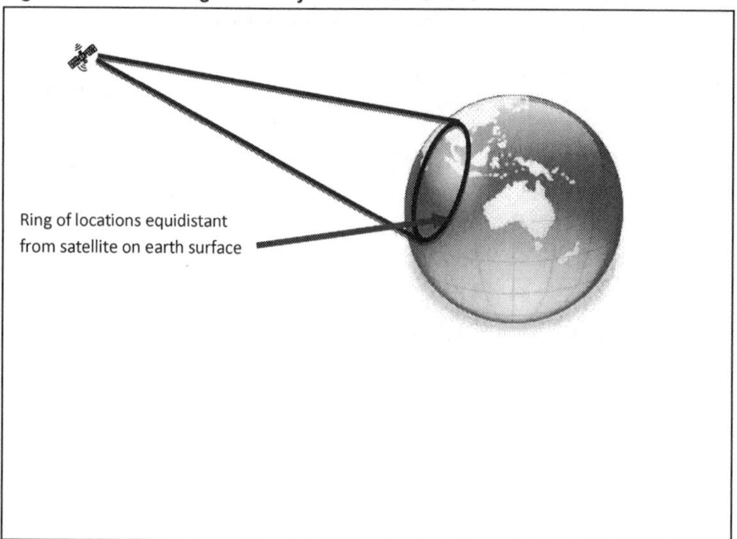

Source: Satellite Comms Working Group

For each completed handshake during flight MH370, the ground station recorded a BTO value which defined a location ring solution (Figure 18).

Figure 18: BTO ring solutions for 9M-MRO

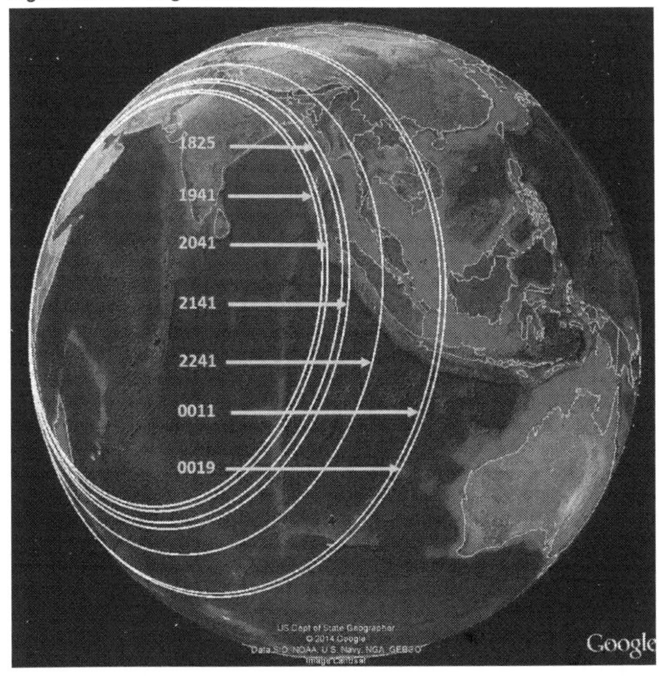

Source: Satellite Comms Working Group

An analysis of the SATCOM system parameters, and empirical comparison between the BTO rings calculated for the time period when the aircraft was on the ground in Kuala Lumpur showed that the tolerance was ±10 km. Figure 19 shows a section of the BTO solution for the transmissions associated with the ACARS message overlaid on the flight track from flight MH370. The distance between the transmission location and the BTO arc is approximately 5 km.

Figure 19: BTO solution arc for transmissions related to last ACARS data

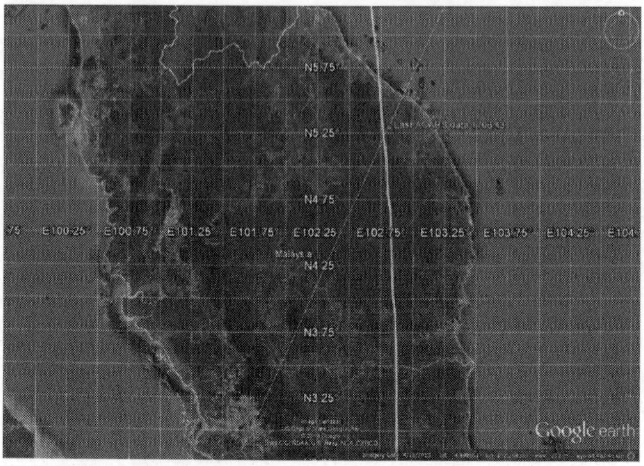

Source: Satellite Comms Working Group

The aircraft estimated paths are therefore constrained to be within 10 km of the BTO defined rings at the time associated with the recorded value. There is no information in the BTO to locate the aircraft at any single point on that ring, however knowledge of the aircraft's prior location and performance speed limitations can reduce the ring to an arc.

Northern and southern aircraft performance limits

Using the remaining fuel reported at the last ACARS transmission and various assumed flight speeds and altitudes, the range of the aircraft could be estimated. The potential search area can be bounded by these performance limits (Figure 20).

The assumptions made for the performance calculations were the following:

- The aircraft was flown at a constant altitude
- The speed selected was operationally achievable for the given altitude
- Aircraft required to cross the arcs at the times defined by the BTO values
- Before the 1941 arc various path estimates were used including an immediate turn south after the last radar point at 1822 and a turn at the north western limit at 1912
- After the 1941 arc straight line segments between the arcs were flown
- Wind effects were modelled
- Modelling did not include individual engine efficiency

Figure 20: Performance limit of the aircraft in yellow - red lines indicate the intersection of the performance limit and the 7th arc.

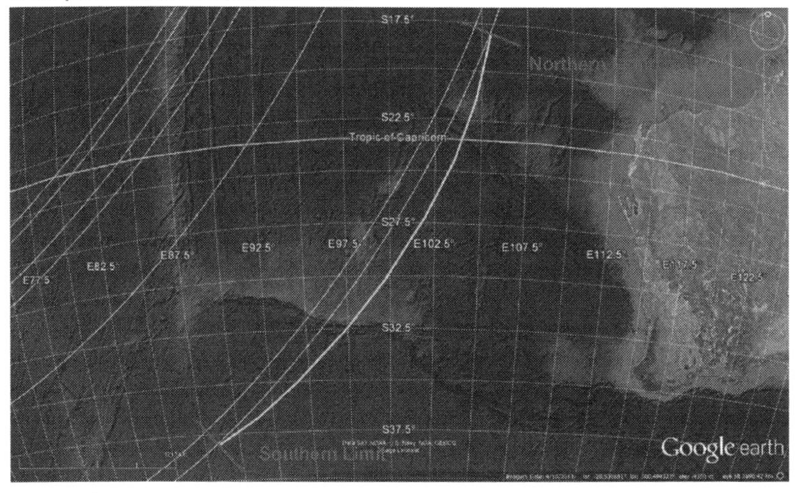

Source: ATSB

1st and 7th handshakes

The 1825 and 0019 SATCOM handshakes were log-on requests initiated by the aircraft. A log-on request in the middle of a flight is not common and can occur for only a few reasons. These include a power interruption to the aircraft satellite data unit (SDU), a software failure, loss of critical systems providing input to the SDU or a loss of the link due to aircraft attitude. An analysis was performed which determined that the characteristics and timing of the logon requests were best matched as resulting from power interruption to the SDU.

Approximately 90 seconds after the 1825 log-on request, communications from the IFE (In Flight Entertainment) system on the aircraft were recorded in the SATCOM log. Similar messages would be expected after the 00:19 logon request, however none were received. This could indicate a complete loss of generated electrical power shortly after the 7th handshake.

Because the location of the 0019 arc is also consistent with estimates of the aircraft range calculated from the remaining fuel quantity provided by the last ACARS transmission, the 7th arc is the focus of the search area.

Using the satellite system information, specifically the location rings determined from the BTO and the current understanding of the cause of the 7th handshake (log-on request) as being related to the fuel exhaustion of the aircraft, the focus of the search area will be along the 00:19 arc. The distance from the arc will be discussed in the section on the search area width.

Burst Frequency Offset (BFO)[16]

The burst frequency offset (BFO) is the recorded value of the difference between the received signal frequency and the nominal frequency at the Ground earth station (GES). The BFO consists of three major components:

---

16 Some additional information regarding BFO analysis is provided at Appendix G: Explanatory notes on BTO and BFO analysis.

- An offset (fixed frequency bias) generated by various components
- Frequency errors related to frequency translation in the satellite
- Frequency errors related to the Doppler Effect on transmissions and associated compensations

The offset could be estimated from the earlier parts of the flight where the location and behaviour of the aircraft was known. For MH370, the estimate was 150 Hz. Due to an observed tolerance of the data of ±5 Hz, the satellite working group used a variety of offsets from 145-155 Hz.

Frequency translation errors are introduced when the transmission frequency is shifted from the L to the C band at the satellite. Translation errors relate to the characteristics of the local oscillators which perform the translation. For example, the oscillators are sensitive to temperature, so when the satellite is in eclipse (shadow of the earth) the oscillators cool down, affecting the frequency translation.

Doppler errors are introduced by relative motion of the aircraft to the satellite, and the satellite to the ground station. The general principle is that when two objects are moving away from each other the frequency decreases and when they are moving towards each other the frequency increases.

The total contributions to the BFO of the transmissions from MH370 are shown in Figure 21.

Figure 21: Total of BFO contributions

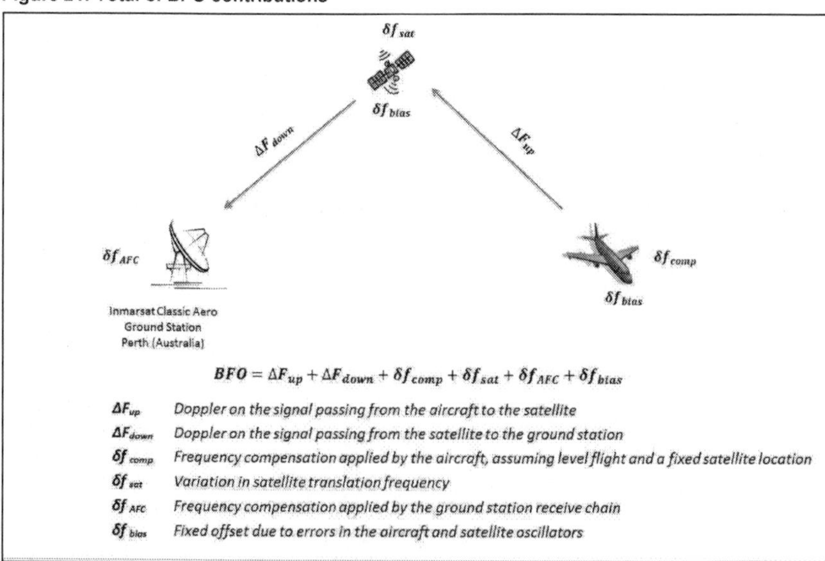

Source: Satellite Comms Working Group

The satellite communication system has controls in place to reduce the changes in frequency in order to ensure that communications are maintained within a channel. Corrections are made on the aircraft and at the ground station for known frequency shifts throughout the transmission. These corrections do not remove all the errors as the magnitude of the offsets are well within the system's normal operating requirements.

The Inmarsat Classic Aero land earth station uses an enhanced automatic frequency control (EAFC) module to correct for Doppler error in the satellite to ground station transmissions and a fixed translation bias.

Inmarsat Classic Aero mobile terminals are designed to correct for Doppler effects on their transmit signals. The method used by the terminal on MH370 is based on computing the speed of the aircraft (using inertial reference system data) in the direction of the satellite; vertical speed of the aircraft is not used. However, the terminal assumes that the satellite is at a fixed location when in fact it is continuously moving due to its inclined geosynchronous orbit (Figure 22). This has the consequence of introducing the following errors:

- The compensation applied by the terminal is calculated along an incorrect direction as the satellite is not at the fixed location.
- No compensation is applied for the relative speed of the satellite in the direction of the terminal.

Figure 22: Satellite motion during geosynchronous orbit

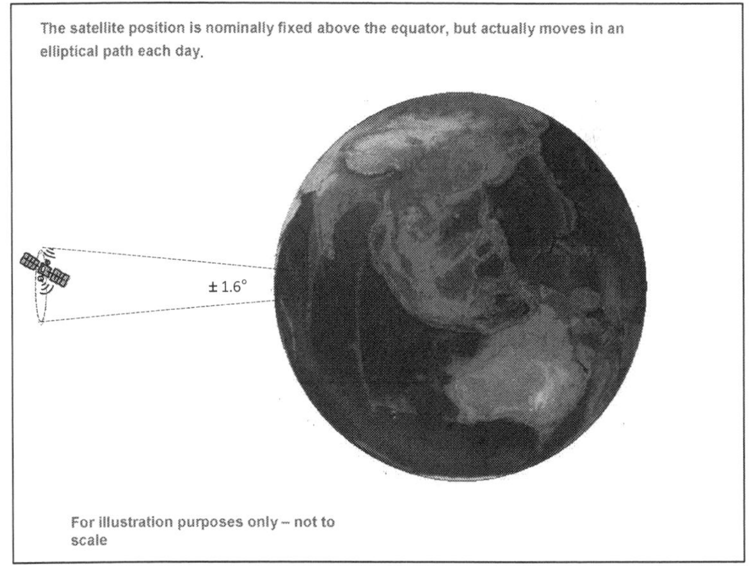

Source: Satellite Comms Working Group

Once the known error associated with the BFO is removed, the remainder is the Doppler Effect associated with the relative motion of the aircraft to the satellite (ΔF_{up}). For a given relative motion, there are many combinations of aircraft speed and heading that will produce the correct frequency change (BFO). There is however a limited range of speeds at which an aircraft can operate and therefore the number of feasible speed/direction solutions is limited (Figure 23).

Figure 23: Simplistic model of velocity component affecting BFO measurements showing directions for various speeds within the possible range

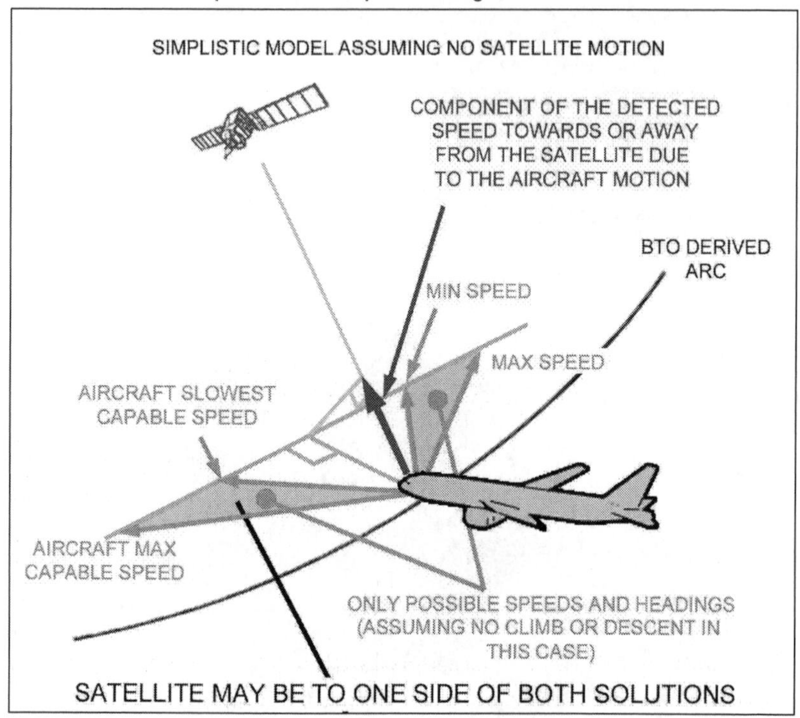

Source: Satellite Comms Working Group

Based on various starting assumptions, the satellite working group analyses used combinations of aircraft altitudes, speeds and headings to generate candidate paths and calculated the BFO values at the arc locations for these paths. These values, compared with the recorded BFO values, provided a measure of correlation.

The following are a selection of results from the BFO analysis. Each analysis used different assumptions.

Analysis A:

Assumptions:

- Starting from locations on the 1941 arc within reach from the last known radar point using possible aircraft speeds
- Constant altitude
- Autopilot modes considered include constant true track, constant true heading, constant magnetic track, constant magnetic heading and great circle (in each case, the previously described drift is allowed about the nominal value)

25

- Speed and heading modelled by a process[17] in which values may drift over time but tend to revert to a fixed (unknown) nominal value
- Wind effects modelled
- Error models used:
- BTO: Gaussian standard deviation of 26 microseconds
  - BFO: Bias uniform (147-152). Random error Gaussian standard deviation 5 Hz
  - Analysis up to 0011 arc
- Generated paths scored according to their statistical consistency with the measured BFO and BTO values

Figure 24: Analysis A results - red / orange/ green paths represent the highest correlation with satellite data

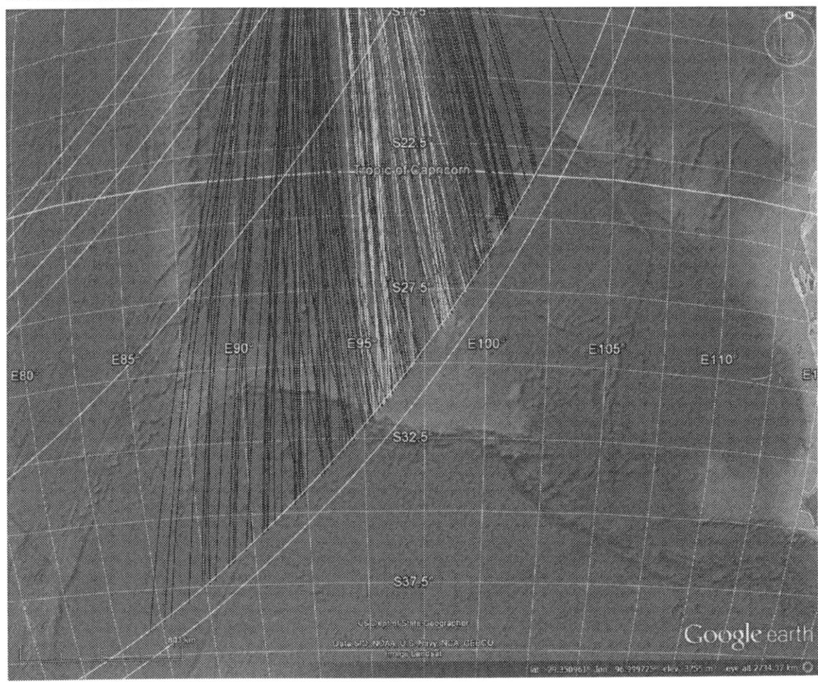

Source: Satellite Working Group

Analysis B

Assumptions:

- Initial track takes a northern hook around the tip of Sumatra
- Constant altitude
- Constant groundspeed
- Heading changes allowed at each arc crossing

---

17 Ornstein-Uhlenbeck stochastic process.

- Straight line segments between arcs

Figure 25: Analysis B results - white paths represent highest correlation with satellite data

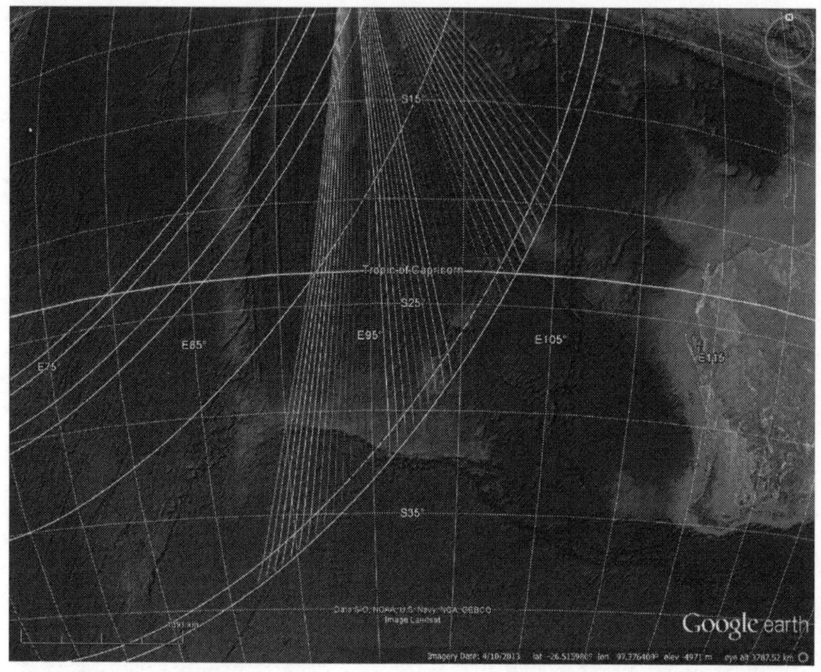

Source: Satellite Working Group

Analysis C

Assumptions:

- Initial track takes a northern hook around the tip of Sumatra
- Constant altitude
- Groundspeed can change at each arc crossing
- Heading changes allowed at each arc crossing
- Straight line segments between arcs

27

Figure 26: Analysis C results: Showing only the top 100 ranked tracks of 5000 candidates

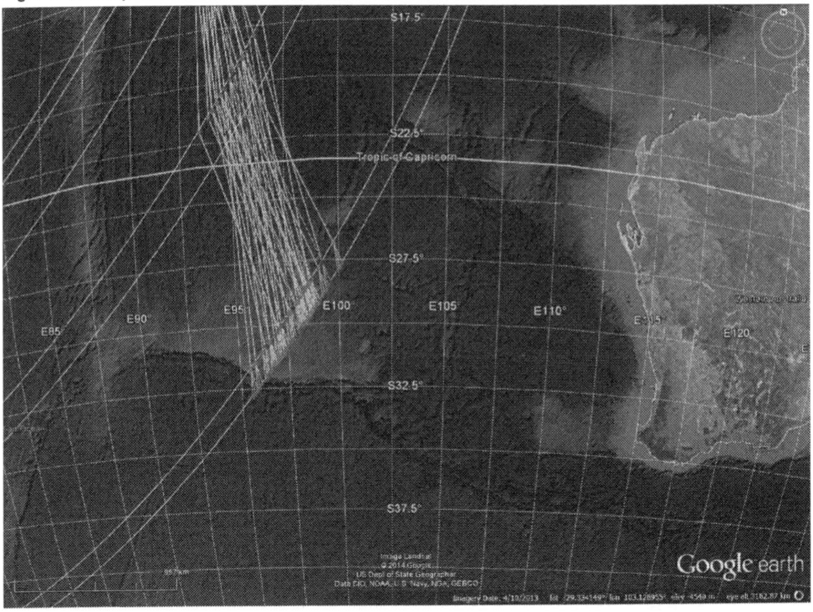

Source: Satellite Working Group

The various results from the analysis were generally in agreement.

From each of the different analyses, the highest correlation paths were compared and each crossed the 7th arc within 450 km of each other. The greatest effect on the paths was from changing the value of the fixed frequency bias. A sensitivity study determined that a change of 1 Hz in the fixed frequency bias was approximately equal to 100 km along the 7th arc. In order to appropriately bound the results, the most northern and southern solutions were used and an error margin of 5 Hz (observed tolerance of the FFB) or 500 km was applied (Figure 27).

Figure 27: Aircraft performance bounds and narrower limits based on the higher correlation area from the BFO analyses with 5 Hz tolerance on fixed frequency bias

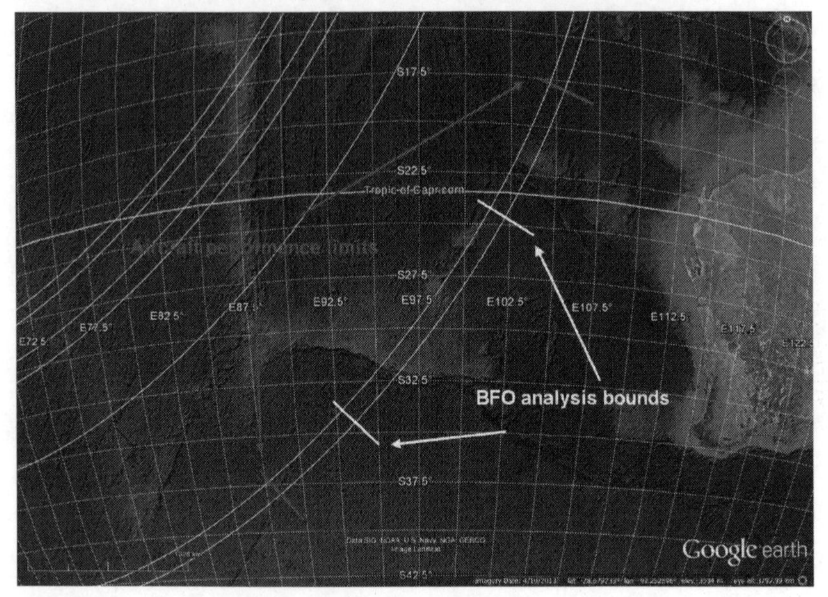

Source: ATSB

Verification and validation of BFO analysis

The BFO analysis was validated by several methods:

- An independent recreation of the satellite communication system model. This simulation was able to prove definitively that the BFO value is influenced by the location, speed and heading of the aircraft.
- Paths were generated starting from the last radar point assuming a single turn followed by a predominantly straight track. These paths were propagated in all directions, unconstrained by the BTO data locations (Figure 28). The BFO, at the times of the handshakes, was predicted for all the paths. In the paths that intersect the measured BFO values (red dots) are cyan and yellow coloured paths ending in the southern Indian Ocean (Figure 29). This was able to confirm that the southern corridor was the only valid solution.

Figure 28: 1000 paths generated, unconstrained by the BTO and BFO values.

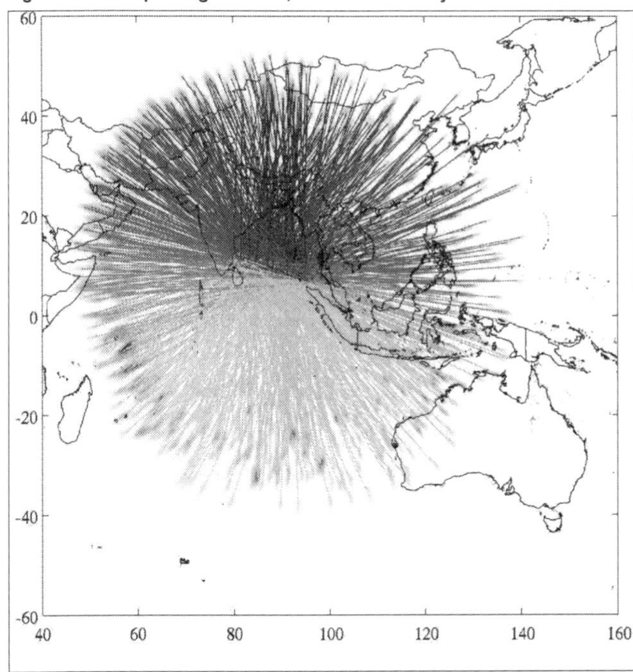

Source: Satellite Working Group

Figure 29: Above 1000 paths predicted BFO - red dots are the recorded values from MH370

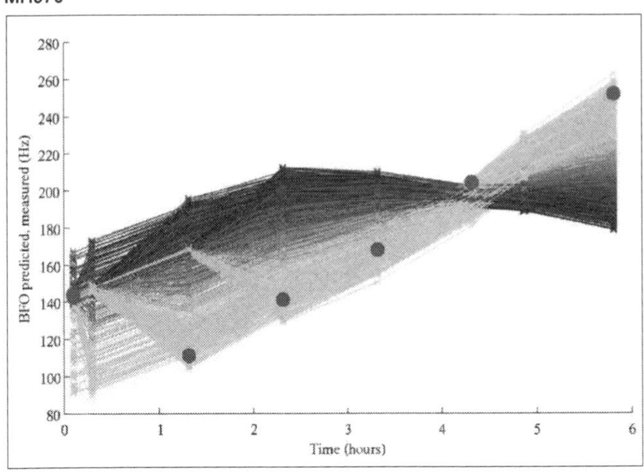

Source: Satellite Working Group

- Using nine previous flights of the accident aircraft (registered 9M-MRO) and 87 other aircraft with the same SATCOM terminal equipment in the air at the same time as MH370, some path prediction analysis techniques were verified. Shown below are two examples of comparative path estimations performed on sister ship flights departing Kuala Lumpur on the same day as MH370. Using only the starting location and an equivalent number, and approximate time spacing, of BFO and BTO values as the accident flight, predicted paths were created and compared against the actual flight paths (Figure 30 and Figure 31).

Figure 30: MH021 07 March 2014 - The red path is predicted path from BTO/BFO values; yellow track is the actual aircraft track

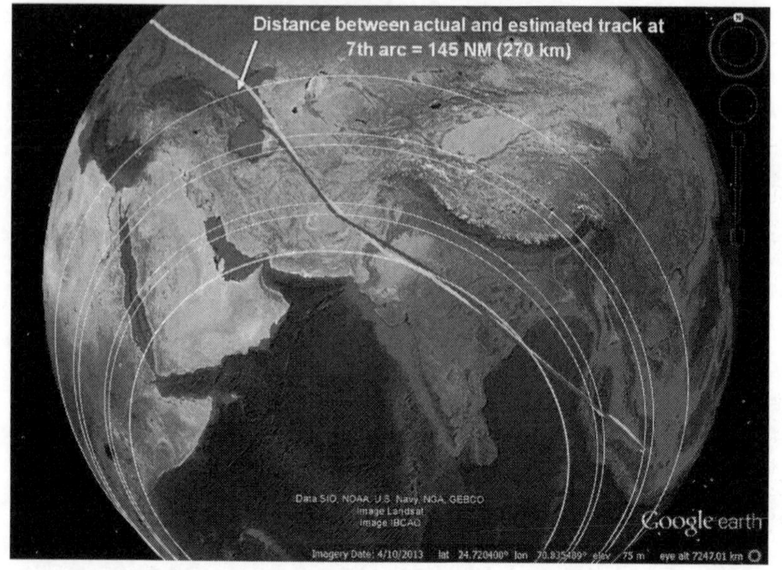

Source: Satellite Working Group

31

Figure 31: MH009 07 March 2014 - The red path is predicted path from BTO/BFO values; blue track is the actual aircraft track.

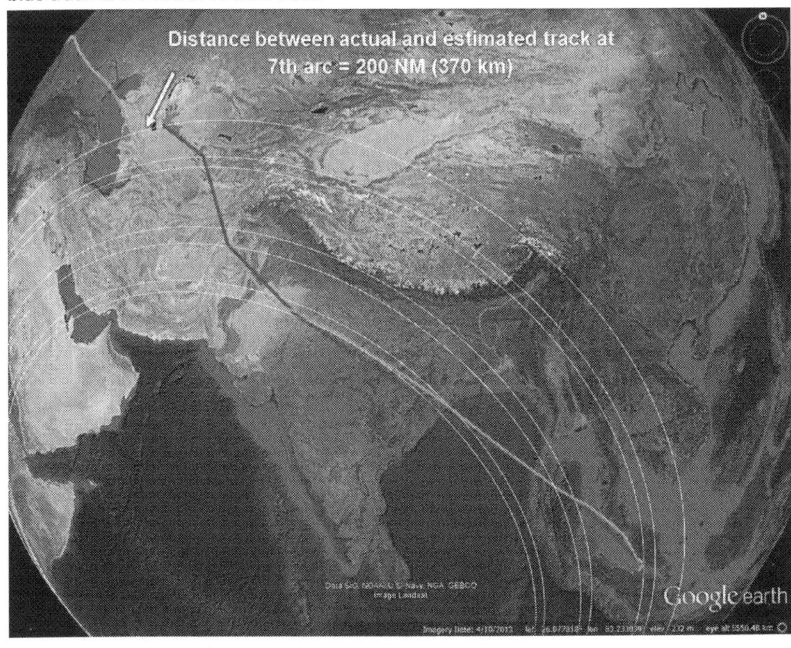

Source: Satellite Working Group

Determining the width of the search area

The width of the search area across the 7th arc is shown in Figure 32.

Figure 32: Description of the width of the search area

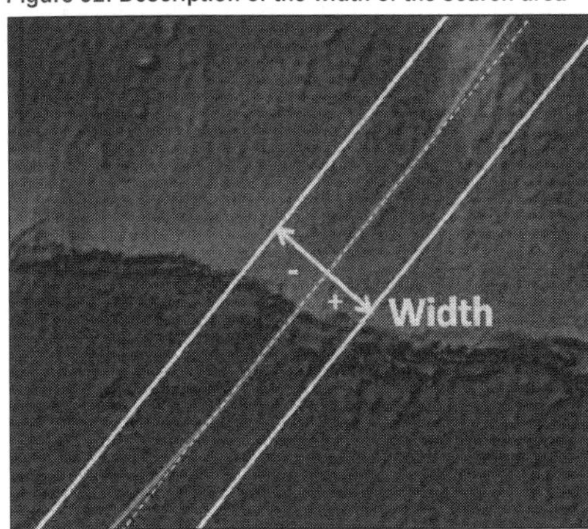

Source: ATSB

The final two SATCOM transmissions from the aircraft at 0019.29 (log on request) and 0019.37 (log on acknowledge) provided the last factual data related to the position of the aircraft. These transmissions placed the aircraft somewhere on the final arc but did not define a particular point on the arc.

There are several reasons why the aircraft satellite data unit (SDU) might generate a SATCOM log on request but an interruption to the aircraft electrical power supply was considered to be the most likely reason.

Aircraft electrical system

The electrical system on the B777 supplies 115 V AC and 28 V DC power. The main power sources are a left integrated drive generator (IDG) and a right IDG, powered by the left and right engines respectively. An auxiliary power unit (APU) can supply power if either or both of the IDGs are unavailable. The SDU was powered by 115 V AC from the left AC bus which was normally supplied by the left IDG. If power from the left IDG was lost, then a bus tie breaker would close and power would be automatically transferred from the right AC bus. Similarly, if power was lost from the right AC bus, power would be automatically transferred from the left AC bus. This power switching is brief and the SDU was designed to 'hold-up' during such power interruptions. To experience a power interruption sufficiently long to generate a log on request, it was considered that a loss of both AC buses or, a disabling of the automatic switching, would be required.

At 00:19, the aircraft had been airborne for 7 hours and 38 minutes[18] and fuel exhaustion was a distinct possibility. When a fuel tank was depleted, the corresponding engine would 'flame-out', spool-down and the electrical generator it was driving would drop off-line and no longer provide electrical power to its associated AC bus. Accident investigations show that when fuel exhaustion has occurred, typically one engine will flame-out before the other. In the case of MH370 it is likely that one engine has flamed-out followed, within minutes, by the other engine.

SDU power-up

Following the loss of AC power on both buses[19], the SDU would have experienced a power interruption sufficiently long to force a shut-down, the aircraft's ram air turbine[20] (RAT) would deploy from the fuselage into the aircraft's slipstream and the APU would auto-start. The APU would take approximately one minute to start-up and come 'on-line' after which time it could have provided electrical power[21] to the SDU. After power became available, the SDU would take approximately 2 minutes and 40 seconds to reach the log on stage evidenced in the SATCOM log at 0019.29.

If engaged, the autopilot could have remained engaged following the first engine flame-out but would have disengaged after the second engine flamed-out. By the time of the SATCOM log on message, the autopilot would have been disengaged for approximately 3 minutes and 40 seconds. If there were no control inputs then it would be expected that eventually a spiral descent would develop. In the event of control inputs, it is possible that, depending on altitude, the aircraft could glide for 100+ NM.

---

[18] A typical flight time from Kuala Lumpur to Beijing was 5 ½ hours.

[19] The earlier SDU log on request at 18:25 UTC was also considered likely to have been due to a power interruption. As this power interruption was not due to engine-flame outs, it is possible that it was due to manual switching of the electrical system. Therefore it is possible that the aircraft's electrical configuration was not in the normal state (i.e. the left IDG powering the left AC bus and the right IDG powering the right AC bus) at the time that the first engine flamed-out.

[20] The RAT provides limited hydraulic and electrical power for instrumentation and flight controls.

[21] The APU is supplied with fuel from the same tank as the left engine. Operation of the APU, after the left engine flamed-out, would be unreliable and would be of short duration before it too flamed-out.

Review of previous accidents

To assist in determining what may have occurred at the end of the flight, a review was performed by the ATSB of a sample of previous accidents. This review included the results of an analysis[22] by the BEA.

The ATSB reviewed three general classes of accidents that were relevant to the cruise phase of flight:

- An in-flight upset generally characterised by:
  - normal radio communications
  - normal en route manoeuvring of the aircraft
  - upset event such as a stall due to icing, thunderstorm, system failure etc
  - pilot control inputs
  - rapid loss of control
- An unresponsive crew/ hypoxia event generally characterised by:
  - failure of the aircraft to pressurise during initial climb
  - loss of radio communications
  - long period without any en route manoeuvring of the aircraft
  - a steadily maintained cruise altitude
  - fuel exhaustion and descent
  - no pilot intervention
  - loss of control
- A glide event generally characterised by:
  - normal radio communications
  - normal en route manoeuvring of the aircraft
  - engine failure/fuel exhaustion event(s)
  - pilot-controlled glide

Examples of these accident types are listed in Appendices C – E.

End of flight scenario

Note: Given the imprecise nature of the SATCOM data, it was necessary to make some assumptions regarding pilot control inputs in order to define a search area of a practical size. These assumptions were only made for the purposes of defining a search area and there is no suggestion that the investigation authority will make similar assumptions.

The limited evidence available for MH370 was compared with the accident classes listed previously.

In the case of MH370, there were multiple redundant communications systems fitted to the aircraft (3 x VHF radios, 2 x HF radios, SATCOM system, 2 x ATC transponders). However, no radio communications were received from the aircraft after 1719.29, 7 hours prior to the last SATCOM handshake at 00:19. Analysis of the SATCOM data also showed that there were probably no large changes to the aircraft's track after approximately 1915, about 5 hours prior to the last SATCOM handshake.

Given these observations, the final stages of the unresponsive crew/ hypoxia event type appeared to best fit the available evidence for the final period of MH370's flight when it was heading in a generally southerly direction:

---

[22] Metron Scientific Solutions Report: *Search Analysis for the Location of the AF447 Underwater Wreckage* 20 January 2011.

- loss of radio communications
- long period without any en route manoeuvring of the aircraft
- a steadily maintained cruise altitude
- fuel exhaustion and descent

This suggested that, for MH370, it was possible that after a long period of flight under autopilot control, fuel exhaustion would occur followed by a loss of control without any control inputs.

Note: This suggestion is made for the sole purpose of assisting to define a search area. The determination of the actual factors involved in the loss of MH370 are the responsibility of the accident investigation authority and not the SSWG.

Also allowing for the fact that a maximum glide distance of 100+ NM would result in an impractically large search area, the search team considered that it was reasonable to assume that there were no control inputs following the flame-out of the second engine. Accordingly the aircraft would descend and, as there would be some asymmetry due to uneven engine thrust/drag or external forces e.g. wind, the descent would develop into a spiral.

As the BEA found in their study, in the case of an upset followed by a loss of control, all the impact points occurred within 20 NM from the point at which the emergency began and, in the majority of cases, within 10 NM.

For the small number of hypoxia cases that were available for review, the starting time of the loss of control was not always as well defined as for the upset cases, so the 20 NM range might not be as applicable. Balancing this was the consideration that, by the time of the final SATCOM log on message, the autopilot could have been disengaged for approximately 3 minutes and 40 seconds and the aircraft would have been descending during that period.

Width of the search area - summary

The position of the aircraft along the final arc was relatively inaccurately known due to the many combinations of starting position, heading, altitude and ground speed that could be matched to the BTO and BFO data.

The search strategy needed to take into account these relative accuracies and minimise the width of the search area as far as practicable to allow a longer search distance along the arc. The uncertainty in the width of the search area should be in balance with the uncertainty in the length of the search area.

The BFO data showed that the aircraft track at the time of final arc was approximately across the arc from North-West to South-East. As a consequence, the search distance to the East (right) of the arc should be larger than the search distance to the West (left) of the arc.

Based on all the above, it seems reasonable to propose a search width of 50 NM (20 NM to the left of the arc and 30 NM to the right of the arc). A 50 NM (93 km) search width would allow a search distance of about 350 NM (650 km) along the arc.

A summary of assumptions to define the width is shown at Table 1.

Table 1: Defining the search width

Probability of including the wreckage site:	Assumptions: (Add ±5 NM to all the distances due to the tolerance in the position of the arc)	Dimensions:	Resultant search length along the arc:	Comments:
Higher	Max. distance unpowered glide B777 from FL350 (120 NM).	± 125 NM (250 NM)	70 NM 130 km	
↓	Max. distance unpowered glide from OEI altitude of FL290 (90 NM).	± 95 NM (190 NM)	103 NM 191 km	Given the uncertainty of where the aircraft crossed the arc, these search widths give impractically small search lengths along the arc.
↓	Realistic distance unpowered glide (60 NM) from FL290 to extend range but no turn back.	+ 65 NM - 20 NM (85 NM)	206 NM 381 km	
↓	• No pilot or autopilot inputs • Use distances from BEA/ATSB study of loss of control accidents (20 NM) plus 5 NM	± 30 NM (60 NM)	292 NM 540 km	Reasonable search width.
↓	• No pilot or autopilot inputs • Use distances from BEA/ATSB study plus 5 NM • Moving in direction of previous track i.e. reduce '–' direction by 10 NM	+ 30 NM - 20 NM (50 NM)	350 NM 648 km	Reasonable search width.
↓	• No pilot or autopilot inputs • Use distances from BEA/ATSB study • Moving in direction of previous track i.e. reduce '–' direction by 5 NM	+ 25 NM -15 NM (40 NM)	437 NM 810 km	The BEA/ATSB case studies generally involve rapidly developing descents and short total upset durations (most cases are < 2 minutes). MH370 may not correlate well with the case studies and the 20 NM distance suggested from the study might not be applicable. A buffer above the 20 NM distance is advisable.
Lower	• No pilot or autopilot inputs • Use distances from BEA/ATSB study • Moving in direction of previous track i.e. reduce '–' direction by 5 NM • Ignore ±5 NM arc tolerance	+ 20 NM -10 NM (30 NM)	583 NM 1,080 km	

Other information considered

Air routes

General

All modern transport category aircraft, such as the B777, have a Flight Management System (FMS). An FMS is an integrated suite of navigation sensors, receivers and computers, coupled with navigation and performance databases. These systems provide performance and guidance information to the cockpit displays and the autopilot. Among other functions, the FMS uses the navigation database for lateral (horizontal) navigation (LNAV) which includes airway[23] and waypoint information[24]. There are two different types of waypoints:

- navigation database waypoints
- pilot-defined waypoints

Before take-off, a flight-plan route will be entered into the FMS. The route typically consists of a standard instrument departure from the origin airport, a series of en-route waypoints, a standard arrival procedure at the destination airport and a missed approach procedure.

The flight-plan can be uploaded automatically using ACARS or manually entered by the crew. In either case, the flight-planned route will be cross-checked by the crew and then must be manually activated by the flight crew. Two routes can be stored in the FMS although only one can be active at any time.

The standard autopilot mode for en-route lateral navigation is LNAV, where the aircraft tracks directly between waypoints along a great circle[25] route and the aircraft heading will be automatically adjusted to allow for the wind (sensed by the inertial reference unit).

In-flight, the flight-planned route can be changed by the crew selecting a different lateral navigation mode or maintaining LNAV and changing the route entered in the FMS. Other lateral navigation modes include:

- heading hold (either a true or magnetic heading can be selected)
- track hold (either a true or magnetic heading can be selected)

With these modes the track or heading is manually selected on the mode control panel on the glare-shield. True or normal reference is selected by the crew using a switch located on the Captain's inboard display panel. Normal reference is the usual setting which references magnetic North, unless the aircraft is operating at high latitudes, in which case the reference will change to true North. True North reference can be manually selected by the crew using the switch[26].

---

[23] An airway is a navigation corridor along a standard air route.

[24] A waypoint is a predetermined geographical position that is defined in terms of latitude/longitude coordinates. Waypoints may be a simple named point in space or associated with existing navigation aids, intersections or fixes.

[25] A great circle is the shortest distance between two points on a sphere.

[26] In the case of MH370, for any possible track, fuel exhaustion would have occurred prior to reaching a latitude at which the aircraft would have automatically selected a true North reference.

Figure 33: B777 LNAV mode and track/ heading hold selectors

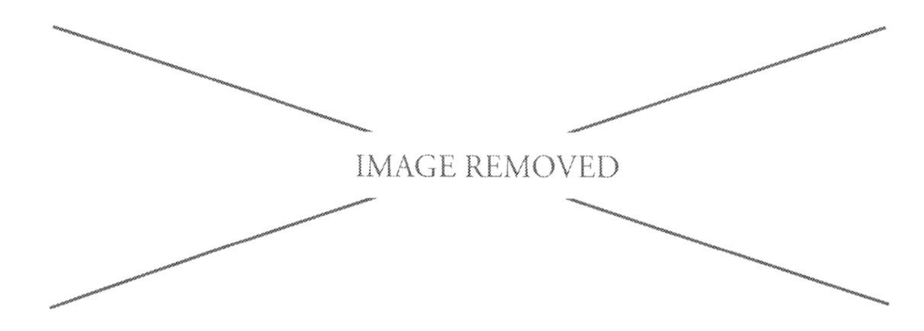

If using LNAV, the crew can enter new waypoints or change/delete existing waypoints. There is complete flexibility in the waypoints that can be entered, for example pilot-defined waypoints can be defined by the following methods:

- place/bearing/distance
- place bearing/place bearing
- along track
- latitude/longitude
- course intersection

MH370

Radar data showed that after take-off MH370 tracked in accordance with its flight-planned route to waypoint IGARI and then turned right towards waypoint BITOD. Secondary radar data was lost shortly afterwards. Primary radar data then showed that MH370 deviated from its flight-planned route.

Primary radar data showed that the aircraft tracked along the Malacca Strait. During this time the aircraft passed close to waypoints VAMPI, MEKAR, NILAM and possibly IGOGU along a section of airway N571.

Southern air routes/waypoints

Air routes and waypoints were then examined to see if there was any correlation with the possible southern tracks for MH370 obtained from the analysis of the SATCOM data. Relevant southern air routes that MH370 may have intersected/traversed were N509, N640, L894 and M641. Waypoints associated with these air routes were also considered as possible points on the MH370 flight path.

N509 ELATI 0200.0S 08957.7E
PORT HEDLAND

N640 TRIVANDRUM
BIKOK 0817.0N 07836.0E
COLOMBO
LEARMONTH
MOUNT HOPE
ADELAIDE

L894 KITAL 2003.0N 06018.0E
MALE
SUNAN 0028.7S 07800.0E
DADAR 0200.0S 07927.1E
PERTH

M641 MADURAI
BIKOK 0817.0N 07836.0E
COLOMBO
COCOS IS

Figure 34: Southern Indian Ocean air routes and selected waypoints

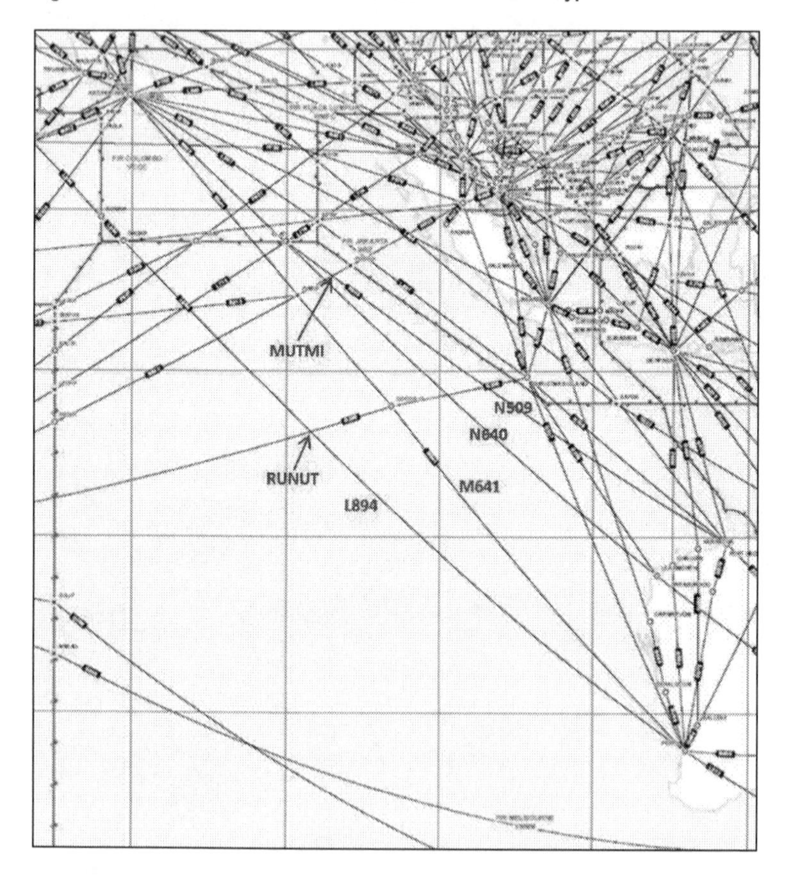

The waypoints at MUTMI and RUNUT were also considered as possible points that MH370 may have crossed. However ground tracks through these points did not correlate well with the most favoured paths generated through the analysis of the BFO and BTO data.

Air routes/ waypoints summary

Although waypoints and air routes were examined and compared to possible tracks derived from analysis of the SATCOM data, there was insufficient evidence to positively determine whether MH370 intersected any waypoints associated with published air routes in the Southern Indian Ocean.

Hydrophones

Low frequency hydro-acoustic signals present in the Indian Ocean were examined to determine whether they could provide any information to help define the search area. These signals were recorded by hydrophones as part of the United Nations Comprehensive Nuclear-Test-Ban-Treaty Organisation (CTBTO) or the Integrated Marine Observing System (IMOS).

Recordings of low-frequency underwater acoustic signals from data loggers and hydrophones off the WA coast were retrieved and analysed by Curtin University's Centre for Marine Science and Technology during the search for MH370.

The ATSB requested the Curtin University Centre for Marine Science and Technology (CMST) and DSTO analyse these signals in an attempt to detect and localise underwater sounds that could be associated with the impact of the aircraft on the water or with the implosion of wreckage as the aircraft sank.

One acoustic event of interest was identified that occurred at a time that may have potentially linked it to MH370. This event appeared to have been received on one of the IMOS recorders near the Perth Canyon (RCS) and at the CTBTO hydro-acoustic station at Cape Leeuwin (HA01). A detailed analysis of these signals has resulted in an approximate localisation for the source that was compatible with the time of the last satellite handshake with the aircraft, but incompatible with the satellite to aircraft range derived from this handshake.

Figure 35: Map showing most probable location for the source of the received sound signals (magenta asterisk) and the uncertainty region (yellow polygon) based on an uncertainty of +/- 0.75° in the bearing from HA01 and a +/- 4s uncertainty in the difference between signal arrival times at RCS and HA01

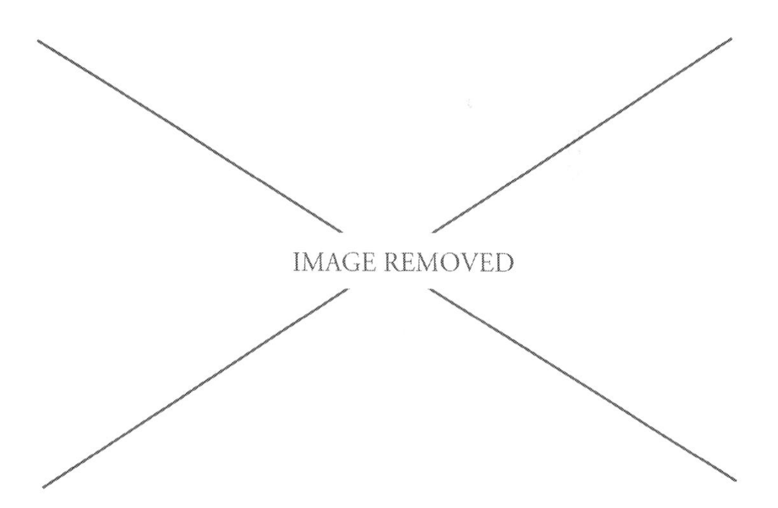

The ATSB greatly appreciates the work and cooperation of Curtin University on this matter. More information regarding these signals can be found at http://news.curtin.edu.au/media-releases/curtin-researchers-search-acoustic-evidence-mh370/. A summary of Curtin University analysis is shown at Appendix B: Hydrophones – Curtin University Executive Summary. The ATSB will continue to discuss any further information with Curtin University for the purposes of the search.

Underwater search area

The ATSB defined underwater search areas using an aggregate of the results from five independent analyses. Individual solutions had provided either a preferred flight path or a range of candidate flight paths spanning a length along the seventh arc. The results showed a high degree of correlation between the preferred paths and the high ranking candidate paths.

The search strategy working group combined this analysis with the location of the 7th arc and width analysis discussed above to derive three search areas. These three search areas were designated wide, medium and priority. The location, size, derivation and position are shown in Table 2 and Figure 36.

Table 2: Designated Underwater Search Areas

Area/ Size	Colour	Latitude lower bound on arc	Latitude upper bound on arc	Width across arc
1 - Priority area	Orange	Priority area definition for the RFT limited to 350 NM (650 km) covering the high probability area based on the ATSB evaluation of the working group results.	Priority area definition for the RFT limited to 350 NM (650 km) covering the high probability area based on the ATSB evaluation of the working group results.	Loss of control study, tolerance of the arc, balance of uncertainties and priority area for RFT of 60,000 km².
60,450 km²		**-32.1**	**-27.4**	**+30 NM, -20 NM**
2 - Medium area	Blue	Spans the highest correlation results from multiple analyses and error margin based on a fixed frequency bias tolerance of 5Hz (5Hz is equivalent to approximately 500 km variation at the 7th arc).	Spans the highest correlation results from multiple analyses and error margin based on a fixed frequency bias tolerance of 5 Hz (5 Hz is equivalent to approximately 500 km variation at the 7th arc).	**Forward of the arc** - Reasonable glide distance (performance of average pilot) starting from 3.5 minutes before final arc (approximately 30 NM) **Behind the arc** - loss of control limit. Both include the 5 NM tolerance of the arc.
240,000 km²		**-34.7**	**-24.4**	**+60 NM,-30 NM**
3 - Wide area	Grey	Southern range performance limit including a possible 100 NM along the arc.	Northern range performance limit including a possible 100 NM along the arc.	Maximum glide range from 30,000 ft including wind effects.
1,120,000 km²		**-39**	**-16.4**	**±100NM**

Source: ATSB

The limited data resulted in a large wide area (grey) needed to represent a high confidence in localising the aircraft. The medium area (blue) was calculated by using the ranking of candidate tracks contained within several of the analysis. Although still of reasonably high confidence, and relatively large, this reduced area does not contain all the possible derived paths.

Figure 36: Underwater Search Areas - Wide (Grey), Medium (Blue) and Priority (Orange) shown in comparison to S3/S5 and red, yellow, green search areas

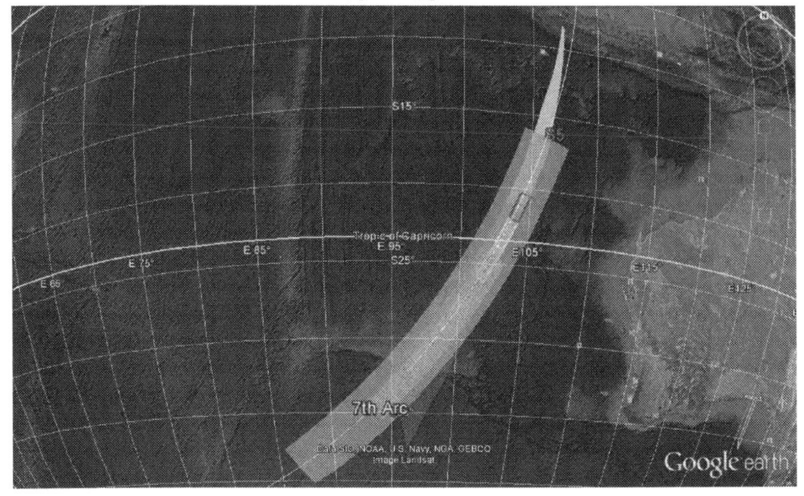

Source: ATSB

Through consideration of the convergence of the preferred paths and highest ranked candidate paths a priority area (orange) was determined. This area is intended to be the priority area for deployment of the underwater search assets obtained through the RFT. Should additional assets become available, then underwater sections in the medium (blue) area may also be searched.

The potential aircraft location, where the derived flight paths cross the 7th arc, is very sensitive to variations in BFO frequency. A 10 Hz variation in the fixed frequency bias can result in the derived flight path at the arc moving 1,000 km.

Work is continuing by the group to define particular areas within the orange priority area in which to commence the underwater phase of the search.

Additionally, work is continuing with incremental refinements in the BFO characterisation in particular the EAFC .The ongoing refinement may result in search assets deployment outside the currently defined priority area (orange) into the medium (blue) area.

A map of the recommended underwater search areas is at Appendix F: Search Strategy Working Group underwater search areas.

Acronyms

AAIB	Air Accidents Investigation Branch (UK)
AC	Alternating Current
ACARS	Aircraft Communications Addressing and Reporting System
ADV	Australian Defence Vessel
AF447	Air France Flight 447
AH	Artificial Horizon
AMSA	Australian Maritime Safety Authority
APU	Auxiliary Power Unit
ATC	Air Traffic Control
ATSB	Australian Transport Safety Bureau
AUV	Autonomous Underwater Vehicle
BEA	Bureau d'Enquêtes et d'Analyses pour la Sécurité de l'Aviation Civile
BFO	Burst Frequency Offset
BTO	Burst Timing Offset
CMST	Curtin University Centre for Marine Science and Technology
CTBO	Comprehensive Nuclear-Test-Ban-Treaty Organisation
CVR	Cockpit Voice Recorder
DC	Direct Current
DSTO	Defence Science and Technology Organisation
EAFC	Enhanced Automatic Frequency Control
FDR	Flight Data Recorder
FFB	Fixed Frequency Bias
FL	Flight Level (altitude in units of 100 ft)
FMS	Flight Management System
FPM	Feet Per Minute
GES	Ground Earth Station
GHz	Gigahertz (1 x 10^9 cycles per second)
GMT	Greenwich Mean Time
HF	High Frequency
IDG	Integrated Drive Generator
IFE	In-flight Entertainment System
IMOS	Integrated Marine Observing System
IOR	Indian Ocean Region
IRS	Inertial Reference System
JACC	Joint Agency Coordination Centre
JIT	Joint Investigation Team
KHZ	Kilohertz (1 thousand cycles per second)
KM	Kilometre
KT	Knot (1 NM per hour)
LNAV	Lateral Navigation
LOC	Loss Of Control
MAS	Malaysian Airline System
MH370	Malaysia Airlines Flight 370
MV	Motor Vessel

NM	Nautical Mile (1.852 km)
NTSB	National Transportation Safety Board (USA)
OEI	One Engine Inoperative
RAT	Ram Air Turbine
SA	Situational Awareness
SATCOM	Satellite Communications
SDU	Satellite Data Unit
SITA	Société Internationale de Télécommunications Aéronautiques
SSWG	Search Strategy Working Group
SW	South West
TPL	Towed Pinger Locator
UK	United Kingdom
ULB	Underwater Locator Beacon
USA	United States of America
UTC	Coordinated Universal Time
V/S	Vertical Speed
VHF	Very High Frequency
Z	Zulu - a time zone reference (interchangeable with GMT & UTC)

List of Appendices

Appendix A: Information used in determining and refining search areas

Dates	17-27 March 2014	28 March – 01 April 2014	02 -28 April 2014	June 2014
Event	Initial Surface Search Area	Refined Surface Search Area	Second Refinement to Search	Proposed Underwater Search Area
Probable Impact area	S1/S2	S3/S4 starting from southerly region of S4	S4/S5 starting at S4/S5 boundary and defined by red/ yellow/green areas	Southerly region of S4
Data used in planning search area refinement	• Fixed satellite location • Turn south occurred at the northern tip of Sumatra • Performance predictions based on speed and range only with no wind consideration • Only positional information from Malaysian primary radar data • Length of arc to the south constrained by maximum aircraft groundspeed • Lateral navigation set to 'track' mode • Two speeds provided 'best fit' with longest and straightest tracks reaching the 6th arc. • Assumed speed/ altitude to last radar point was final ACARS values	• Greater confidence in increased speeds from primary radar thus increased fuel burn • More confidence that 7th arc was fuel exhaustion point	• Based on the satellite timing data, the aircraft will be located near the 7th arc. • The aircraft passed close to a NW point at 1912. • The measured Doppler profile closely matched that expected from an aircraft travelling in a southerly direction. • One analysis showed that the best fit for the Doppler frequency was at a ground speed of 400 kts, with slightly 'less' best fits at 375 and 425 kts. A Monte Carlo style analysis, using a number of different starting positions on the 2nd arc also gave a best fit at 400 kts. A most probable speed range of 375 to 425 kts was selected. • One analysis used a combination of aircraft performance and Doppler data, obtained from the satellite, to generate a range of probable best fit tracks. This work was supported by a Root Mean Square analysis that took account of a number of variables. • Flight planning carried out by MAS independently showed that there was sufficient fuel onboard the aircraft to reach the positions determine by the analysis. •The length of the arc that defined the most probable area was obtained from the overlay of the results of all approaches. •Given the probable battery life of the Dukane beacon, and the number of assets available to conduct the underwater search, it was decided to break the underwater search area into three smaller areas. • The width of the areas was defined by the probable position of the 7th arc, half of the glide range (40 NM) and the area the towed detector could cover before the Dukane battery expired. • The area that was crossed by air route M641 was classified as red (Priority 1), the next two priorities, yellow and green, were then defined moving south along the arc from this position.	• Effects of an eclipse on the satellite during a period of MH370 flight taken into consideration • Refined EAFC model • Flight path from 2nd arc at 1941 • Candidate paths with zero BTO tolerance • Candidate paths within BFO tolerance of 10Hz

Appendix B: Hydrophones – Curtin University Executive Summary

The Australian Transport Safety Bureau (ATSB) asked the Centre for Marine Science and Technology (CMST) to analyse signals received on underwater sound recorders operated by CMST that form part of the Australian Government funded Integrated Marine Observing System (IMOS), and on hydro-acoustic stations operated by the Comprehensive Nuclear Test Ban Treaty Organisation (CTBTO) in an attempt to detect and localise underwater sounds that could be associated with the impact of the aircraft on the water or with the implosion of wreckage as the aircraft sank.

One acoustic event of particular interest has been identified that occurred at a time that could potentially link it to MH370 and appears to have been received on one of the IMOS recorders near the Perth Canyon (RCS) and at the CTBTO hydro-acoustic station at Cape Leeuwin (HA01).

A detailed analysis of these signals has resulted in an approximate localisation for the source that is compatible with the time of the last satellite handshake with the aircraft, but incompatible with the satellite to aircraft range derived from this handshake. There appear to be three possible explanations for this discrepancy:

1. The signals received at HA01 and RCS are from the same acoustic event, but the source of the signals is unrelated to MH370.
2. The signals received at HA01 and RCS are from different acoustic events, which may or may not be related to MH370.
3. The signals received at HA01 and RCS are from the same acoustic event, and the source of the signals is related to MH370, but there is a problem with the position line determined from the satellite handshake data.

Of these, the first explanation seems the most likely as the characteristics of the signals are not unusual, it is only their arrival time and to some extent the direction from which they came that make them of interest.

If the second explanation was correct then there would still be some prospect that the signal received at HA01 could be related to the aircraft, in which case the combination of the HA01 bearing and the position arc derived from the satellite handshake data would provide an accurate location on which to base a search. However, the analysis carried out here indicates that, while not impossible, this explanation is unlikely.

The third explanation also seems unlikely because of the intense scrutiny the satellite handshake data has been subjected to, However, should the arc defined by the handshake data be called into question, the various timing and acoustic considerations discussed here would suggest that a reasonable place to look for the aircraft would be near where the position line defined by a bearing of 301.6° from HA01 crosses the Chagos-Laccadive Ridge, at approximately 2.3°S, 73.7°E. If the source of the detected signals was the aircraft impacting the sea surface then this would most likely have occurred in water depths less than 2000m and where the seabed slopes downwards towards the east or southeast. These considerations could be used to further refine the search area. If, instead, the received sounds were due to debris imploding at depth it is much less certain where along the position line from HA01 this would have occurred.

Appendix C: Accident case studies – loss of control accidents

Date:	Location:	Reg:	Type:	Operator:	Upset Duration (mm:ss):	Altitude Loss (ft):	Average V/S: (fpm)	Max. Distance from start of emergency (NM):	Type of Loss of Control:
23-May-06	Helendale, CA, USA	N600XJ	Lear 24B	Pavair Inc.	02:00	23,000	11,500	N/A	Undetermined LOC.
25-Oct-99	Aberdeen, SD, USA	N47BA	Lear 35	Sunjet Aviation	02:30	48,900 Planned: 39,000	> 30,000	N/A	Hypoxia, fuel exhaustion. 'Payne Stewart' flight. Spiral and 'severe' descent.
01-Jun-09	Atlantic Ocean (500 NM from shore)	F-GZCP	A330-203	Air France	03:18	37,924	11,500	5	Stall.
22-Mar-94	Near Novosibirsk, Russia	F-OGQS	A310-308	Aeroflot	02:36	33,100	12,000	3	Roll upset, spiral and spin. Child at controls.
03-Mar-91	Colorado Springs, CO, USA	N999UA	B737-291	United Airlines	00:10	1,000	6,000	1	Rudder hard-over.
03-Mar-74	Near Paris, France	TC-JAV	DC-10-10	Turkish Airlines	01:12	9,000	7,500	11	Control damage. Cargo door failure.
12-Feb-63	Near Miami, FL, USA	N724US	B720B	Northwest Airlines	00:30	19,000	> 30,000	< 10	Extreme turbulence, overspeed.

Date:	Location:	Reg:	Type:	Operator:	Upset Duration (mm:ss):	Altitude Loss (ft):	Average V/S: (fpm)	Max. Distance from start of emergency (NM):	Type of Loss of Control:
01-Dec-74	Near JFK airport, NJ, USA	N247US	B727-251	Northwest Orient	01:23	24,800	16,500	< 20	Pitots blocked, stall and spiral dive.
26-May-91	Near Bangkok, Thailand	OE-LAV	B767-329ER	Lauda Air	00:29 (inflight break-up ~10,000 ft)	24,700	> 30,000	N/A	Asymmetric thrust. Thrust reverser deployed in flight.
07-Dec-95	Near Grossevichi, Russia	RA-85164	TU-154B	Aeroflot	00:57	31,000	32,000	8	Roll upset, spiral. Fuel imbalance.
19-Nov-01	Near Kalyazin, Russia	RA-75840	IL-18V	IRS Aero	00:59	26,000	26,000	4	Dive from cruise and spiral.
21-Dec-02	Near Penghu Islands, Taiwan	B-22708	ATR72	Trans Asia	00:40	18,000	27,000	2	Icing and stall.
16-Aug-05	Near Machiques, Venezuela	HK-4374X	MD-82	West Caribbean	03:30	31,000	12,000	17	Stall during cruise.
22-Aug-06	Near Donetsk, Ukraine	RA-85185	TU-154M	Pulkovo	02:46	39,000	14,000	3	Stall during cruise and spin.

Date:	Location:	Reg:	Type:	Operator:	Upset Duration (mm:ss):	Altitude Loss (ft):	Average V/S: (fpm)	Max. Distance from start of emergency (NM):	Type of Loss of Control:
01-Jan-07	Makassar Strait, Indonesia	PK-KKW	B737	Adam Air	01:45	35,000	20,000	9	Roll upset. IRS malfunction.
15-Jul-09	Near Qazvin, Iran	EP-CPG	TU-154M	Caspian Airlines	01:30	24,000	16,000	5	Roll upset and spiral.
12-Nov-01	New York, USA	N14053	A300-605R	American Airlines	00:24	2,300	5,750	1.5	Vertical stabiliser failure.
10-Oct-85	Near Sydney, Australia	VH-IWJ	IAI 1124	Pel-Air Aviation	00:25	5,000	20,000 (last 9 seconds)	< 5	Simulated emergency instrument flight conditions check at night. Loss of SA.
09-Apr-08	Near Sydney, Australia	VH-OZA	SA227-AC	Airtex	00:30	4,340	10,400	< 2	Spatial disorientation at night. AH unpowered.
03-May-05	Near Stratford,New Zealand	ZK-POA	SA227-AC	Airwork (NZ)	~ 01:20	22,000	15,000	< 2	Steep spiral descent, overstress and break-up. Fuel trimming using rudder.
26-Jan-90	Near Meekatharra, Australia	VH-MUA	MU-2B-60	Great Western Aviation	~ 02:00	21,000	10,500	< 5	Icing & stall. Aircraft entered a spin. Steep, near vertical, descent.
07-Oct-07	Near Nanches, WA, USA	N430A	C208A	Kapowsin Air Sports	~ 02:00	15,000	8,000	3	Hypoxia and stall. Pilot conscious but hypoxic.

Appendix D: Accident case studies – unresponsive crew/ hypoxia accidents

Date:	Location:	Reg:	Type:	Operator:	Upset Duration (mm:ss):	Altitude Loss (ft):	Av. V/S: (fpm)	Max. Distance from start of emergency (NM):	Loss of Control:
25-Oct-99	Aberdeen, SD, USA	N47BA	Lear 35	Sunjet Aviation	02:30	48,900 Planned: 39,000	> 30,000	Unavailable.	Hypoxia, fuel exhaustion. Loss of control. 'Payne Stewart' flight. Spiral and 'severe' descent.
14-Aug-05	33 km NW Athens, Greece	5B-DBY	B737-31S	Helios Airways	11:52	N/A	No LOC	0849:50 FL340 left engine flame-out. 0851:40 Start of descent. 0859:47 7,000 ft right engine flame-out. 0903:32 Impact.	Hypoxia, fuel exhaustion. Under the partial control of a cabin crew member.
04-Sep-00	Qld, Australia	VH-SKC	Beech 200	Mining Charter Flight	Unavailable	5,000	Unavailable	Unavailable. Gradual steady descent over a period of hours.	Planned cruise level was FL250. Observed at FL343. Hypoxia, fuel exhaustion. Low level loss of control. No CVR or FDR.
07-Oct-07	Near Nanches, WA, USA	N430A	C208A	Kapowsin Air Sports	~ 02:00	15,000	8,000	3	Hypoxia and stall. Pilot conscious but hypoxic.

Appendix E: Accident case studies – a sample of accidents involving a glide

Date:	Location:	Reg:	Type:	Operator:	Duration (mm:ss):	Altitude Loss (ft):	Av. V/S: (fpm)	Max. Distance from start of emergency (NM):	Comments:
14-Oct-04	Jefferson City, MO, USA	N8396A	CL-600	Pinnacle Airlines	20:30	41,000	2,000	81	Dual engine flame-out. 2154:36 Stick-shaker. 2215:06 Impact.
23-Jul-83	Gimli, Canada	C-GAUN	B767-233	Air Canada	17:00	28,500	1,700	39	'Gimli Glider'. Fuel exhaustion. High for landing and side-slipped.
24-Aug-01	Azores, Portugal	C-GITS	A330-243	Air Transat	19:00	34,500	1,800	65	Fuel leak, fuel exhaustion.
16-Jan-02	Serenan, Indonesia	PK-GWA	B737-300	Garuda Indonesia	~ 4:00	18,500	4,600	~ 35	Dual engine flame-out due to water/hail ingestion.

Appendix F: Search Strategy Working Group underwater search areas

53

Appendix G: Explanatory notes on BTO and BFO analysis

This appendix provides some explanatory notes on the BTO and BFO calculations used by the satellite communications group. The organisations within the group worked independently using different techniques but collaboratively came to a consensus on the results of their analysis.

BTO Analysis

The BTO measurement comprises two components: a bias component caused by fixed delays in the system, plus a variable component caused by the time taken for the outbound radio wave to pass from the GES to the aircraft and the inbound radio wave to make the return journey. This allows a simple equation to be developed relating satellite to aircraft distance to timing delay.

$$Range_{(satellite\ to\ aircraft)} = \frac{c.(BTO - bias)}{2} - Range_{(satellite\ to\ Perth\ LES)} \qquad (1)$$

where

bias is a fixed (and constant) delay due to GES and AES processing
c is the speed of light

To determine the bias value, and to get an indication of the accuracy of the technique, signals exchanged between the GES and aircraft, historical values were analysed with the known aircraft location.

BTO Example

An example of this would be to use the values in the 30 minutes prior to take off. During this 30 minute period the satellite moved 122 km. Table 1 shows the location of the satellite, aircraft and GES during this period, expressed in an Earth Centred Earth Fixed (ECEF) coordinate system where the centre of the earth is the origin, the z-axis is due North and the x and y axes are in the equatorial plane with 0° and 90° longitude respectively. Note: this example uses a simplified ellipsoid Earth model.

Table 1: BTO Calibration Geometry

Terminal	Location (km)			Lat	Lon
	X	Y	Z	°N	°E
GES (Perth)	-2368.8	4881.1	-3342.0	-31.8	115.9
AES (KLIA)	-1293.0	6238.3	303.5	2.7	101.7

Time	Satellite Location (km)			Dist to Satellite	
(UTC)	X	Y	Z	GES (km)	AES (km)
16:00:00	18118.9	38081.8	706.7	39222.7	37296.0
16:05:00	18119.6	38081.5	727.9	39225.0	37296.4
16:10:00	18120.3	38081.2	748.7	39227.3	37296.7
16:15:00	18120.9	38080.9	769.2	39229.6	37297.1
16:20:00	18121.6	38080.6	789.4	39231.8	37297.4
16:25:00	18122.2	38080.3	809.1	39233.9	37297.8
16:30:00	18122.9	38080.0	828.5	39236.1	37298.1

17 measurements taken during this 30 minute period can be processed to estimate the fixed timing bias. The mean bias of -495,679 μs is then used to predict the path length from the measured data (Table 2 right hand columns), showing a high degree of consistency. The peak error out of all 17 measurements is 17.7 km in the distance from GES to AES and back, equivalent to less than 9 km in the distance between the satellite and the AES.

Table 2: BTO Calibration (Kuala Lumpur International Airport)

Time (UTC)	BTO (μS)	Path (km)	Transmission Delay (μs)	Bias (μs)	Predicted Path (km)	Error (km)
16:00:13	14820	153037	510478	-495658	153044	-6.3
16:00:17	14740	153037	510478	-495738	153020	17.7
16:00:18	14780	153037	510478	-495698	153032	5.7
16:00:18	14820	153037	510478	-495658	153044	-6.3
16:00:23	14740	153037	510478	-495738	153020	17.7
16:00:23	14820	153037	510478	-495658	153044	-6.3
16:00:32	14820	153037	510478	-495658	153044	-6.3
16:09:37	14840	153048	510514	-495674	153050	-1.7
16:09:47	14840	153048	510514	-495674	153050	-1.7
16:11:04	14840	153048	510514	-495674	153050	-1.7
16:11:13	14860	153048	510514	-495654	153056	-7.7
16:27:59	14920	153068	510581	-495661	153074	-5.5
16:28:16	14860	153068	510581	-495721	153056	12.5
16:29:17	14860	153068	510581	-495721	153056	12.5
16:29:42	14920	153068	510581	-495661	153074	-5.5
16:29:50	14940	153068	510581	-495641	153080	-11.5
16:29:52	14920	153068	510581	-495661	153074	-5.5
			Average:	-495679		

With the bias value determined from the ground measurements the in-flight measurements can be processed to determine the satellite to aircraft distance at each measurement point.

Additional information

The signals at 18:25:27 and 00:19:37 were both generated as part of a Log-on sequence after the terminal has likely been power cycled, contrasting with the other messages which were generated as part of a standard 'Log-on/Log-off Acknowledgement' (LLA) exchange. Each power up sequence starts with a Log-on Request message which has been found to have a fixed offset of 4600 μs relative to the LLA message exchange by inspecting historical data for this aircraft terminal. The subsequent messages during the Log-on sequence have variable delay, and so are not helpful in this analysis. This means that the BTO data for 18:25:34 and 00:19:37 should be ignored, but that corrected BTO values of 12520 and 18400 μs may be derived from the Log-on Request messages at 18:25:27 and 00:19:29 respectively.

BFO Analysis

Unlike the timing calculation, which predicts the location of the aircraft relative to the satellite from the BTO measurement, the frequency calculation works backwards, taking the aircraft location and velocity at a given time and calculating the BFO that this would generate. This enables the likelihood of potential flight paths to be evaluated, depending on how well the projected BFO values align with the measured values during the flight.

The BFO may be calculated by combining the contributions of several factors:

$$BFO = \Delta F_{up} + \Delta F_{down} + \delta f_{comp} + \delta f_{sat} + \delta f_{AFC} + \delta f_{bias} \quad (2)$$

where

ΔFup	is the Doppler on the signal passing from the aircraft to the satellite
ΔFdown	is the Doppler on the signal passing from the satellite to the GES
δf comp	is the frequency compensation applied by the aircraft
δf sat	is the variation in satellite translation frequency
δf AFC	is the frequency compensation applied by the GES receive chain
δf_{bias}	is a fixed offset due to errors in the aircraft and satellite oscillators

BFO Example

The uplink and downlink Doppler may be calculated from the relative movement of the aircraft, satellite and GES using the signal frequencies of 1646.6525 MHz (uplink) and 3615.1525 MHz (downlink). The satellite location and velocity are accurately documented by Inmarsat for satellite station keeping and collision avoidance activities and a selection are shown in Table 3 for the key times used in the analysis.

Table 3: Satellite Location and Velocity (ECEF)

Time	Satellite Location (km)			Satellite Velocity (km/s)		
(UTC)	x	y	z	x'	y'	z'
16:30:00	18122.9	38080.0	828.5	0.00216	-0.00107	0.06390
16:45:00	18124.8	38079.0	884.2	0.00212	-0.00114	0.05980
16:55:00	18126.1	38078.3	919.2	0.00209	-0.00118	0.05693
17:05:00	18127.3	38077.6	952.5	0.00206	-0.00120	0.05395
18:25:00	18136.7	38071.8	1148.5	0.00188	-0.00117	0.02690
19:40:00	18145.1	38067.0	1206.3	0.00189	-0.00092	-0.00148
20:40:00	18152.1	38064.0	1159.7	0.00200	-0.00077	-0.02422
21:40:00	18159.5	38061.3	1033.8	0.00212	-0.00076	-0.04531
22:40:00	18167.2	38058.3	837.2	0.00211	-0.00096	-0.06331
00:10:00	18177.5	38051.7	440.0	0.00160	-0.00151	-0.08188
00:20:00	18178.4	38050.8	390.5	0.00150	-0.00158	-0.08321

The aircraft terminal adjusts its' transmit frequency to compensate for the Doppler induced on the uplink signals by the aircraft velocity. Aircraft heading and ground speed are used to calculate the Doppler shift the signal would experience if the satellite was at its nominal location over the equator. This only partially compensates for the Doppler associated with aircraft velocity as it does not allow for vertical movement (which introduces discrepancies when the aircraft is climbing/ descending) and the satellite is rarely at its nominal location: these small errors are immaterial to the communications performance, but do affect the BFO. This is δf_{comp} in equation 2.

Signals received by the satellite are translated in frequency, amplified and relayed to the GES. The satellite translation frequency is derived from an ultra-stable oscillator which is maintained in a temperature controlled enclosure to improve its stability, nevertheless its temperature (and hence frequency translation) varies throughout the day. During eclipse periods when the satellite passes through the earth's shadow, the satellite temperature drops significantly resulting in a further variation in translation frequency. Such an eclipse occurred during the flight of MH370 starting at 19:19 and ending at 20:26. The changes of satellite oscillator frequency with time are represented by δf_{sat} in equation 2.

The GES translates the frequencies it receives from the satellite to an Intermediate Frequency (IF) before passing them to the equipment that demodulates and processes them. The translation frequency it applies is controlled by an Automatic Frequency Control (AFC) loop to compensate for the downlink Doppler. The AFC loop works by monitoring the absolute frequency of a reference signal transmitted through the satellite, and using these measurements to determine the appropriate translation frequency to apply over a 24 hour period. The hardware used to implement this AFC loop in the Perth GES only partially compensates for the downlink Doppler, and the translation frequency cannot readily be deduced by arithmetic calculation, however its effects can be measured. This is δf_{AFC} in equation 2.

The final component in the frequency calculation is a fixed bias component related to the aircraft and satellite oscillator errors. Whilst manufactured to high tolerances, the oscillators on the aircraft and the satellite exhibit small fixed frequency errors which result in a bias value appearing in the BFO associated with any particular terminal. As the value is constant it can be determined through calibration measurements when the aircraft location and velocity are known. This is δf_{bias} in equation 2.

A key problem in solving equation 2 is determining the values of δf_{sat} and δf_{AFC} at the arc crossing times. This was resolved by measurements taken on a fixed frequency L Band reference signal that was transmitted from Inmarsat's GES in Burum (Netherlands) through the 3F1 satellite and received in the Perth GES, where its final frequency was recorded after passing through the EAFC controlled down conversion chain. These measurements allowed the combined value of δf_{sat} and δf_{AFC} to be determined at the appropriate times, as documented in Table 4.

Table 4: Satellite and AFC values

Time UTC	(δf sat + δf AFC) Hz
16:30:00	29.1
16:42:00	27.6
16:55:00	25.8
17:07:00	24.1
18:25:00	10.7
19:41:00	-0.5
20:41:00	-1.5
21:41:00	-18.0
22:41:00	-28.5
00:11:00	-37.7
00:19:00	-37.8

Tables 5 and 6 present an example BFO calculation during the early phase of flight MH370 when the aircraft location, ground speed and heading are known. They illustrate the sensitivity of the BFO frequency calculation to heading and latitude errors, showing that the calculation works and that it is reasonably sensitive to errors in aircraft location and heading.

Table 5: BFO Sensitivity to Aircraft Heading Errors					
Measurement		Heading			
Parameter	-25°	True	+25°	Unit	Notes
Time	17:07	17:07	17:07	UTC	
Aircraft Latitude:	5.27	5.27	5.27	°N	
Aircraft Longitude:	102.79	102.79	102.79	°E	
Aircraft Ground Speed:	867	867	867	kph	
Aircraft Heading:	0	25	50	°ETN	
Bias Component:	152.5	152.5	152.5	Hz	From Calibration
Aircraft Freq. Compensation:	108.9	489.5	777.8	Hz	Calculated (for 64.5°E satellite)
Uplink Doppler:	-75.3	-459.4	-756.8	Hz	Satellite and aircraft movement
Downlink Doppler:	-75.1	-75.1	-75.1	Hz	Satellite movement
Satellite & EAFC Effect	24.1	24.1	24.1	Hz	Measured
BFO (predicted):	135.1	131.7	122.5	Hz	
Measured BFO:	132.0	132.0	132.0	Hz	Measured
Error:	3.1	-0.3	-9.5	Hz	Close match at true heading

Table 6: BFO Sensitivity to Aircraft Latitude Errors					
Measurement		Latitude			
Parameter	-5°	True	+5°	Unit	Notes
Time	17:07	17:07	17:07	UTC	
Aircraft Latitude:	0.27	5.27	10.27	°N	
Aircraft Longitude:	102.79	102.79	102.79	°E	
Aircraft Ground Speed:	867	867	867	kph	
Aircraft Heading:	25	25	25	°ETN	
Bias Component:	152.5	152.5	152.5	Hz	From Calibration
Aircraft Freq. Compensation:	398.3	489.5	577.1	Hz	Calculated (for 64.5°E satellite)
Uplink Doppler:	-367.9	-459.4	-547.5	Hz	Satellite and aircraft movement
Downlink Doppler:	-79.5	-75.1	-70.7	Hz	Satellite movement
Satellite & EAFC Effect	24.1	24.1	24.1	Hz	Measured
BFO (predicted):	127.5	131.7	135.5	Hz	
Measured BFO:	132.0	132.0	132.0	Hz	Measured
Error:	-4.5	-0.3	3.5	Hz	Close match at true latitude

58

Zaharie Ahmad Shah's brother-in-law Asuad Khan at Penang International Airport.
Photo: Geoff Taylor.

Fariq Abdul Hamid's home in Shah Alam.
Photo: Ewan Wilson

Zaharie Ahmad Shah lived in the luxurious gated community Laman Seri in Shah Alam.
Photo: Ewan Wilson

The lane in Shah Alam where Fariq Abdul Hamid lived.
Photo: Ewan Wilson

People arrive outside Kuala Lumpur International Airport.
Photo: Ewan Wilson

The train arrives at area C in the Kuala Lumpur International Airport terminal.
Photo: Ewan Wilson

The Surau Al-Mawaddah mosque, about 30m from Fariq Abdul Hamid's house.
Photo: Ewan Wilson

A Malaysia Airlines aircraft at C1 departure gate where MH370 departed from.
Photo: Ewan Wilson

A departures screen at Kuala Lumpur International Airport indicates another cancelled flight to Beijing for the embattled Malaysia Airlines.
Photo: Ewan Wilson

The departure lounge at C1 where MH370 passengers waited for their flight to be called.
Photo: Ewan Wilson

Made in the USA
Middletown, DE
03 August 2019